The Blue Bottle Craft of Coffee

THE
Blue Bottle Craft of Coffee

Growing, Roasting, and Drinking, with Recipes

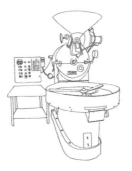

James Freeman, Caitlin Freeman, and Tara Duggan
Photography by Clay McLachlan
Illustrations by Michelle Ott

TEN SPEED PRESS
Berkeley

CONTENTS

Introduction / 1

INTRODUCTION

I have had opinions about coffee ever since I can remember. The seeds were planted when I was four or five and my parents let me open their green can of MJB Coffee with a can opener. I felt so adult—dangerous tools and cans of coffee! I loved the moment when the can opener pierced through the metal and there was that hiss as the air rushed out of the vacuum-sealed chamber. All of the aroma came out in a whoosh, and it smelled incredible. I begged my parents for a taste, but they refused.

My parents' coffee setup was seriously considered, emphatically defended, and brutally misguided. We lived in Fieldbrook, a Northern California town in rural Humboldt County, where my dad worked for the State Board of Equalization and my mom was a homemaker. They had a Corningware plug-in percolator with a light blue cornflower design—a classic. My parents put in the coffee the night before and set the lamp timer that my dad bought at the hardware store so all of us would wake up to that gurgling sound. As I got older, I realized that it was the sound of coffee dying. They drank it with extra-rich milk.

I begged and begged them to let me try the coffee, and after my prolonged campaign, they finally let me take a sip. Of course, I was repulsed. I couldn't believe how terrible it tasted compared to how good it smelled. It turns out that the whoosh of coffee aroma coming from the can was the best moment that the coffee had. The maximally cheap, underdeveloped, preground coffee never had a chance of tasting good. This experience stayed with me much longer than it would have had the coffee been delicious—the tension between smelling something great and having it taste horrible gnawed away at me over the years. I couldn't shake the feeling that there was supposed to be more to the experience of drinking coffee.

It took a few years to heal from that experience, and in some ways the bafflement never went away. But things got better when my oldest sister married and moved to Santa Cruz, where I would go and visit. Her husband was born in Italy, so, as a rebellion to my parents' ways, they drank Medaglia d'Oro, which they prepared in a Mr. Coffee machine. My mother, of course, did not approve.

They would drink pots and pots of coffee, and they were cool and young enough to be different from my parents. Instead of talking about road conditions, sales tax, and grammatical errors, they talked about Solzhenitsyn, J. D. Salinger, and Jerry Brown. They drank coffee with half-and-half and sugar, which made the coffee itself beside the point. At their house, coffee was social. I was about twelve when I started drinking it, and it was fun to participate in this cultural exchange. I felt grown up drinking coffee and talking about the issues of the day.

But drinking coffee with my sister did not make me cool. Au contraire. As I got older, I became increasingly dedicated to playing the clarinet. To give you an idea of how nerdy I was, in the ninth grade I gave up playing Dungeons & Dragons so I could spend more time practicing my clarinet. One day in high school a group of kids pushed me up against some lockers and called me "Flute Boy." I almost said, "Well, actually . . . ," like I was going to correct them for accusing me of playing the wrong instrument.

When it came time to go to college, I enrolled in the University of California at Santa Cruz so I could study clarinet with renowned musician Rosario Mazzeo, who lived in Carmel, about an hour away. I was working very hard, about four or five hours a day with Rosario in Carmel, plus taking a full load of courses toward a philosophy degree, which required lots of reading and writing. I started drinking a lot of coffee—a lot of bad coffee.

When I was working on a paper for a college course, I averaged about one cup of coffee per completed page of the paper. It was less for pleasure and more a pharmacological necessity, and it only escalated as I started working as a musician. If you have to play in an eight o'clock opera and it's a four-hour show, you need coffee.

Santa Cruz actually had a few cafés with drip coffee bars at the time, and I used a plastic cone at home. I didn't have very much money, but every once in a while I went to this store that that sold Chemex and French press pots and coffee beans from different origins. Their offerings seemed exotic and unobtainable. When I had a little money left over from a gig, I would try a few things. That was the first time I had the chance to buy coffee from specific places. Hmm, coffee from Kenya? Interesting.

After college, I went to New York to study with Kalmen Opperman, another famous clarinet teacher, and then worked as a professional clarinetist for eight years, including while I was in graduate school at the San Francisco Conservatory of Music. I became part of what is called the Freeway Philharmonic, a group of around 150 people who live in and around San Francisco and play for regional symphonies nearby, in smaller cities throughout Northern California, such as Monterey, Napa, and Modesto. Since each symphony only had a five- or six-week season, we tried to patch together a living by playing in several different orchestras.

In tandem with my music career, my interest in coffee continued to grow. I got into roasting coffee at home, using a perforated baking sheet in the oven. Once in a while I would get on a plane to perform outside of California. Back then, if you were going to Phoenix and wanted to drink good coffee, you had to fend for yourself. (This may still be true.) I would pack beans and a Zassenhaus hand grinder, and sometimes I'd even take them on the plane with my little French press and ask the flight attendant for hot water.

I feel like everything that has worked out for me in coffee didn't work out for me as a musician. As clarinet player, I was saying yes to jobs I didn't want and not winning auditions to jobs I did want. I was getting enough work to live, but it wasn't my favorite work. I was driving 30,000 miles a year in a series of beat-up used cars.

The moment when it crystallized for me was in early 1999. Due to the vicissitudes of my freelancing schedule, I ended up playing Holst's *The Planets* three times with three different orchestras in a six-month period. Maybe you know that piece. There are recycled versions of it in everything John Williams swiped for the Star Wars movies and everything bombastic and shallow you've ever been annoyed by in every action movie of the last twenty years, plus the horrible Phrygian raised fourth that was everywhere in early twentieth-century English classical music (I'm talking to *you*, Gordon Jacob, and *you*, Edward Elgar). *The Planets*, along with Carl Orff's *Carmina Burana*, had been grating on me more and more with each passing year of being a musician. Playing *The Planets* with three orchestras within a year, this time as clarinet two in the Modesto Symphony, made me realize that if I played it one more time, I would go on a rampage and hurt people with my clarinets. I needed a plan B, and coffee was all I could imagine.

However, there was a brief interlude. At the tail end of the dot-com boom, some friends asked me to come work for MongoMusic, a website similar to Pandora's personalized Internet radio service. The basic concept was "Tell us what songs and artists you like, and we'll stream you music you'll enjoy." Imagine this big wall with impressive dials and flashing lights, but behind it squirrels on treadmills frantically trying to keep the lights on. We were the squirrels—squirrels with headphones on. A different song was piped in every thirty seconds, and then we did a very fast, cursory, musical analysis.

I'd never had a nine-to-five, Monday-to-Friday kind of job before. As a musician, I had practiced all day and performed most weekend nights. Now I had a salary, got paid every two weeks, and didn't have to drive to Modesto. It was what I needed. But it lasted all of seven months, then guys wearing tan pants and polo shirts started showing up. Turns out they were from Microsoft. They shipped us up to Seattle, where Mongo became MSN music. Pretty soon, they figured out how to automate what the squirrels were doing, and I was laid off right after September 11, 2001.

Losing that job was how I got started in the coffee business. At that point, I didn't want to sell coffee drinks—that came later. I wanted to roast and sell coffee beans. I was roasting coffee at home, experimenting with different beans and roasting levels, and I realized I needed a commercial space dedicated to roasting.

I saw a "For Rent" sign on Telegraph Avenue in Oakland's Temescal district and called the number on the sign. It turned out the landlady had a fairly large space that was too expensive for me. But she was intrigued with what I was proposing, and she said she had a little potting shed that was available, right off the patio of the restaurant Doña Tomás. It was 186 square feet, and she proposed $600 a month rent. I didn't know rents were negotiable, so I agreed.

I started building it out, even though I didn't have much money. I went to Idaho and bought a little red Diedrich roaster. I remember opening the crate, seeing the roaster, and being astonished that this would soon be my career. I put it at one end of the shed and installed a three-tub sink, one of the many sinks required by the health department.

All of those early experiences were so vivid. As the coffee roasted, I dumped out small amounts of it at one-minute intervals, or even twenty-second intervals, and brewed them. It was an amazing process of self-education and discovery. Basically, I was figuring out what I thought was delicious. I had this image of how I wanted things to taste, and I was trying to make that happen.

I got up early because I had to stop roasting when the restaurant opened for dinner at five. It would get really hot in the shed, so I kept the door open, and I usually blasted opera from my little stereo. As soon as the roaster was installed in the space, I began to develop roasting profiles and blends for my first farmers' market in mid-August 2002. Later, when business started picking up, I roasted all day on Sundays and Mondays, since the restaurant was closed those days. The roaster could only roast 7 pounds (3 kg) at a time, and once, before I moved to my roasting facility in Emeryville, I did fifty-three batches in a row, at 17 minutes a batch; it's a company record that still stands.

At that time, I ordered all of my beans from Royal Coffee, a green coffee importer and supplier Blue Bottle still uses for some of our coffees. I would drive down to the warehouse in Emeryville and load two or three bags of coffee into my Peugeot station wagon. It still seemed

so mysterious. I would think, "That came from Yemen? Astonishing!" "That came from Ethiopia? Amazing!" As I opened a bag, I'd wonder what the coffee was going to be like. The more I think about it now, the more I realize it was a little crazy to just show up and act like a coffee roaster because I say I am—to get set up in that little shed, schedule inspections, and get them checked off. It feels like I established a legitimate, viable business entity mostly through luck and stubbornness.

Now that I was paying rent, I had to start selling coffee. Plus, my son, Dashiell, had just been born to me and my first wife. My goal was to have a stand at the Saturday San Francisco Ferry Plaza Farmers Market but you have to work your way up, and the first market I could get into was the Old Oakland Farmers' Market, on Fridays.

To do some outreach, I went to the Ferry Plaza market and gave bags of my coffee to my favorite vendors: chocolatier Michael Recchiuti, Berkeley's Acme Bread, and Miette Cakes. This was back when the Saturday market was smaller and still a precursor to today's Ferry Plaza Farmers Market, and back when the now-famous Michael Recchiuti and Miette didn't yet have permanent stores.

One day when I was at the Oakland market, it was so slow that I mostly just sat there reading Adam Gopnik's *Paris to the Moon*. Then I got a call from one of Caitlin's partners at Miette. She said she had an espresso cart and wanted to use my coffee.

Yes! I thought. I would be selling an extra 4 pounds (1.8 kg) of coffee a week. Awesome!

When I started making the coffee drinks for Miette, I impressed upon them, perhaps too emphatically, that coffee was very difficult to make properly. So eventually they sold me the cart. (I found out later that they had chosen my coffee primarily because they thought the bag was cute.) While Miette was operating the cart, I would swing by their kitchen to provide training on technique, and I met Caitlin during my first trip. At the time, we were both involved with other people, and our romance wouldn't begin for almost a year, but I remember thinking what a strange creature Caitlin was. She was fast and pragmatic and cute and tough. She would wear vintage dresses to sell cakes at the farmers' markets and would constantly text her partners using an early smartphonelike device called a Sidekick. I nicknamed her "the baker from the retro-future." All of the Miette bakers, especially Caitlin, were sources of such fascination for me—I had never imagined the existence of women so earthy, ambitious, dedicated, and young, all at once. Eventually, both my and Caitlin's single-minded focus on our businesses took the inevitable toll on our relationships, so we would get together every so often, as confirmed bachelors, to compare notes on our lives and our newly single existences.

After a few weeks of helping Caitlin and her crew make coffee at the Berkeley Farmers' Market, I bought their espresso cart and started running the cart at the market twice a week.

Slowly, people started taking notice of my coffee. At the time, it was still rare to have short, well-extracted shots of espresso and milk that wasn't super hot or bubbly. Plus I was trying different extraction techniques and using different beans, blends, and roast profiles for the espressso. I also had a wobbly wooden drip bar that I would make all the brewed coffee on: very laboriously, one cup at a time. People thought that was crazy. They were not accustomed to waiting. These days it's more common for people to pay attention to the details while making coffee—and there are more people making coffee that doesn't flow out of an airpot—but at that time it was unusual. Some people were interested, and some thought it was ridiculous. That's probably still the case.

At the end of 2003, renovation of the Ferry Building was complete and the market had moved to the adjoining plaza. Shortly thereafter, I heard there was finally an opening for a coffee cart at the market. I had to come in and give a blind tasting. I didn't know that another roaster had been invited to give a tasting at the same time. He had a very polished presentation, with immaculate totes stacked on a hand cart. A hand cart! Why didn't I think of that? They took our coffees to a tasting panel in another room. A week later I found out that I got in.

My spot was off to the side, in what was then a dead zone near a rotisserie chicken truck. I had one employee who came to help an hour before the market started; otherwise it was just me, my Peugeot wagon, and the cart.

I remember a couple of drizzly Saturdays in December when things were really quiet. Then, one Saturday in January the weather got nicer. It was right before the winter Fancy Food Show, which is always held in San Francisco, so there were a lot of chefs and food people in town. I looked up, and suddenly there were fifteen people in line.

It's basically been like that ever since.

People would wait a long time for their coffee. They must have found it unusual, watching a couple of people to take forever to make one drink. It must have looked arduous and fascinating. Ultimately, they liked the product. But it was all so puzzling to me. Perhaps that was because of the overall context of my life. I was exhausted all the time. When I wasn't selling coffee, I was roasting it. At the same time, I was getting divorced and taking care of my boy. It was all so intense, and also kind of wrenching. Everything was so new.

At the farmers' market, I was plunged into a community of people unlike anything I'd experienced. I had friends in the classical music world, but that world tended to be chilly and formal. The food community was very warm, and everyone was so curious about what I was doing. I wanted to explain to my friends in the classical music world about these strange, demonstrative people who spend so much time outside and will hug you for almost no reason. Plus, it's such a sensual world, in part because you're feeding people. That shift in my life was breathtaking. I was doing hard physical labor, and I was surrounded by people who were so excited about what they were doing and what I was doing.

I like how tangible everything is in coffee. With the clarinet you practice, practice, practice and rehearse, rehearse, rehearse. When you perform, you're training essentially invisible muscles to manufacture a vibrating column of air. Coffee is tangible. I am actually able to change the brain chemistry of my customers. Making an espresso is a performance that lasts ninety seconds and then you're done. You go on to the next performance. You may get applause or you may get boos, and then you move on.

After a few failing and unsuave attempts to interest Caitlin in more than just "hanging out," I managed to convince her that I needed a date to accompany me to observe the coffee service at a new wholesale account. The account was the restaurant Aziza, now a Michelin-starred San Francisco legend, but at the time it was a relatively unknown spot in San Francisco's Outer Richmond District. The chef/owner, Mourad Lahlou, was trying to break out of the Arabian Nights school typical of Moroccan restaurants by emphasizing scrupulous sourcing and modern cooking techniques. That was September of 2004, and although there was a certain amount of skepticism over what a cute, young baker was doing with such an uptight, old guy, Caitlin and I have been together ever since.

After things started taking off at the Ferry Plaza Farmers Market, I wanted to open a café, but I didn't have enough money to do that. However, I had a friend who owned a building in Hayes Valley, near San Francisco's Civic Center, and he said I could set up a kiosk in the garage of his building. I got a permit and opened the Blue Bottle kiosk in January 2005. That was the first Blue Bottle location open every day.

I didn't know if it was going to work. The kiosk was on a dead-end alley that smelled like pee. I used credit cards and a little savings to start the business. I should have had more money, and I should have had more experience. I should have worked at a café at least once before starting the business!

After a few months, the Blue Bottle kiosk started to get a lot of attention, and not just for the improbability of the location but because we were doing things in ways that were unusual for a San Francisco café at the time. No sizes, no flavors, a six-drink menu, the first PID-controlled La Marzocco espresso machine in California, all shots pulled thick and short, all drinks steamed to order, latte art on every milk drink, strict monitoring of coffee freshness, and no airpots! All of the drip coffee was ground and brewed to order using a drip bar of our own design. Now it's not so hard to find shops like this in many parts of the country (absent the pee-smelling alleyway), but at the time it was unusual.

Somehow it worked. Three years to the day after we opened the kiosk, we opened our first café at San Francisco's Mint Plaza. Within a year, we opened cafés at the Ferry Building and the San Francisco Museum of Modern Art, as well as new roasting facilities and cafés in Oakland and Brooklyn—two roasting facilities and four coffee shops inside a year. After that, we opened cafés in the Rockefeller Center, Chelsea, and Tribeca, and a kiosk on the High Line— all in Manhattan.

If I'd had any background in the coffee business or business in general, I never would have started the company. I probably would have said, "It's too hard. It's not practical. There's no way you can make a profit working so slowly." But I think the fact that I didn't have preconceived notions about it meant I was freer to take a leap and do something more personally meaningful.

Ignorance is bliss. It's like how people who aren't native English speakers have ways of speaking that are charming, even if not technically correct. For example, when you sell coffee, you're supposed to have sizes—small, medium, and large, or perhaps tall, grande, venti, and so on, right? I had no sizes, and I refused to make coffee in large batches and put it an airpot. Coffee gets stale within minutes of brewing it. Plus, if people are confronted with a spigot, they don't get to have the experience of seeing how the coffee is constructed.

Instead, I decided that, at Blue Bottle, we would grind your coffee, put it in a filter, and slowly pour water over it. We will construct your coffee. —J.F.

GROW

For those of us raised with the idea that coffee is a dark powder that comes in a can, it's easy to forget that coffee actually comes from a fruit that grows on trees and is subject to seasonality and harvest cycles. Though green coffee—the term for unroasted coffee beans, which come in various shades of jade green—can be held much longer than roasted beans, coffee should preferably be consumed within a year of harvest, though that can vary depending upon how it's packed, shipped, and stored. Once we run out of a coffee from a particular harvest, that variety is gone until the next harvest. There are cafés in Japan that feature coffees aged twenty years or more, and Italian roasters sometimes age certain beans for their espresso, but these are the rare exceptions.

Fortunately, coffee is harvested almost year-round in the world's various coffee-producing regions, which extend from well-known areas in Latin America and Africa to lesser-known regions in Taiwan and India. Hawaii is the only U.S. state with the right climate for commercial coffee production, so for most of us, coffee growing is a fairly distant and mysterious thing. This chapter will cover the basics of how and where coffee is grown, looking at how farmers and millers transform the juicy red berries from the coffee tree into green coffee beans. Then I'll offer a more in-depth look at a few of my favorite coffee-growing regions, as well as two growers Blue Bottle works closely with: Lorie Obra in Hawaii and Aida Batlle in El Salvador. I'll also discuss issues such as organic certification and how we get access to some of the world's best coffee, such as the online auction called Cup of Excellence.

Coffee Growing

The two main types of coffee that are harvested for consumption are arabica, from the species *Coffea arabica*, and robusta, from the species *Coffea canephora* (formerly known as *Coffea robusta*). Arabica, which is of much higher quality than robusta, accounts for around 70 percent of the coffee grown worldwide, and those of us in specialty coffee work almost exclusively with it. At Blue Bottle, the only exception are a few robustas—principally certified organic robustas from India and Madagascar—that we use to add depth and an oily body to one espresso blend. So I'll focus on arabica here.

Coffea arabica is native to Ethiopia and was the first coffee to be grown commercially. Within this species, there are thousands of varieties—called varietals in the coffee trade. Typica and Bourbon are two of the most widely grown varietals.

PLANTING AND FARMING

Coffee beans are the seeds inside the fruit of the coffee tree, which is actually more of a shrub. While it can grow quite tall, it is usually trimmed down to around 6 to 10 feet (1.8 to 3 m). The tree has oblong leaves, and its fruit, called the cherry, is about the size of a cranberry and has an outer skin that is dark red when ripe. Underneath the skin is the pulp, or mucilage, a sticky substance surrounding the coffee bean that is so high in sugar that it tastes sweet if you bite into it (and it's caffeinated!). Each coffee cherry usually contains two coffee beans, each with a flat side; peaberries are a naturally occurring mutation in coffee cherries that contain only one round coffee bean in each cherry. In any case, the beans are wrapped in parchment, a thin papery layer that must be removed during processing, and under that is the silverskin, an even thinner layer that comes off, for the most part, during roasting.

The ideal growing conditions for arabica coffee are a constant moderate temperature, a latitude between approximately 10 degrees north and south of the equator, and an altitude approximately 3,000 feet to 6,000 feet (915 m to 1,830 m), though coffee is grown successfully at lower altitudes. The higher the coffee is grown, the more slowly it develops and the denser the beans become, which can create more interesting flavors. Much like wine grapes grown under "stressful" conditions in great growing regions, the challenge of altitude forces coffee plants to focus their energy on developing seeds, rather than more extensive vegetative growth, which would be the plant's inclination under less stressful circumstances.

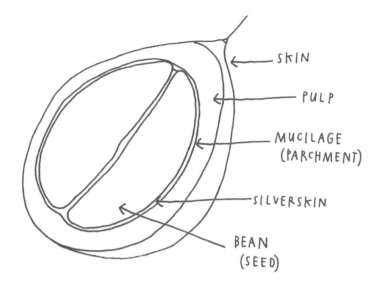

SKIN

PULP

MUCILAGE
(PARCHMENT)

SILVERSKIN

BEAN
(SEED)

Depending on climate and elevation, coffee might be grown under shade trees, which can protect both the coffee plants and the native bird species, explaining the origin of the term shade-grown. However, coffee is also traditionally grown without shade in Brazil and in places with a lot of natural rainfall, such as Hawaii.

Trees start producing fruit at around three to four years of age. At this point, they're given fertilizer and pruned regularly for easier harvest and higher yields. Irrigation is uncommon in coffee farming, which is why rainfall, storms, and drought can have a huge influence on the worldwide coffee market.

HARVEST

Coffee is different from other fruit trees in that the plant continues to produce flowers and newly ripe cherries throughout the fruiting season, even on the same branch, which results in repeated crops—and requires a lot of hand labor for harvest. In some regions the fruiting season lasts only a few months, while in others, such as Brazil—one of the few places where mechanical harvesting is common—it lasts for about six months. Harvest timing and duration also vary depending on altitude.

Because the fruiting season can last so long, some trees or branches will be full of red cherries, while others will have a mixture of blossoms, green or pink (underripe) cherries, dark red (ripe) cherries, and brown (overripe) cherries. Harvesting only ripe coffee cherries well is a skill and directly relates to higher coffee prices. So if roasters choose to buy excellent, well-harvested coffee, the farmers have an incentive to offer a premium to the best pickers. Therefore, careful harvesting can directly lead to increased standards of living for both farmers and their pickers.

Yields average around 2 to 3 pounds (0.9 to 1.4 kg) of green coffee per tree per year. Each 100 pounds (45 kg) of coffee cherries results in about 20 pounds (9.1 kg) of green coffee.

Processing

Most small farmers send their coffee cherries to a mill, where they enter the next stage of their journey: processing. In this important step, the green coffee beans are removed from the fruit and dried to prepare them for transport. In most cases, the harvest from small farms is processed with the cherries of other nearby farms, whereas larger growers often do their own processing. However, the increased demand for single-origin microlot coffees means that some small farms do their own processing or strictly supervise the processing of their beans, keeping them separate from those of other farms (for more on this, see the profiles of Lorie Obra on page 26 and Aida Batlle on page 35).

The two main processing styles used in the coffee industry are washed, also called wet, and natural, also called dry. Washed beans are washed or soaked in water to remove the outer pulp before drying, whereas natural processing means the beans remain in the cherry for drying. Within those two basic categories, there are many variations.

The style of processing that's chosen varies according to local tradition and has a lot to do with access to water. For example, natural processing is traditional in the Harar region of Ethiopia, where water is scarce. On the flip side, natural processing doesn't work well in rainy climates because it requires a long drying period. Farmers who pay a lot of attention to processing also vary their methods depending on what works best with specific varieties and what their customers want.

WASHED COFFEE

Washing, or wet processing, results in coffees with higher acidity and more consistency, and these are among the reasons why this is the most common processing method. The basic process goes like this: the cherries are sent through a pulping machine, which removes the outer skin, leaving the sticky mucilage, or pulp, still clinging to the beans. The beans are then soaked

in water, and often gently agitated during this stage. They are then allowed to ferment for a period of time that ranges from hours to a day or two, during which time the pulp falls off. (Note that all fermentation and drying times vary greatly depending on the type of equipment used and the weather, so these are all approximations.)

After fermentation, the beans are rinsed and washed and then allowed to dry, either in the sun on patios or raised beds, or in a mechanical dryer, usually for a period of four to eight days, depending on sunlight and climate.

Kenya-style processing is similar to wet processing, with a longer fermentation period—often with an additional rinsing and soaking period that results in coffees with high acidity and elegance. The cherries are pulped and then fermented for eight to sixteen hours. Next, the beans are washed, then soaked in clean water, usually for six to twelve hours, but sometimes as long as forty-eight hours.

NATURAL COFFEE

Natural processing, or dry processing, is the original way of processing coffee. In this method, coffee cherries are dried whole on raised beds, mats, or patios. Some farms in Brazil let the coffee cherries dry on the tree and then harvest them when they resemble small prunes. Because the beans remain inside the fruit as it dries, this results in a very noticeable difference in aroma and flavor. For example, this is how Ethiopian natural coffees develop the fruity flavors and blueberry scents they are known for. Natural processing also results in coffee with more body and less acidity.

This method does not come without risks. If the beans rest in the wet fruit for too long, the fruit will ferment and get moldy or impart a sour, yeasty taste to the coffee, so frequent raking is necessary during the drying period, which usually lasts around three weeks. The beans are then either stored in their skins for a period of months or hulled right away in a machine or by hand to remove the dried outer skin and the inner parchment.

Natural coffee is a somewhat controversial topic in today's coffee world. Some coffee professionals claim that natural processing is wrong because it allows reabsorption of some of the coffee fruit into the coffee seed, creating a characteristic fruit bomb flavor profile that can either hide subtle faults or obscure subtle virtues. Personally, I've had both stunningly refined dry-processed coffees and lurid, bombastic, overpowering dry-processed coffees, and I would be loath to live in a world where coffee scolds limited our access to them.

PULPED NATURAL COFFEE

Popular in Brazil, pulped natural processing is a cross between wet and dry processing. It is also known as honey processing, the word *honey* referring to the sweet pulp. As in wet processing, the cherries are pulped, removing the outer skin but leaving the mucilage attached to the beans. But then instead of soaking, the beans are spread on large tables to dry for anywhere from five days to two weeks, with the mucilage still surrounding them. The resulting coffees are more consistent in quality than dry-processed coffees and tend to have similar characteristics, such as a lot of body and low acidity. However, they don't develop vivid fruit notes of dry-processed coffees.

WET HULLING

Wet hulling is a version of pulped natural processing used widely used in Sumatra, where it is called *giling basah*. It results in coffees with heavy body and low acidity. The process starts like pulped natural processing, except the coffee is only dried for about a day with the mucilage attached. Next, the beans are washed, partially dried again, and then hulled to remove the parchment before the beans finish drying.

FINAL STEPS

After the first phase of processing, using one of the above methods, which is somewhat confusingly called wet milling as a whole, the coffee beans are usually stored for one to three months to help balance out their moisture levels. Then they enter a phase called dry milling, when the parchment is removed and they are sorted by size. This serves two functions: first, roasters like coffees of even size and density because this makes roasting easier. Second, larger beans often fetch a premium because the coffee is thought to have been harvested from riper cherries and might cup better. After sorting, storage time can vary, but the coffee beans should ideally arrive to customers within one year of harvest, preferably sooner.

IN DEFENSE OF BLENDS

A blend is a combination of coffees from different countries or regions, whereas a single-origin coffee is from one country, one region, one farm, or even one part of a farm. The notion of which is more desirable—a blend or a single-origin coffee—has seesawed throughout the history of coffee. Right now the single-origins have it. But focusing only on rarified single-origin coffees is like being at a restaurant with only Grand Cru Burgundies on the wine list. A good restaurant's wine list includes hearty house reds, approachable whites, and different types of wines at different price points. Sometimes people want something simple, consistent, and delicious. That's what a good coffee blend can do.

The main reason we blend is to achieve a consistently delicious flavor. The first blend was probably Mocha-Java, in which a winey, bright coffee from Yemen (which at the time shipped from the Red Sea port of Al-Makha, or Mocha) was added to the heavy, thick coffees being shipped out of Dutch coffee holdings in Java. As commercial coffee roasters came on the scene, their desire to create proprietary blends that would taste the same throughout the year led to more focus on blends than on the origins of the green coffee itself. This allowed coffee companies to "cheat" and increase their margins by sneaking in cheaper, lesser-quality coffees and hoping to cover them up with careful blending. As large companies producing commodity-grade canned coffee used cheaper and cheaper raw materials, the degradation in quality soon became evident. When Peet's came on the scene in the late 1960s, commercial blends had sunk to such a nadir of quality that Peet's blends, made from carefully selected high-quality coffee chosen to have enough acidity to withstand very dark roasting, were revelatory.

Coffee blending for espresso has been a fixture in the Italian market since the introduction of the espresso machine (see page 111). Whether out of economic constraints or the desire for a simple, delicious, muted flavor profile, Italian coffee companies have been putting time and energy into the careful development and maintenance of their espresso blends for decades. Espresso coffees have been blends from their inception, and for good reason. As mentioned on page 24, espresso really took off in Italy after World War II due to the scarcity of high-quality green coffee. Coffee roasters combined lower-quality beans, including robustas from Africa, with slightly better-quality coffees from Brazil. Both coffees had lackluster acidity, reasonably thick body, and a lot of potentially off flavors, and if made like a modern pour over, might yield a pretty frightening cup. However, espresso extraction tends to increase the perception of acidity and body and mute funky qualities. So one of the reasons espresso extraction evolved is that Italians figured out how to use modest ingredients to make something delicious, the same way they reinvented basic cornmeal into polenta and, when they had no chocolate, created gianduja using sugar, cocoa powder, and hazelnuts.

At Blue Bottle, we offer several espresso blends and brewed coffee blends that highlight diverse flavors, and all are extremely popular. We put forethought and energy into maintaining a consistent flavor with excellent coffee, even as the availability of specific beans changes seasonally. Although we are thrilled with the dazzling array of vibrant single-origin coffees we source, we realize that many of our customer come to us for delicious, comforting consistency, and our blends achieve precisely that.

The question everyone working in coffee is asking today is how we want our coffee to taste. We have unparalleled options in terms of green coffee and an unprecedented customer base. Do we want something to taste as consistent as possible from week to week and year to year, or something that's constantly different? Sometimes people come into our shops, god help them, before they've had coffee. Sometimes they're seeking reassurance. They don't want bell pepper notes one morning and evocations of watermelon Jolly Rancher the next. They want something that's going to be delicious and suit their preferences whenever they buy it. Then there are the people who want novelty, excitement, and surprises; they are the ones who tend to be drawn to single-origins.

What can get lost in the discussion is that maintaining a blend year after year is expensive and requires a lot of forethought and skill. You have to make buying decisions six or seven months in advance—and then you have to write checks based on what you think you're going to use in a blend. You have to be resourceful in managing the alchemy as different coffees interact in different ways. With single-origin coffees, the situation is much more straightforward: when you run out, you buy something else.

The focus on single-origins is valuable and timely. These days we have a lot more access to quality lots of single-origin coffees that should be showcased on their own. There are some coffees that are so distinct, so brilliant, and so inspiring that they absolutely need to display their qualities unmediated by the influence of other coffees. Single-origin coffees also allow the efforts of the farmer to be better noted and rewarded. All of that said, there is definitely a place for blending: to make coffee drinkers happy by giving them a specific, repeatable experience tailored for a particular and enduring context.

Getting to Know Coffee from Three Favorite Regions

I try to avoid generalizing about coffee. But then again, let's generalize. Beans from particular places are sought after because of certain characteristics they are known for. So rather than exhaustively covering all of the coffee-producing regions around the globe, let's focus on three of my favorite coffee-growing countries.

ETHIOPIA

ETHIOPIA

Ethiopia is the birthplace of coffee. In fact, the English term *coffee bean* probably comes from the Ethiopian word *bun*, for coffee, and Kaffa, a region where the arabica bean is a native plant. Ethiopia, which ranks sixth in production among coffee-growing nations, is the source of some of the most memorable coffees I've had. Some of Ethiopia's best-known coffees are named for the region they come from, such as Yirgacheffe in Sidamo, which gets its distinctive floral notes from the coffee varietals, terroir, and traditional wet processing, and Harrar, which is dry processed and tends to have distinctive, bright fruit flavors.

Because Ethiopia is where coffee originated, it has more indigenous coffee varietals than any other nation. Whereas the rest of the world grows a handful of varietals originally smuggled out of Ethiopia and nearby countries, Ethiopia has over one thousand. Imagine if there were one thousand varieties of tomatoes at the farmers' market! Because of the huge variety, there's always a fascinating new Ethiopian coffee to try, something incredible you've never tasted before.

Ethiopia has a rapidly growing local market for its coffee; about half of the coffee grown in Ethiopia is consumed in Ethiopia. An internal market builds the economics of the coffee industry in that country. As more people in Ethiopia drink Ethiopian coffee, the nation's coffee farmers will benefit, not just because of increased demand, but also because they receive more direct feedback about quality.

Meanwhile, many more varieties of coffee are now being exported from Ethiopia's various coffee-growing regions. Some are great, and some not so great, so it's much more difficult to generalize about taste profiles from specific regions than it used to be. The big organic co-ops produce so many different lots, and the only way to get coffee that meets Blue Bottle's standards is to constantly do cuppings, or evaluative tastings, of the current offerings. (For details on cupping, see page 63.) Blue Bottle buys a lot of coffee from the Yirgacheffe region, both dry and wet processed. I adore these wet-processed coffees when they're at their best; they are delicate and floral, with an underlying body and sweetness similar to Moscato d'Asti, an Italian sparkling white wine.

With so many dazzling coffees coming out of Ethiopia, and increasing investment in identifying great varietals, I believe we are only starting to see how wonderful the possibilities of Ethiopian coffee are. And on top of all of this, Ethiopia's organic certification options and coffee processing infrastructure are among the best in the coffee-growing world.

ETHIOPIAN CUP CHARACTERISTICS There's a lot of dry processing in Ethiopian, which yields the classic blueberry profile, both in nose and in the cup, that Ethiopian coffees are known for. Even the wet-processed coffees can have amazing, delicate flavors, such as jasmine and stone fruit, with baking spices. However, the flavor of these wet-processed coffees is more subtle, and it's easier to roast out some of the more delicate qualities.

VARIETALS: Because of the huge number of coffee varietals in Ethiopia, the country has a numerical system in which the type of bean is referred to by a number, rather than a name of the varietal, as is the case in other countries. However, there may be several varietals present in any given bag of Ethiopian coffee, even one labeled single-origin.

TALKING ABOUT ACIDITY

The word *acidity* is a wedge that can separate coffee professionals from their customers. As coffee professionals, we need to use this word a lot, but we try to use it internally. When customers hear or use that word, it's typically as a pejorative. They hear acidity and think, "My tummy hurts!" They think about sharp, unpleasant flavors that actually aren't directly related to the pH level of the coffee; rather, they're related to compounds that develop as a result of poor brewing, holding coffee for a long time, or careless roasting of poor-quality green coffee.

At Blue Bottle, when we speak to customers about acidity, we try to use words like *bright*, *snappy*, or *lively*. Technically, when coffee professionals use the word *acidity*, we aren't talking about the pH level, but the presence of particular acids that are the same as those in lemons, berries, vinegars, and other "lively" foods. All of that said, coffee professionals generally revere these compounds more than most of our customers do, so we have to be careful that we don't let acidity become the primary driver in our decision to buy a coffee.

BRAZIL

As the world's largest coffee producer, Brazil is responsible for a lot of the stuff that comes in cans; it's also had a huge role in the evolution of espresso, traditionally a humble blend of Brazilian beans. But in our buying trips to Brazil, we are seeing a new generation of farmers, often second- or third-generation farmers, who are studying coffee roasting and service in Europe and the United States, cupping intensively, and producing high-quality coffees that will be widely sought out as vibrant and distinctive single-origin coffees, not just beans that serve as a pleasant base in an espresso blend.

Coffee was first planted in Brazil in the eighteenth century, and commercial cultivation began in the 1800s around São Paulo. Early plantations relied on slave labor and then immigrant (almost-slave) labor after slavery was officially outlawed. The rapid growth of Brazilian coffee farming in the nineteenth century, which caused massive deforestation, also led to Brazil's near domination of the market. The country produced 80 percent of the world's coffee for a time in the early 1900s, a number that has since fallen to around 30 percent. Coffee played a huge role in the industrialization of Brazil.

So much of the style and character of Brazilian coffee is about its processing—the pulped natural method that's native to Brazil. Because of the large scale of production, reliable weather, and lack of shade canopy, in the early days most Brazilian coffee was dry processed, and there is still a lot of dry processing in Brazil. But pulped natural processing has been an important part of Brazil's relationship with espresso, which came into fashion in Italy in the postwar years, when all the country had access to was low-grade dry-processed Brazilian coffee and rubbery-tasting robusta from North Africa. The pulped natural process turned out to be a preferable form of processing because it tends to create a heavier body and to mute acidity, adding a sweetness and refinement typically not present in dry-processed Brazilian coffees. In the 1980s, spurred on by large companies like Illy, even more coffee farms began to use pulped natural processing to get a more consistent product geared toward espresso extraction.

When the Cup of Excellence (COE) auction (see page 34) launched in Brazil in 1999, it helped spur a subculture of attention to the highest-quality coffee. Over the last decade, COE has rewarded farmers for diligently cupping and separating the best coffees into microlots to get the best prices. A meticulous domestic café culture is still in its infancy there, and the vast majority of the better-quality beans are still exported. However, since Brazil's economy is rapidly growing, more of the best Brazilian coffee is consumed internally. Interestingly, it is illegal to import non-Brazilian coffee into Brazil, so the range of coffees the increasingly affluent internal market can enjoy is limited by law. It remains to be seen how that will affect the growth of high-end cafés in Brazil.

Certified organic farming is still very rare for Brazilian coffee. Because almost all of the Brazilian coffee Blue Bottle buys is organic, we tend to deal with a tiny subset of farms that we've grown to appreciate over the years.

BRAZILIAN CUP CHARACTERISTICS The majority of Brazilian coffee is grown at 1,800 to 4,000 feet (550 to 1,220 m). As a result, Brazilian coffee tends to have a softer, more muted flavor than those grown at higher elevations, and this quality is heightened by natural and pulped natural processing. It has a lovely, round, gentle quality and is rarely strident. It has sweetness—molasses and sugary tones—without many fruity notes. Good Brazilian coffee is comforting, likable, and seldom polarizing.

VARIETALS: In addition to classic varietals, such as Bourbon and Typica, Brazilian hybrids include Icatu, which tends to have low acidity and chocolate flavors; Mundo Novo, which is sweet and has high yields; and Catuaí, which has a brighter flavor.

THE LEGACY OF SUMATRA

Owing to the influence of Peet's Coffee, a lot of coffee drinkers, especially in Northern California, adore woody, peaty coffees from Indonesia and particularly from Sumatra. Early on in establishing Blue Bottle, I decided to not offer a single-origin Sumatran coffee because I realized that no one would buy anything else! So much of the cup character comes out of the processing that it is hard to find lots that have enough character to offer as single-origin coffees.

Instead, at Blue Bottle we love the deep cello-section notes of clean Sumatran coffees and rely on them to provide the depth that we like in our espresso and brewed coffee blends. However, for the last few years, we've been roasting single-origin coffees from a project in the Toraja region of Sumatra's nearby neighbor Sulawesi. These coffees are fully washed and have so much brightness and so much depth that they overpower a delicately calibrated blend. Plus, they really need to stand on their own to be appreciated.

EL SALVADOR

In El Salvador, coffee growing has a violent history that began in the late nineteenth century, when foreigners took over lands from native peoples. During the Salvadoran Civil War, from 1980 to 1992, the guerrilla movement was driven in part by the plight of exploited farm workers. A lot was lost during the war, but some people theorize that one result of the turmoil was preservation of more of the old coffee varietals that might otherwise have vanished. Because the war went on for twelve years, farms didn't have a chance to modernize, so they continued to grow many of the old varietals.

One of the qualities that keeps me coming back to great coffee from El Salvador is substantial body that doesn't overshadow the complex flavors. I love the juxtaposition of density and vitality in the best Salvadoran coffees.

As in most coffee-growing regions, the majority of the coffee farms in El Salvador are at lower elevations and produce commodity-grade coffee. However, El Salvador does have reasonably good infrastructure at high elevations, decent access to the deepwater Pacific port of Acajutla, great microclimates, and farmers dedicated to preserving the delicious but lower-yield Bourbon and Pacas varietals. These factors come together to create some of my favorite coffees.

EL SALVADORAN CUP CHARACTERISTICS What I love about great coffees from El Salvador is the way their complexity and sweetness is meshed with a heavy, silky body.

Blue Bottle is lucky to be able to obtain a small amount of a beautiful coffee from El Majahual, in the Los Naranjos region in El Salvador, managed by Aida Batlle (see page 35). It tends to have has notes of brown sugar and sometimes plum, butter, and toffee—a complex cup that's tangy and has a long molasses finish. When we're at the farm at the right time, we can often get El Majahual beans in as many as four different processing types: washed, dried, pulped natural, and the variation of the wet-hulling process Aida calls "Sumalvador."

VARIETALS: Key varietals grown in El Salvador are Bourbon, Typica, and Pacas. Pacas is a Bourbon mutation that has a bright flavor with floral characteristics and a heavy body.

Farmer Profile: Lorie Obra, Hawaii

Since so much of the world's coffee is grown in faraway countries, at Blue Bottle we've been excited to have the chance to work with a coffee grower in our own backyard, so to speak. Lorie Obra of Rusty's Hawaiian, a 12-acre (4.9-hectare) farm on the Big Island's southern edge, has experimented extensively with processing to produce some truly astonishing results. I visited Rusty's in the past and recently decided to go back to learn more about the farm's growing and processing methods.

Rusty's is located on the slopes of the Mauna Loa volcano in the Big Island's Ka`u District, about 60 miles (97 km) from the Kona coffee region. At about 2,000 feet (610 m), the farm is at a relatively high elevation by Hawaiian standards.

Lorie is part of a group of Ka`u coffee growers who are building the region's reputation. She and her late husband, Rusty, founded the farm in 1999 after relocating from New Jersey, where they had worked as a medical technologist and a chemist. They wanted to be near Rusty's parents, who used to work for a sugar plantation that dominated the area until it closed in 1996. Lorie said they originally thought they might open a Dunkin' Donuts franchise or a bed and breakfast—until they visited a friend's new coffee farm, part of an initiative to convert abandoned sugar fields to coffee growing. As she reports, "We saw the farm and the trees loaded with red-ripe cherries. Without even saying anything to each other, we knew deep in our minds and in our hearts that this was what we were going to do."

The couple secured their lease on a lot on the southern slope of Mauna Loa, surrounded by mountains and wild sugarcane and with a wide view south toward the Pacific. Using seedlings donated from family friends in Kona and Ka`u, and mostly volunteer labor, they planted seven thousand trees over 9 acres (3.6 hectares). Since the closest mill was in Kona, they decided to do the processing themselves, which meant buying specialty equipment, including a pulper, a huller, and even a small roaster. Because both had a background in science and had worked in laboratories, they were aware of all of the variables that might affect quality and wanted to control everything.

Soon, Rusty was approached by other new coffee farmers to head up the growing Ka`u Coffee Growers Cooperative. Grower William Tabios confided to Rusty that he didn't think he could make it as a farmer. Rusty assured him that good times were ahead. Sure enough, in 2007 the Specialty Coffee Association of America ranked Tabios's beans sixth-best in the world, and he and other Ka`u growers, including Lorie, have continued to receive that type of recognition.

Unfortunately, Rusty didn't live to see the progress of the cooperative or his own farm. Diagnosed with cancer, he urged Lorie to get rid of the farm because he thought it would be

too hard for her to carry on by herself. When he died in 2006, she wasn't able to find someone to take over the farm's lease, and she managed to keep the operation going.

In 2008, the owner of their land brought in several coffee experts to meet with the Ka`u growers, including roast master R. Miguel Meza, of Paradise Coffee Roasters in Ramsey, Minnesota. Miguel became Lorie's mentor, and she started sending green coffee samples to him back in Minnesota, representing different processing times, down to the number of hours of fermentation.

Soon thereafter, Miguel moved to Hawaii to work for Hula Daddy Kona Coffee in Kona and began visiting Lorie on the weekends, helping her identify her trees and conduct more experiments and teaching her how to cup. Demand for her coffee increased, and Lorie was still doing everything, from picking to shipping. Fortunately, her daughter, Joan Obra, and son-in-law, Ralph Gaston, both journalists, decided to move out from California to help her with the farm. Miguel also relocated to Ka`u, and soon Pete Licata, a U.S. barista champion, soon joined them. In addition to running Rusty's, they also are partners in Isla Coffee, a company that develops custom lots of coffee by working with farmers in Hawaii, Taiwan, and elsewhere.

Rusty's has won numerous honors that have helped Lorie sell a lot more coffee, and she thinks that they would make Rusty happy. "His vision was to bring Ka`u coffee up alongside other great coffees of the world," said Lorie, who has a bracelet tattoo with Rusty's name set inside a lei of coffee leaves and cherries. "I want to be a part of this Ka`u coffee revolution and bring Ka`u coffee up there. I have strived very hard to attain that."

Hawaiian coffee is relatively expensive, primarily because labor costs are high compared to elsewhere in the world. But when you see the high-quality production at Rusty's, the cost seems reasonable. Lorie tells her pickers to select only the cherries with full color, similar to selecting the best strawberries at the farmers' market. She doesn't want those that are green, half ripe, or browns (which means overripe).

One person working to Lorie's standards can pick about 12 pounds (5.5 kg) of ripe cherries per hour, enough to produce about 2 pounds (0.9 kg) of finished roasted coffee. On top of that, add the several hours of processing that goes into each batch.

"Hawaiian coffee is not overpriced," says Miguel. "It's just the rest of the world's coffee is undervalued."

Each year Rusty's produces about 1 pound (0.45 kg) of green coffee from each of its roughly six thousand trees (they have thinned the orchard since the initial planting). Most of the farm is devoted to four varietals: Guatemala Typica, Yellow Caturra, Red Caturra, and Red Bourbon. Harvest in their part of Ka`u, called Cloud Rest, usually lasts from November to May, but Lorie can purchase fresh coffee cherries from other Ka`u growers most of the rest of the year, depending on their elevation. Lorie personally processes all of the cherries—from her own farm or other farms—using her methods and high standards.

After the cherries are picked, they go to Lorie's house in Pahala, a small town about ten minutes down the mountain from the farm, for processing. Processing always begins on the same day as harvest, which means Lorie—and often Miguel, Pete, Joan, and Ralph—tend to work late for eight to ten months of the year.

Lorie varies her processing methods depending on the varietal, weather, and customer demand. The first step she takes for any processing method is to "float" the cherries, which means to immerse them in water, a common practice in the industry. Any cherries that float to the top are removed because they contain low-density beans that didn't develop well and will lack flavor and sweetness. Then, unlike many of her competitors, Lorie and the rest of the crew meticulously sort through the remaining cherries to discard any that are overripe or underripe, or that simply aren't the perfect shade of full red or yellow. After sorting, Lorie begins processing.

PROCESSING

Like most people in the coffee trade, Lorie uses wet processing most often. To begin, she pours the cherries into her pulper and uses a garden hose to spray water through the machine. The machine removes the skin from the cherries, spitting out coffee beans covered in sticky pulp. She transfers the slippery, slimy beans into buckets filled with cold water and leaves them to ferment overnight. After much trial and error, she has found that about eight to ten hours of fermentation is the right amount of time for her coffee; it also gives her a little time to sleep.

In the morning, the beans sit in a thick brownish soup. Using a pool pump, Lorie sucks out the liquid and rinses the beans with fresh water. At this stage, the pulp has separated and the beans, which have a gritty, sandpapery feel, are spread on waist-high wire drying racks set up around Lorie's yard, each with a corrugated vinyl cover that can be deployed when it rains. The beans dry in the sun for five to eight days.

For dry, or natural, processing, Lorie spreads the cherries on the drying racks immediately after sorting and lets them dry until they reach a moisture level of 10 to 11 percent; typically three weeks. The amount of time depends on the weather. To prevent mold and unwanted fermentation, Lorie rakes the cherries frequently during drying. During the third through fifth day, when the skins have turned leathery and are no longer fragile, she rakes the cherries as often as once per hour.

For pulped natural processing, after the cherries have been pulped, they are spread on the racks to dry. During the first day they must be raked every twenty minutes for even drying and to prevent mold from developing. Joan often sets up her laptop in the backyard so she can work between rakings. After that, they need to be raked only twice per day, and the full drying period is about five to ten days, depending on the weather.

FINAL STEPS

After wet, dry, or pulped natural processing, the beans are placed in special bags in a shed. Wet-processed and pulped natural beans are stored for three months, and dry-processed beans are stored for four to five months. As Lorie says, "My coffees need their beauty sleep." Miguel explains that this extra step prevents the coffee from having a grassy, astringent flavor.

In all cases, the goal is to have the beans roasted within nine months of picking. When the beans are ready to ship, they go through the hulling machine, which removes the parchment, and then they are sorted to remove small and defective beans. After sorting, the green coffee is inspected and certified by the Hawaii Department of Agriculture and shipped or flown to customers. One big advantage for customers in the United States is that Rusty's shipments don't have to go through customs, unlike coffee from other parts of the world, and this greatly speeds delivery.

THE CUP OF EXCELLENCE

When you look at the big shift that has happened in the coffee world over the past decade, the Cup of Excellence (COE) has been an influential part of it. Now the world's most prestigious international coffee auction, it was created in 1999 when a group of roasters wanted to improve access to great coffee from previously unknown growers.

The COE has been instrumental in building worldwide awareness of the distinctiveness of single-origin coffees. The high prices even for the lower-placing lots (which are often still beautiful and rarefied coffees) allow coffee farmers to see that there is a market for quality coffee. As opposed to charity-based programs, the COE is a quality-based program where the rewards are greater in accordance with the caliber of the coffee.

The vast majority of coffee growers around the world bring their coffee to a central mill for processing, where it gets mixed with other coffees from the same region. With COE, which aims to find the best coffees from specific member countries in annual competitions, any farmer can enter his or her coffee beans, no matter how small the operation. Since the first competition in Brazil, it's increased to eleven countries, mostly in Central and South America.

After farmers send in their samples for consideration in a COE competition, the coffees are cupped five or six times, first by a national jury composed of residents of the country, then by an international jury of mostly coffee roasters. The winners are ranked, with the first through third getting the most attention, and then all of the coffees are placed in an online auction. Interested bidders receive samples of green coffee before the auction.

Blue Bottle bought its first COE lot in 2006, the year we began bidding. We now usually bid in four to six COE auctions a year and hope to get at least one lot in most of them. Lot sizes vary from year to year and country to country, but often the lots are quite small—around 2,000 pounds (900 kg). When we cup the samples we're considering for bidding, we list the coffees by farm name and not numerical ranking, so we don't know how they placed in the competition. More often than not, there are one or two coffees that we absolutely adore, and it's up to our green coffee buyer to juggle the often competing demands of cash flow and desire when the Internet auction begins. Coffee buyers from all over the world sit down simultaneously at their computers and bid on their favorite lots. A single lot of coffee has been priced at over $100,000. (Interestingly, if that lot would have been sold on the commodity market that year, it would have sold for $7,500.) So in many cases, roasters bid together rather than take the whole lot. We have the disadvantage of being one of the smaller coffee companies bidding on entire lots, and paying in dollars instead of yen works against us as well. Sometimes we get our hearts broken when we're outbid on a particular favorite, but we usually luck into a few great lots every year. I expect that as we grow, we'll be able to buy, roast, and serve more of our favorite COE coffees.

COE means great coffee, and the COE logo is something our customers now look for. Also, COE auctions are a great way to get employees excited and involved. Once the samples are roasted, we have open cuppings, with side-by-side tasting of the various samples, for all our employees. Then we feature a smaller subset of our favorite lots at public cuppings. Usually the coffees will have a common thread that lets people start to get a handle on "Brazil-ness" or "Rwanda-ness," even though there's a lot of diversity among the submissions from any given country.

Farmer Profile: Aida Batlle, El Salvador

When you can trace your family's coffee growing lineage back four generations, it might seem predetermined that you will become a coffee farmer. But when Aida Batlle was six, she and her family fled El Salvador to escape its civil war, and she grew up in the United States.

In the summer of 2002, Aida, who had settled in Nashville, went to El Salvador to visit her parents, who had previously moved back to oversee the family's coffee farms. Coffee prices were at their lowest point in many years, and her father seemed overwhelmed. Suddenly she knew she was going uproot her life in the United States and become a farmer. "My parents looked at me like I was crazy," she says.

Aida wanted to learn as much as she could about the coffee trade, so she started attending lectures and sought help from the Salvadoran Coffee Council. She heard about the Cup of Excellence and decided to enter coffee from two of their three main farms in the first El Salvador COE, which took place in 2003. She was shocked when one of their entries won first place.

Before their COE win, her family had never cupped its own coffees or even tasted them. Aida became the first woman to win first place in a COE and her coffee's price—$14.06 a pound for green coffee—also set a record. Aida had quickly become one of the world's most celebrated coffee growers.

Aida now is in charge of the family's four farms (three of them named for places in Africa): Tanzania, located at 4,180 to 4,530 feet (1,275 to 1,380 m); Mauritania, at 4,590 to 5,250 feet (1,400 to 1,600 meters); Los Alpes, at 5,085 to 6,150 feet (1,550 to 1,875 m); and Kilimanjaro, at 5,185 to 5,645 feet (1,580 to 1,720 meters). Aida is also a consultant and oversees picking, sorting, and overall quality of the lots she chooses at two other farms, El Majahual in Los Naranjos, at 4,920 feet (1,500 m), and Plan de Batea in Cerro Verde, at 4,590 to 4,920 feet (1,400 to 1,500 m).

When she took over the farms, Aida instituted organic practices right away and got organic certification in 2005. Farming organically results in a significantly lower yield than conventional farming and so does using older varietals, which are also more susceptible to disease. Yet Aida has stayed loyal to traditional varietals, such as Bourbon, which her great-great-grandfather first introduced to El Salvador. The Mauritania farm grows all Bourbon, Kilimanjaro has mostly Kenya and Bourbon, Los Alpes has Typica and Bourbon, and Tanzania, a newer addition to the family farms, has almost all Bourbon.

"In El Salvador in this day and age, it's hard to stick with the older varietals with the cost of production being as high as it is, and if you're not in the market to have direct trade with a roaster, you depend on an exporter or mill to sell your cherries to," says Aida, who started Aida Batlle Selections to help connect other quality local growers to roasters.

People in the industry who have visited Kilimanjaro have said its Kenya (spelled Kenia locally) coffee trees might be the prized African varietal known as an SL-28, based on its cup profile and the way the plant looks, though Aida has never had the trees tested. Kilimanjaro was one of the only farms in the area with Kenya trees, and some of the trees were uprooted and stolen during Aida's first COE.

Aida has a farm manager for each of the farms, and each farm employs at least ten people year-round, plus seasonal pickers. After the coffee is harvested, the mill sends a truck to pick up the cherries. Aida or a staff member is constantly on site to monitor the processing. She is always looking to experiment, mostly based on suggestions from customers.

One of her innovative practices is offering customers something like a menu, with the same coffees processed several different ways. Each experiment is very small, using about 25 pounds (11.3 kg) of cherries, which amounts to about 5 pounds (2.3 kg) of beans, and customers have to preorder. Aida doesn't allow her coffees to be blended with those from other farms, and the only blend she offers is called Aida's Grand Reserve, a mix of peaberry coffees (see page 15) from three of the family's farms.

After Solberg & Hansen of Oslo, Norway, purchased Aida's first-place COE lot back in 2003, she went to visit the café so she could see her coffees in the cup. She had never seen latte art and was intrigued. "I can do everything perfectly, the exporter can do everything right, and so can the importer and then the roaster. But really everything hangs on the barista," says Aida, who later received barista certification from the Barista Guild of America to deepen her knowledge of what happens to her coffee after it leaves the farm. It is this kind of attention to detail that continues to earn her reverence from the international coffee community.

Farmers such as Aida and Lorie set an impressive standard. Their care and dedication is abundantly evident in the coffee. And when coffee comes into our roastery in such good condition, we realize that the only people who can ruin the farmer's excellent work is us. So we try to stay inspired by their example and pour all of the resourcefulness and care that we can summon into making something delicious. In the next chapter, I'll explain what we do to turn their agricultural product—green coffee beans—into a memorable and compelling beverage.

WHAT IT TAKES TO BE ORGANIC

Almost 85 percent of the coffee we roast at Blue Bottle is certified organic, and our roasteries are certified organic too. Organic certification is expensive, cumbersome, and bureaucratic, both for farmers and at our roasteries. So why do we think it's worthwhile? It's not just about pesticides.

At the farm level, the downsides to organic certification are high cost, limitations placed on water treatment, and first-world bureaucratic expectations placed on third-world environments. But the positive impact of a successful organic program is undeniable: authentic documentation of the coffee's cleanliness and sustainability at every step in its journey from seedling to cup. For coffee to be certified organic, all of the elements of the entire chain, from farm to washing station to shipper to holding warehouse to roastery, is regularly inspected, and the scrutiny extends far beyond just measurable pesticide residues. Practices examined and documented include environmentally correct water treatment at the farm, not using chemical-based cleaning supplies, and not using genetically modified (GMO) seeds, to name just a few.

Even when small farmers can't afford the steep fees for organic certification, they can adopt organic practices. This is where having a direct relationship with growers is invaluable. Even though Blue Bottle's priority is to use certified organic coffee in our blends and as many of our single-origin coffees as possible, the most important criteria is purchasing single-origin coffees from farmers we admire and whose practices we respect. That said, we do mention that we will happily pay more for the coffee if the farmer progresses toward organic certification.

If a roaster buys certified organic coffee but hasn't gotten the roastery certified, then he or she can't call it organic. Is that fair? Well, yes. If a roaster uses toxic cleansers, doesn't clean equipment properly between batches, or isn't keeping adequate records to assure that certified organic coffee is consistently present, measurable residues can be introduced into previously clean coffee. I'm always leery when I hear baristas in other shops describe a coffee as "better than organic" or "as good as organic" because it implies that there's some kind of sliding scale within organic certification. There isn't. Coffee is either certified organic or it's not. All of us along the chain work very hard to keep our records perfect and our environment clean in exchange for the privilege of showing a seal that demonstrates an unbroken chain of inspection and quality all the way back to the coffee seedling.

ROAST

After coffee is painstakingly cultivated, harvested, processed, rested, shipped, cleared through customs, delivered to the contract warehouse, and finally arrives at one of Blue Bottle's roasteries, we get a chance to open a bag and roast it. If it's a coffee we have cupped—the industry term for an evaluative tasting—and selected at its origin, we are especially excited to see how it has traveled. First we roast samples of the coffee using a variety of roast levels and roasting profiles using our tiny Probat sample roasters, which have a capacity of 0.5 pound (227 g). We cup all of the variations over several days, and once we have a consensus about which roast profile we are most excited about, given the intended context for the coffee, we pass the beans on to the roasting team. It's their job to bring out everything we discovered in the samples and then add gravitas and dignity, like a great actor bringing an interesting role to life. The production roast illuminates the coffee in unexpected ways, so we never know exactly how the combination of skilled human labor and old gear—in the form of our vintage roasters—is going to manifest, but the results are always distinctive and personal.

Roasting is all about choosing your recipe to determine the flavor profile of the beans. Not to romanticize it, though that temptation is always there, the beans are taken on a journey. As we take these steps, we imagine qualities that we're attempting to bring out or suppress in the roasting.

Roasting begins with the tools we choose. I started out roasting coffee at home on a perforated baking sheet in the oven. It created a lot of smoke, so I had to wait until my ex-wife (who was a singing teacher and therefore had certain needs regarding her household air supply) was out of the house. I loved the taste of the coffee I got from roasting at home. At the time (the late 1990s), commercial coffee roasters didn't indicate the roast date on the bag, and I became obsessed with how the coffee I roasted at home would change as the days progressed. That coffee was palpably different on the third day after roasting compared to the fourth—imagine! This was before the Internet was ubiquitous and methodically took the joy out of personal discoveries like these, so I felt like an explorer. The pleasure I got from coffee I roasted myself was uncanny.

When I was first thinking about starting a coffee roasting business, I imagined setting it up in my Oakland backyard—building an adobe oven that would house a perforated metal drum, heated by a separate firebox. I thought I had it all figured out: where I would store the wood, what to use for the drum (the enamel-coated steel drum of a KitchenAid clothes dryer), how the oven would work, and how the roasted beans would cool. I bought books on constructing an adobe oven. I found a source for ceramic flue piping, I sketched plans, and I made shopping lists. I wanted the rotation of the drum to be powered by a series of gears and chains that could be attached either to a bicycle or a treadmill, the latter so my German shepherd, Ivy, could power the roaster. This was a serious plan—as serious as anything I had ever thought about. I was captivated by it. I would go for a run around Lake Merritt with Ivy, and I could feel it: standing outside in my backyard, building a fire, taking turns with Ivy on the treadmill, showing up at Whole Foods Market or a farmers' markets in my Peugeot wagon filled with coffee, and saying, "Voilà! Here is the coffee that you've been waiting your whole life to buy."

It was frustrating when I found out that people thought this was a ridiculous plan. I called a woman I knew who worked for the planning department in Oakland, and she underscored that it was a ridiculous and illegal plan. My conversation with a fellow at the Alameda County Public Health Department was similar, except he wasn't as nice about it.

Undaunted, I bounded into the offices of Royal Coffee in Emeryville. Royal is one of the most respected coffee brokers in the United States. I was absolutely positive I would be hailed as an innovator. A dog-powered, wood-fired, backyard coffee roastery—genius! Oddly enough, I wasn't ushered ASAP into the office of the boss to expound on my brilliant idea. There was, however, a very nice, understanding man who apparently had a lot of experience dealing with crazy people. After I told him my plan, he fixed me with a kindly gaze and said,

"Maybe you should look into some of the commercial manufacturers of coffee roasters. There is a fine one located in Sandpoint, Idaho." I felt the air go out of my dog-powered roaster idea. A few days later, I booked a flight to Spokane, rented a car, drove to Sandpoint, and, by the weekend of the Westminster dog show, was learning how to roast on the Diedrich IR-7 from none other than Stephen Diedrich himself.

When I meet people now and they tell me about their insane or terrible plans for starting a food business, I recognize that look. It was my look. I know that soon enough someone from the Alameda County Public Health Department or other such entity will come into their lives and burst their bubble, so I try to be understanding. I nod my head and smile and let them tell me about their ridiculous plans.

At Blue Bottle, we now roast in older drum roasters made by the German company Probat in the 1950s. I like old gear—old espresso machines, old bass clarinets, old opa-scopes, old stereos—but I may like old coffee roasters best. There is something humbling about using an

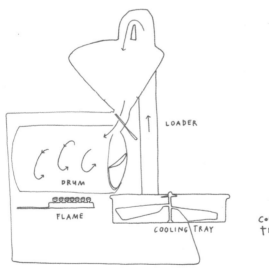

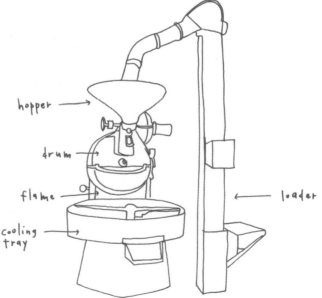

industrial machine that has been operating almost continuously since the 1950s. It reminds me that good workers have been roasting good coffee on simple, durable machines for a long time. We don't get up any earlier, we don't work any harder, and we aren't any smarter, funnier, or happier than all of the people who have been using this machine over the last sixty years. Like the roasters before us, we are trying to make a delicious product on this big, simple machine.

When using a drum roaster, in which coffee beans spin in a metal drum as they are roasted, there are two basic ways of heating the beans: conduction or convection. Conduction is the transfer of heat between matter: when beans touch the warm roasting drum or when warm beans touch other beans, raising their temperature. In convection, heated air moves through the mass, heating the beans. Both types are present at all times; however, depending on the stage of the roast and the type of coffee, the roaster chooses which type of heat to emphasize.

People often think about roasting in terms of how the color of the beans changes. Yes, the coffee changes color when it's roasted—from green to yellow to various degrees of brown—but how that color is arrived at determines the flavor of the coffee. If you cook a whole chicken at 700°F (371°C) and pull it out of the oven after 7 1/2 minutes, it's going to be dark on the outside and raw on the inside. The same thing can happen with coffee.

During roasting, the heat dries out the beans and converts starches into sugars. Although this process is usually referred to as either the Maillard reaction or caramelization, interchangeably, the two are really quite different. The Maillard reaction is the type of reaction that causes meat to brown or colors the crust on bread. It involves a reaction between sugar molecules and amino acids and produces more savory umami flavors than sweetness. Caramelization occurs at higher temperatures than the Maillard reaction and involves only sugar molecules. Paradoxically, increased caramelization results in decreasing sweetness but increasing complexity.

In terms of coffee roasting, we're hoping to hit that spot where the coffee will still be sweet but with a pleasantly savory and bitter complexity starting to develop. Undershooting that point by a little will result in coffee that's bland but sweet. Undershooting it even more allows astringent, sour, grassy notes to remain, a quality coffee professionals refer to as underdeveloped. Overshooting the spot we are aiming at emphasizes the toastiness of the coffee flavors, much the same way that slightly too much time in the toaster makes the character of different types of bread hard to distinguish from each other. Even more time in the roaster will emphasize the carbon flavors of coffee, like the way the char of burned steak overpowers the taste of the meat inside.

The important thing to remember is that the roaster chooses this optimum point of flavor development. It isn't an objective decision, despite the school of thought that there are intrinsic qualities locked in coffee that roasters merely illuminate—that we are blessed with a privileged insight into some truth of coffee that others can't hope to understand—like David somehow locked in that piece of marble, and Michelangelo chipping away to find him. But I don't think that's true. Roasting is, by definition, manipulation. While the quality of the raw materials helps determine the quality of the finished product, roasting is about making choices: which qualities in a coffee do you want to highlight, and which do you want to suppress? When I cup our coffee, I think about pleasure and context: Is this coffee delicious and interesting? Are we bringing out an appropriate flavor for the context intended for it? Have we failed to elicit something potentially appealing?

In this chapter, I'll explain the steps involved in commercial coffee roasting as we approach it at Blue Bottle. I'll also help you develop a hands-on appreciation for the process by explaining how you can roast coffee at home, using a method that is almost primitive in its simplicity. Then I'll help you become even more intimate with your coffee by doing what roasters do every day: cupping.

At Blue Bottle, we make coffee at the roastery in almost every sense of the word "make," but the coffee is also making us. That act of ontological transformation initiated by drinking coffee, especially drinking coffee that we have roasted, is central to what we do and how we think. We, and thousands of our customers, expect our coffee to be delicious. But coffee is also transformative—it makes us smarter, healthier, funnier, more charming. If it's a drug, then it is the *best* drug. Good coffee makes us curious about pleasure. It makes us who we wish to be.

Roasting Day

The roasting day starts early. Coffee is an *ante meridiem* business and usually starts in the dark. At Blue Bottle's roasteries, the roasters arrive before anyone else—before the janitors, the delivery drivers, the baristas, or the accountants. It's hard to get up at 4 a.m. It's something that never gets easy. For me, no matter when I got to bed, I always felt a sense of dread when the alarm went off at 4 a.m. Classic Kierkegaard, straight out of *The Concept of Anxiety*: animals are slaves to their instincts and hence feel no responsibility, but humans are free and therefore constantly aware of their failure to live up to their responsibilities to God—or to Coffee. When the alarm goes off at 4 a.m. and your body is crying out in the dark for more sleep, that feeling of anxiety and responsibility can immobilize you or animate you. Every working morning, roasters choose to animate their terrible feelings of anxiety, dread, and responsibility and face the daunting task of roasting coffee. That first decision to get up in the morning is a mirror of all the hard and lonely decisions that must be made for the rest of the roasting day.

Four a.m. There's a reason Bergman called it the hour of the wolf. But we need to get coffee roasted, and this is how we do it.

STARTING THE DAY

At 5 a.m., you arrive at the roastery. Maybe another roaster is already there, maybe not. It's quiet—as quiet as the place will be for the next twelve hours. And cold. The first thing to do is turn on the roaster. The switches are a little newer than the Probat itself, which was built in the 1950s, in a retro-industrial style, almost like something in a Wes Anderson movie. The switches are cold to the touch and difficult to turn. Every morning that seems surprising. The first switch turns on the motor that drives the roasting drum, and the second one turns on the gas.

When you throw the first switch, there's a juddering as the speed of the drum catches up to with the speed of the motor. That's the first moment of uncertainty in a day filled with moments of uncertainty. After a few seconds, the juddering calms down to a quiet, rhythmic hum, like an old clothes dryer. It's comforting, and feels like sipping hot chocolate on a cold, blustery day while waiting for your jeans to dry.

When you throw the second switch, there's an insistent and suspenseful clicking for twenty to forty seconds and you wonder if this is the morning the pilot won't light the burners. But then the burners light, just like they did yesterday, and just like they will tomorrow. There's a reassuring whoosh that brings the first small satisfaction of the day—the roaster is on.

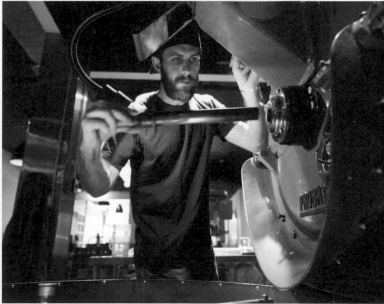

WARMING UP THE ROASTER

Next, the roaster needs to heat up. At Blue Bottle, our roasters are simple machines. Imagine a drum much like the one inside a clothes dryer, powered by an electrical motor and rotating over an open flame fueled by natural gas. Hot air moves through the drum and is vented out the back (see page 43). The drum is made of cast iron and is heavy. It has so much thermal mass that it usually takes thirty to forty minutes to reach the roasting temperature, depending on how cold the day is. But if you're standing next to it, you can feel a little heat radiating outward within a few minutes. To me, it always feels soothing but tentative, maybe like prehistoric wolves felt inching closer and closer to the caveman's fires.

Once you're satisfied that the roaster is turning and heating up, it's time to make a cup of coffee. Now you're faced with another key decision: Choose a coffee from yesterday's roast that you're concerned about? Or choose a coffee that will be reassuring? The best scenario is to choose a coffee that you're worried about and have it be glorious. The worst is to seek reassurance from a coffee that you thought you nailed yesterday and have it raise more questions than it settles. Is the flavor flat? Not sweet enough? Once again, we suffer at the hands of our own choices. Regardless, coffee must be made.

While you wait for the machines to warm up and drink your cup of coffee, you review the roasting sheet. The office took orders for coffee yesterday and entered them in the computer. The coffee will be roasted today and delivered tomorrow morning. You look at that sheet and think about which coffee you're going to roast in which roaster and when; you want to start by roasting the components for blends, so the baggers can work on them when they come in at 8 or 9 a.m. Maybe you'll do a batch of Sumatra for a brewed-coffee blend, or a Brazilian coffee for an espresso blend—something you know really well. You drink your coffee. You start doing the math and start weighing out batches in buckets. You check the samples from the day before: look at them, smell them, and finally pop a few beans in your mouth and crunch them like cocktail peanuts. The cupping will come later, when more people arrive for work. For now, this taste of crunchy coffee beans is the second indication of how well things went yesterday. Are the beans tasty? Fragrant? Promising? You look at notes from the day before, and if someone else was roasting, you learn something about that person's state of mind. Was the machine making a funny sound? Were they having difficulties? Were they nailing it?

LOADING THE MACHINE

Now the machine is up to temperature and ready to roast. This is the exciting part. You pick up the bucket with the first batch of beans and send it up the loader. Much like a miniature grain elevator, the loader mechanically moves the green beans up to the hopper and then deposits the beans into the drum. You press a button and slide a slider that separates the hopper from the drum, then the sound of the machine goes from fairly quiet to louder and more rhythmic.

According to baby books, the womb is noisy place. There's a loud rhythmic churning, a swooshing kind of white noise. Yet what increases the baby's stress levels (again, according to the baby books) isn't the noise or the churning, but arrhythmic moments of quiet. The Probat turns at about sixty-two rotations per minute. That's a human rhythm—a lot of hearts beat at that speed, my own included. Once green coffee goes in the roaster, there's a repeated, rhythmic whooshing that's relaxing. Roasters internalize this peaceful noise and rhythm, and anxiety increases when it disappears. You live in dread of these moments of quiet—moments that tell you something bad might be happening or is just about to happen. But in the early morning hours, before anyone starts the stereo, before the bagging machines get turned on, before the forklift is running, the espresso machines steam milk, or the janitor power washes the sidewalk, that's what you hear—the womb.

The beans roast through a combination of conductive heat (contacting the drum and each other) and convective heat (the flow of warm air through the drum). In the process, the beans gradually lose water content and begin to undergo chemical reactions, their precise nature determined by the amount of heat, air, and moisture. You know where you want this coffee to go, so you set the timer and then take notes, recording batch size, varietal, and other crucial details.

Earlier in the day, the drop temperature—the internal temperature of the roaster when you drop the coffee into the drum—will be a little higher than later in the day because of the lower air temperature in the warehouse in the morning and the huge thermal mass of the roaster itself. If the drop temp is too high, you'll scorch the beans when they are in a very vulnerable position—at cool room temperature and holding their maximum water content. Scorching robs the coffee of some of its vitality and thins the texture, so a drop temp that's too high is a bummer. But if the drop temp is too low, that's bad too. It can slow the roast to the point of flattening the flavor. In effect, the coffee bakes and steams in a humid environment, rather than roasting.

For every varietal, you want to find the drop temp that enhances the qualities that make that particular coffee special. For example, altitude can correlate with density, and denser, high-elevation coffees, say from Ethiopia, often taste better when roasted with a higher drop temperature. On the other hand, a lower-elevation coffee from Brazil can't take as much heat, so you would drop the Brazil at a lower temperature than the Ethiopian.

At Blue Bottle, when roasting coffee we are always thinking about how the coffee will be used. We roast espresso differently (not necessarily darker) than coffee we plan on brewing by pour over, for example. Coffee used in a blend is often roasted differently than the same coffee if we intend to use it by itself. How we determine those differences is the result of cupping the coffees, experiments in our lab, and feedback from baristas. Sometimes, we actually want a little less vitality from a coffee. For example, we tend to use Guatemalan coffees from co-ops in our espresso blends. These coffees are very dense, high-altitude coffees and have a lot of inherent vitality. Because the espresso extraction process can emphasize brightness to uncomfortable levels (think of warm grapefruit juice in your cappuccino), we roast those beans at a lower drop temp and for a longer time than if we were roasting them to be consumed as an unblended pour over. Note that the longer roasting time doesn't mean we're roasting the beans darker. The results of the two different roasting profiles could look exactly the same, but one might be perfect in an espresso, whereas the other would be much too sharp.

BOTTOMING OUT

Once the beans are loaded, you're waiting for the roaster temperature to bottom out, indicating completion of the first stage of the roast. The green coffee is at about the ambient temperature of the warehouse, usually around 60°F (16°C) in our unheated Oakland space. So the thermal mass of the coffee brings the much greater thermal mass of the roaster down from about 380°F (193°C) to its lowest point—usually 180°F to 190°F (82°C to 88°C), depending on the weather and batch size. The amount of time it takes to get to the lowest point tells you how much energy you'll need to put back into the coffee to get it though the roast. If you reach the lowest point at 2 1/2 minutes, that's a gentler curve than 1 1/2 minutes, which means that you are in danger of baking instead of roasting. You write down the time when the temperature bottomed out. (The key to being a good roaster is systematically doing three things: taking good notes, cupping your coffee, and cleaning your machine.)

Once the bean temperature hits the bottom of the curve, it's going to climb, and your job is to keep it from climbing too fast. If you put too much heat into it, that will suck air through the drum, drying the coffee too quickly. You want the temperature to rise smoothly and gradually to get to what's called first crack.

ARRIVING AT FIRST CRACK

First crack is the coffee roaster's term for a chemical reaction that occurs as coffee begins to reach the "drinkable" stage. Much like the chemical reaction that pops corn, the audible popping, increase in bean size, and decrease in bean density that occurs in coffee at that stage of the roast is the result of the moisture trapped in the coffee boiling off and forcing its way outside the coffee bean, rupturing the cell walls.

For the first few minutes of the roast, it looks like nothing is changing. But the beans are warming up, and soon the moisture will start to boil away. After 3 or 4 minutes, the small, hard, green coffee beans start to take on some color and smell like popcorn or warm, damp hay. It's a gentle, grassy, youthful aroma. This can be a great stage of the roast—if you're off to a good start. It's like having a smart four-year-old who is out of diapers but still almost all potential. It feels boundless and positive.

Because the coffee is steaming and losing water, it's important to make sure that air is moving through the drum, otherwise the humidity level in the drum can get too high. About 5 minutes into the roast, the coffee starts to turn yellow-gold. With some coffees, this is when you first smell attributes that you want to be able to taste in the finished product. At this point, you might pull the tryer, which allows you to get a sample of the beans inside the roaster, and smell them—just out of sheer pleasure, because it smells like something great is about to happen.

You're still applying a lot of heat, but you're starting to think ahead. You're going to have to walk a tightrope in a few minutes.

The temperature is still climbing, and the coffee is becoming an increasingly darker brown. It's starting to smell less like hay and toast and more like coffee. The beans are still kind of ugly and wrinkly but soon will puff up. First crack is an endothermic reaction, which means that it depends on the coffee absorbing heat, so you have to make sure you're still adding heat to the system. On the machines at our roasteries, with most of our coffees first crack happens at around 9 to 11 minutes in. If you've been careful, the beginning of first crack comes on subtly: a gentle pop or two, then nothing for a few seconds, then a few more pops—more often, louder, and more insistent.

Right around first crack is when the creativity of the roaster starts to matter. You start pulling the tryer more often, and you think about the profile you're aiming for and the last time you cupped this coffee. At Blue Bottle, the goal for most of our coffees is vitality: a strong, integrated personality that displays a perspective on the coffee that thrills us. The short period of time before, during, and after first crack—approximately 120 seconds total—is when we are most consumed with changes in roasting variables. We want the temperature of the coffee to continue to rise, but we want to manage the rate very carefully. If the temperature rises too quickly, momentum will carry the coffee past where we want it to be. But if there isn't enough heat, the temperature will stay the same for too long or, worse, fall, either of which can result in a coffee with a flat, boring flavor. At the beginning of the roast, we may allow the temperature to climb by 5°F (2.7°C) in 20 seconds, but toward the end we may tease the heat so that we add 5°F (2.7°C) over the course of 90 seconds, while still ensuring that the heat rises steadily, without stalling or leveling out. If we know we have decent momentum going into first crack, striking a balance between stalling and climbing helps us manage the tension between developing depth and maintaining sweetness.

SECOND CRACK

Second crack is the coffee roaster's term for the exothermic chemical reaction that occurs after first crack. As opposed to first crack, second crack produces its own heat, which can quickly sweep a roast past the point of being too dark. Any coffee labeled "French" or "Italian" roast is coffee that has most likely been roasted well into second crack. Depending on the type and quality of the green beans and the skill of the roaster, the coffee tastes more of toast, and perhaps carbon, than of its origin. Having said that, a generically "toasty" flavor profile is the object of a legitimate desire for a certain taste and even though we choose not to roast that darkly, we are never scornful of customers voicing a wish for a "French" roast.

DUMPING THE BATCH

After a patient and contemplative start, you need to finish the roast very succinctly. The momentum of the heat in the beans means you can't just set a target final temperature. You must account for the thermal mass and its momentum in deciding when to dump the batch. You have to bring maximum concentration to the task during the last 20 seconds of the roast, remaining alert to all of the sensory information that will inform your decision. You're looking for signs that the beans are plumped up, and beautiful aromas that remind you of the last great batch you cupped. At the same time, you try not to let pressure or indecision cause you to overthink and freeze. You want to drop the batch when your mind and body team up to say, "Now!" If you let your mind say, "But on the other hand . . . ," you've choked, and the coffee probably won't be what you were hoping for.

You dump the coffee, then click on the fan and agitator arm to speed the cooling of the coffee. You open the door and there's a puff of smoke. You feel the heat on your face. How the coffee looks and smells tells you a lot about whether the roast turned out how you'd hoped. The smell is the first cue: Did you nail it? If it smells like toast wafting down the hallway while you're still lying snug and warm in bed, mingled with the dregs of the glass of strawberry Quik you left on the bedside table the night before, the answer is a most emphatic yes. If you get a stronger scent of toast mingled with the pungent smell of inflatable pool toys on a hot day, or the briny hit of opening a can of low-end olives at a smoky party you probably don't want to be at in the first place, then you know you didn't do your best for that coffee. Even after it is dumped from the drum, the coffee continues to roast in the cooling tray until it cools down, for about the next 4 minutes, but that first smell doesn't lie.

As the agitator arm spins the beans around to cool them, the temperature near the roaster rises. You can feel the heat on your face as you walk around the roaster. The fan sounds different because the bearings are under less pressure and it changes the sound in the room. As we've discussed, the sonic environment is an important part of the roaster's sensory world.

When the bearings sing a different song—a song that is about there being no coffee in the drum—we roasters relax, knowing that on some level, we are free to concentrate less severely.

TAKING NOTES

Once the coffee is cool, you put it in a bin. Then you weigh it and compare its weight before and after roasting. Because roasting cooks out some of the water in the coffee, each batch loses about 13 to 18 percent of its weight. To determine the water loss for each batch, you subtract the roasted weight from the unroasted weight and divide that number by the unroasted weight. That's your percentage, and you write it down. Is it 14 percent or 14.5 percent? And if it was 14.8 percent yesterday, why is it different today? You keep track of all these numbers—the drop temp, the time to first crack, and percentage of water loss—so that, if this batch turns out great, other roasters can duplicate your results.

The beans for the next few batches have been weighed out, so you grab a bucket and pour it in the hopper. You turn up the heat and wait for the drum to reach the target drop temp before loading in the beans. Meanwhile, you empty the current batch into a tub, weigh it, drop in a label, and send it on its way. Next, it will go through a destoner, where any little bits of foreign matter (that is, stones, coins, bullet casings, bits of cement) are removed by vacuuming calibrated to pick up matter with the density of coffee, not the density of metal or rock. Then the baggers will put it bags, pack the bags in handsome gray totes, and load them in the delivery vans.

Tomorrow, that coffee will be cupped—by the roasters and by the training staff, by managers and lead baristas, by random visitors in the cupping room, and perhaps by the general public if that coffee gets into a public cupping. Everyone will methodically take notes on cupping forms. And when you arrive the next morning and make that first cup of coffee, perhaps you'll cup that coffee and revisit your notes to see how you did and whether you want to do anything differently.

FINISHING

If you're working the roaster for a long time, it's easy to forget that the coffee you're creating will go somewhere. You aren't engaged in a rote exercise or, like Sisyphus, forever rolling the same boulder uphill. The bags of coffee you create are going to take a trip in the next few days. They'll be delivered to the shops. People will buy some to take home or give as gifts (but hopefully not to put in the back of the freezer to "save" for a special occasion; see page 54 for more on this point). People will wake up in the dark and pad to their kitchen needing strength, and the reassurance that something delightful is about to happen—and hoping that this small chore of making coffee might set the tone for a day filled with difficult, wonderful things.

As a coffee roaster, your life is divided in roughly 17-minute segments—enough time to load the green coffee, roast it, dump it, cool it, and send it on its way. That means you have about twenty-five chances in an average day, 125 chances in a week, and 6,500 chances a year to make something beautiful.

ROASTED COFFEE'S SHORT LIFE SPAN

At Blue Bottle, every single day customers ask how they should store their coffee. And every day we tell them to buy a small amount, put the bag in a cool cupboard, and come back and buy more when they run out. Unless you go to a lot of trouble, freezing isn't an effective way of making coffee flavors last. The freezer is good at taking moisture out of an environment to prohibit bacterial growth. But we want the delicate balance of moisture in the coffee beans to remain! Also, water condensing on icy roasted coffee when it is pulled from the freezer gets reabsorbed into the beans, making them duller tasting. Coffee has a life span: after being roasted, it gets more interesting for up to nine days after roasting—fuller, more complex, and generally more enjoyable. After that time, there's an inevitable decline. Coffee oxidizes. The flavors become less vibrant, and eventually the coffee tastes dull. It's stale. There's really nothing you can do about it.

Darker roasts are more perishable. Those tend to have a palpable decline within seven days after being roasted. Lighter roasts take longer to get to their peak and to become stale, especially light roasts of dense, well-harvested, well-processed, high-elevation coffee. We like to sell coffee to our customers no later than forty-eight hours after roasting. That way our customers have the amazing opportunity to participate in the life span of their coffee, experiencing it ascending to its peak and discovering when it starts to decline.

Ground coffee is even more fragile. Espresso dulls ninety seconds after being ground. Courser grinds last a little longer: twenty minutes to an hour. That's why Blue Bottle doesn't sell preground coffee. Every now and then customers get mad because we won't grind their coffee for them. It kills us to be the bad guy, but we know in our hearts that the coffee won't be very good after twenty short minutes. How could we willingly sell a product to someone knowing that it will be disappointing before they can even get it home?

How to Roast Coffee at Home

Putting coffee on a perforated baking sheet in the oven is one of the most basic ways to roast it at home. You can buy complicated roasting tools and machines, but this is a good way to try home roasting without making a major investment. The result is fairly rustic; you wouldn't want to use this method with the most rarefied Panama Geisha. However, this simple method is an empowering process, and it could save you a lot of money. Sweetmarias.com sells green beans and roasting equipment, and they have a wide selection. They also offer an online library of resources that they aptly call a "virtual coffee university" and copious details on home roasting. (And they're located in Oakland, which means they rule.)

Be sure to take notes along the way so you can reproduce your method later if you like how the coffee turns out. Keep in mind that it's normal for the beans to be unevenly roasted when you use this method. The trade-off is that you can get an increased complexity with a lot of different roast levels.

When you're first starting, it helps to have a reference color in mind. When I started roasting coffee at home, I kept a handful of roasted coffee beans in a white ceramic bowl and compared the color of the coffee on the baking sheet to that in the bowl. Right away, I learned that the coffee continues to darken a bit after removing it from the oven, so when the coffee wasn't quite as dark as

my sample, I pulled the baking sheet out of the oven. After a while roasting the same varietal, you'll get a sense of what color translates to what flavor. One thing to keep in mind: the reference coffee will change as the days progress, so you can't use any given sample for very long.

In general, in my first roasting of a particular type of coffee, I aim for a medium brown that resembles a light mahogany. (Aside from color, another way to assess when coffee is roasted to a medium level is if oil is visible, like little pin pricks, on the surface of the beans five to six days after roasting, but of course you can't use that indicator while roasting.) When picturing the ideal medium brown, I think of the little wooden rocking chair that I've had my whole life and passed down to my son. It's a color I can see with my eyes closed. Maybe your medium brown is the soft Corinthian leather seats of the 1976 Chrysler Cordoba in which your older sister took you, petrified, to the principal's office after a lighthearted seventh-grade prank went terribly awry. I think we all have a medium brown that we can see with our eyes closed. What's yours?

WHAT YOU'LL NEED
Gram scale
Perforated baking sheet that is the size of a cookie sheet and will fit in your oven. Because
    it's important for the coffee to be no more than one bean deep, if your oven (and hence,
    baking sheet) is particularly small, you should adjust the size of your batch.
150 g (5.3 ounces / about 1 cup) green coffee beans
2 medium or large metal sieves
Stopwatch or timer that shows seconds

Place a rack in the center of the oven. Preheat the oven to 500°F (260°C) for 30 minutes or more, using an oven thermometer to ensure the temperature is accurate. Just like Blue Bottle's Probat coffee roasters and La Marzocco espresso machines, your oven has significant thermal mass, and the longer you allow it to preheat, the more stable the temperature will remain when you open the door during roasting.

If you have a gram scale that weighs to tenths of a gram, now is the time to use it (so that later you can most accurately determine the percentage of weight the coffee loses during the roasting process). Weigh out 150 grams (5.3 oz) of coffee beans, and spread them in a single layer over the center of the baking sheet, extending over no more than one-half to two-thirds of the baking sheet. (If spread all the way to the edges of the pan, the beans tend to singe around the edges.) Have the sieves at hand, turn on any vent fans, open any windows, and consider turning off the smoke alarm in the kitchen. (But if you do, remember to turn it back on after roasting.)

Put the pan in the oven, close the oven door, and start the stopwatch.

If you have a reasonable view through the glass of your oven door, you can observe the coffee's progress. If you have an old oven with no glass or poor visibility through your glass door, resist the temptation to open the door too often, as this will allow too much heat to escape. Open the door no more than every 90 to 120 seconds at first, increasing the frequency only as the roast progresses. Don't open the door for more than 4 to 5 seconds at a time, using a good flashlight if need be to quickly observe the coffee. Here's a timeline of how the roasting should proceed.

2 TO 3½ MINUTES: The beans will take on a brighter, more intense green color.

3½ TO 4 MINUTES: The coffee will start to turn yellow. Write down when this happens. Open the oven and agitate the baking sheet to bring in the outer beans to the center.

5½ MINUTES: The coffee will start to take on a light brown color, but the beans will still be small and wrinkly. Agitate again if the outer beans are getting dark more quickly.

7 OR 8 MINUTES: You will start hearing the first crack, which sounds similar to popcorn popping. Write down when this happens.

20 TO 30 SECONDS PAST FIRST CRACK: Agitate the pan.

45 SECONDS PAST FIRST CRACK (AT AROUND 9 MINUTES): Fast popping means that the coffee is changing dramatically. At that point, it's just a matter of taste. You will learn to associate the accelerando of the pops with a taste profile that you either enjoy or don't, and, hence, can adjust in future batches. Toward the end of the first crack, the popping will decelerate and there will be a moment of silence prior to second crack. The more momentum the roast has, the shorter the moment will be before second crack.

Take the coffee out before you think it's done, just like a steak. It will continue to cook by virtue of its own thermal mass.

Preferably on a back porch or other outdoor area, carefully pour the coffee into one of the sieves. Holding both sieves at arm's length and a foot or two apart (see bottom left photo, opposite), pour the coffee from one sieve into the other sieve. The chaff, which is the remnants of the silverskin beneath the parchment, will blow out as you pour. Continue pouring the roasted coffee back and forth until it feels only warm to the touch, ideally no more than 4 minutes. Hopefully you haven't spilled much or any coffee during the cooling process. Assuming you haven't, weigh the beans, subtract that number from the initial weight, and divide the difference by the beginning weight to get the percentage of weight lost. Write that down, so you can start tracking the percentage of weight lost, as this correlates very strongly with the degree of roasting.

Depending on the roast level you choose and the type of beans you use, the flavor of your coffee will evolve over the next 5 to 10 days. But there's no need to wait if you'd like to drink it sooner.

Cupping and Describing Coffee Flavors

Coffee roasters spend a lot of time cupping, which is the industry term for evaluative coffee tasting. Cupping allows us to assess and select coffees from samples we receive from brokers or growers. It's also how we determine what roasting level to use for each variety of coffee. Plus, it allows us to do quality control on the coffees we roast over and over again.

A repetitive exercise that involves sniffing, sipping, and slurping, cupping is a ritual that frames our day. Several of us get together to cup at least once in the morning and once or twice later in the day. After you've been cupping for a while, you develop a sensitivity to the tiniest differences between samples of coffee, even between batches of the same coffee roasted the same way on different days or by different people.

There have been times in the history of coffee when cupping was more about finding out if a coffee had faults before buying a shipment of it. Did the bags sit in the sun for a week while the freighter was delayed? Is there an off flavor or aroma that means the coffee was poorly harvested or processed? But these days many roasters cup not just to see what faults can they can sense, but what positive attributes are present. The increases in availability of good information from farms, ease of traveling to countries of origin, and access to customers willing to pay a premium for extraordinary coffee are responsible for this exciting shift.

Simultaneously, cafés and other venues have begun to offer public cuppings, and cupping notes have become quite elaborate. It's become a geeky subculture. What I like about cupping is that it's social. In the coffee roasting business, you're always cupping with people, bouncing ideas off each other, and often coming to a consensus.

When cupping, coffee professionals use taste descriptors like *vegetal*, *pineapple juice*, or *cedar*. But the way that I talk about the flavors in coffee to the public is influenced by my belief in the futility of language when it comes to adequately communicating sensory experiences. This is a direct result of my experience as a musician. Musicians are trained through a combination of language and demonstration. As the years progress, language starts to stand for a sensory experience. But this process (the objectification of the subjective) takes a long time to develop. If a musician next to me were to say, "That was too metallic," I would know exactly what was meant. But an outsider who happened to overhear that comment probably wouldn't understand the specific sensory experience we were referring to; in that context, the word *metallic* wouldn't make sense. How could it? The language was attached to that sensory experience only after countless incidents in which playing note X with tone Y yielded *metallic*.

It's the same with the language of cupping. I cup with our green coffee buyer almost every day. If we both use the word *cedar* to describe something we taste in a coffee, we have a sense of what is meant because we have built a shared sensory vocabulary over years of working together. The cupping form that we use for Blue Bottle cuppings has a list of dozens of descriptors that we've grown to understand and use as our common sensory language—a vocabulary that's evolved alongside continued cupping. Here are a few examples:

- TREES: cedar, redwood, holly, pine, fir
- CHOCOLATES: dark, white, milk, waxy
- FLOWERS: jasmine, rose, lilac, honeysuckle
- NUTS: peanuts, almonds, hazelnuts, walnuts
- FRUITS: bananas, blueberries, strawberries, honeydew melon
- SPICES: black pepper, ginger, coriander, vanilla
- DEEPLY EVOCATIVE BUT OUT OF THE BLUE: inflatable pool toys, Vespa exhaust, Bazooka gum, Goodwill store leather jacket

Assuming that the general public can immediately grasp a sensory vocabulary that takes time and training to develop is a mistake. If I use the word *cedar* in the language I put on our bags to sell to the public, one of two things is going to happen: either people won't taste cedar and will then think they must be stupid, or they won't taste it and will then think I must be stupid. Either way, people aren't happy and someone is stupid.

So instead of using coffee descriptors like *Christmas marzipan* or *dried Philippine mango* for Blue Bottle's descriptions on labels, online, and elsewhere, I tell stories about our coffees and try to capture what kind of state the coffee puts me in—in other words, what it *feels* like to drink the coffee. I don't think of this as marketing or trying, in a calculated way, to manufacture a desire. I think of it as sharing my joy for a coffee in a personally meaningful way.

Giving up on language to accurately communicate the taste of coffee is liberating. Having done so, I can approach the problem obliquely, as for the Amaro Gayo Washed:

> As a brewed coffee, the Amaro Gayo Washed is a remarkable sonata of baking spices and aromatic woods. Imagine a grand piano. Now imagine playing a descending F major arpeggio over several octaves. Now imagine that, instead of sounds, the piano produces alternating aromas of cinnamon, nutmeg, cedar, and maple. Now imagine buying a bag, going home, and making a careful pour over of the Amaro Gayo. Optional: imagining slippers, the Times Style section, grapefruit macarons, and napping Irish setters.

Alternatively, I can approach the problem elliptically, loading up so many adjectives that customers are amused, or dazzled, or infuriated at the Proustian excess of language:

> As a pour over, the Amaro Gayo Natural exudes a naive sumptuousness. The aromas of vanilla, weak fruit punch, and strawberry lip gloss combine to place

some of us back at the junior prom. As an espresso, it is compact, creamy, puzzling, and somewhat stern, like watching, at close quarters, your unpredictable grandfather eating profiteroles in his ancient, tobacco-smelling cardigan. It likes cooler temps, faster extractions, ounce and a quarter shots, clean living, and Penderecki on the stereo.

Even if some people do feel a bit infuriated or perhaps bemused, at least no one feels stupid. As part of the evaluative language of coffee at Blue Bottle, we do ascribe objective-seeming numbers, based on the Specialty Coffee Association of America's cupping forms, to certain attributes of the coffee we cup. Their language and system evolved as a method of attempting to impartially evaluate crops of coffee so that forward contracts for large lots of coffee could have a way of ensuring a specific, presumably desired, quality for the buyer. While there are a lot of coffee professionals that, once "calibrated" (the industry term for, essentially, being on the same page with each other), can generally agree on ranking a coffee an 86 compared to a 90 or an 82, we are hesitant to take this system outside the cupping room. The reason is that an objective-seeming numerical cupping score is exactly that: a snapshot of how a coffee cups, rather than how it may taste in a specific context.

WHY YOU NEED A GRAM SCALE

Throughout this book, we have provided the volume measures most U.S. cooks are familiar with, although it isn't in keeping with our own methods or our recommendations. But you, Caitlin, and I are going to make a deal: we will put volume measurements in our recipes if you promise to ignore them and buy a gram scale. Gram measurements are more accurate, and we think using them will improve your experience as a coffee drinker and baker—and therefore improve your life.

So let's face it: you need to go the extra mile and buy a gram scale if you don't already have one. Why? Volume is a less accurate way of measuring things than mass is. That's not an opinion; it's physics. Consider flour: 1 cup of sifted flour weighs significantly less than 1 cup of unsifted flour. Another clear example is brown sugar: a firmly packed cup of brown sugar

weighs significantly more than a loosely packed cup. And clearly, when roasting and preparing coffee at home, it's worthwhile to make a modest investment in a gram scale so you can easily track percentage of weight lost, and make an excellent pour over. Look at it this way: If you're going to go to the trouble to bake cakes or roast coffee at home, why not do so accurately? If you're going to buy good coffee and attempt to make it well, why be approximate?

Escali and Oxo have some good gram scales, but we're partial to the American Weigh AMW-2,000-gram scale. It weighs to tenths of a gram, has terrific battery life, is rugged, isn't bad-looking, and has a setting that disables the auto-off feature that can frustrate the slow, deliberate pour-over artist that so many of us strive to be.

Cupping at Home

You can cup at home—but don't cup by yourself and write about it on the Internet. Coffee is social, and cupping coffee at home should be something you share with humans, preferably humans you like. Putting on a cupping at home is a terrific way to get to know what kinds of coffee you like and learn to identify flavors and characteristics. The great part about cupping coffee is that it allows you to discover that it isn't difficult to differentiate among coffees. I see it at Blue Bottle's public cuppings all the time: people are astonished and beaming when they find that they can easily distinguish a Brazilian coffee from a Sumatran. It's empowering to realize that you know more than you thought you did. That said, it's best to set yourself up for success at first. Start out with no more than four coffees, all single-origins from different regions. Avoid blends, and also avoid extremely dark roast coffees, since higher roast levels tend to make the origin characteristics harder to discern. Later, you can geek out with a side-by-side cupping of washed Yirgacheffes. Make sure to use water that tastes good enough to drink on its own.

WHAT YOU'LL NEED

18 grams (0.65 oz) each of three or four types of coffee beans, plus 9 to 20 grams (0.3 to 0.7 oz) of each for priming. In order to control for measurement or other process errors, you are going to cup two samples of each coffee.

Gram scale

Coffee grinder

6 to 8 identical porcelain cups that hold 180 to 240 milliliters (6 to 8 fl oz) and are preferably wider at the top, such as cappuccino cups or small soup bowls

Good-quality water

Soup spoon for each taster

Empty dish for the wet grounds

PRIME THE GRINDER. This step clears out any remaining grounds from another coffee. Take a small handful (9 g, or 0.3 oz if you are really dedicated to imperial units) of the first coffee you're cupping and run it through the grinder, then throw that away.

GRIND THE COFFEES. Weigh out 9 grams (0.3 oz) of the first coffee and grind it at a medium-coarse setting, somewhere between a pour-over grind (see page 79) and a French-press grind (see page 83). Repeat without priming for the second sample of that varietal and place another 9 grams in a second cup. Repeat for each type of coffee, priming the grinder before grinding each variety. Label the cups.

SMELL. Take a whiff of each dry sample with your mouth open—this helps bring more aromas to the palate.

ADD WATER. Heat about 50 fluid ounces (1.47 l) water to 205°F (96°C), using a kettle or other vessel that is used only for heating water. Slowly pour the hot water over each sample. Pour to same level in each cup. The cupping ratio we use at Blue Bottle is 17 parts water to 1 part coffee, so you'll need about 150 grams of water for each sample cup to follow our ratio precisely. Conveniently, 1 gram of water is 1 milliliter of water by volume, so that comes to 150 milliliters (5 fl oz) of water per cup. Let sit 3 to 5 minutes. Meanwhile, place the soup spoons in a tall glass and fill with the remaining hot water.

SMELL AGAIN. After pouring the water, smell each sample again with your nose 1 inch (2.5 cm) above the cup. (I almost always get coffee on my nose.) Try to note the differences and similarities. Have the aromas of the dry coffee changed in any way? It's easier to compare and contrast than to come up with brilliant observations like "I smell olives."

BREAK THE CRUST. After the coffee has brewed for 3 to 5 minutes, break through the layer of coffee grounds that has formed on top, which is trapping most of the aromas. Use the spoon to break through the crust and away from you, releasing as much trapped gas as possible. As you break, inhale deeply, again with your nose to the bowl. Rinse your spoon in the glass of hot water between coffees so you don't cross-contaminate the samples.

REMOVE THE CRUST. Using one or two spoons, scoop off the top crust and put in a dish. Try to remove all of the coffee grounds from the surface so they don't end up in your mouth. For very light roasts, most of the ground coffee will sink to the bottom, so there won't be much to scoop. Again, be sure to rinse the spoons between coffees.

TASTE. Take a spoonful of coffee and slurp sharply. This aspirates coffee over your palate, helping bring in all of the flavors and aromas. (In the traditional machismo of the cupping room, whoever slurps the loudest is the baddest, so work on your loud slurp.) Pay attention, compare, and contrast, but don't share your thoughts with others until they're done tasting. If you say, "Interesting . . . roasted bananas," everyone will say, "Exactly! Bananas!"

REPEAT. Go through several rounds of tasting as the coffee cools. You're going to notice new things each time. This process also helps you realize that piping hot coffee may not always be the most interesting or flavorful.

DRINK

I believe coffee should be prepared one cup at a time and consumed right away, no matter what technique you chose. The most low-tech way to make coffee, and one of my favorite methods, is the pour over. It feels elemental, sort of like cooking over an open flame: just coffee, water, a cone, and a filter. You grind the coffee, weigh it, put it in the cone, and pour water over it—slowly so the coffee has enough time to absorb the water and the water can extract the correct solubles from the coffee.

At Blue Bottle, we put a lot of energy into pour-over coffee in our cafés, and I do the same in this book because it's one of the most basic, approachable, and effective ways to make a beautiful cup of coffee. But whether you are making a pour over or an espresso, the elemental process is extraction—which simply means hot water dissolving the compounds that are in roasted coffee. First the grinder breaks the coffee beans down into much smaller pieces with varying surface areas. Then these surface areas are exposed to hot water. The hot water dissolves particles from the coffee grounds' exposed surface area, creating brewed coffee. If the ground coffee is underextracted, you'll miss out on a lot of flavor, and if it's overextracted, water may leach unpleasant properties out of the coffee that mask its deliciousness. How the coffee is ground, the water temperature, and the amount of time the ground coffee is exposed to water are all crucial factors in extraction. In this chapter, I'll show you how to work toward mastering those variables for a few recommended methods of preparing coffee.

I'll explain how to make beautiful pour-over coffee, step-by-step. I'll also explain how to choose a grinder, use a nel drip, and a siphon, and even an ibrik for Turkish coffee, if you decide to explore those methods. Then I'll delve into the murky waters of trying to write about making espresso. You may not leave the discussion convinced that you should buy a home espresso machine. But if you choose to go that route, I'll tell you how best to do it.

Making coffee is a simple art, yet it also has so many aspects: practice, precision, and the sheer pleasure of making something you know you're going to enjoy. It's an expanding universe of wonderfulness; you never run out of things to get better at.

Brewed Coffee Techniques

Would you cook a good steak in the microwave? Why would you let a machine make your coffee? Letting a machine brew your coffee is like putting popcorn in a microwave and pressing "popcorn." It takes the power away from you. If you buy good coffee and want to prepare it well, you have to choose a method that lets you express your dedication, skill, and enthusiasm. Plug-in brewers are not that method.

Most plug-in coffee brewers don't heat the water sufficiently for optimum brewing, and they tend to leach off-flavors from the cheap plastic tubing typically used. Even the best of these machines give you no control over flow rate and dispersion patterns, resulting in some areas of the grounds being overextracted and others being underextracted. In general, the grounds don't get fully saturated, and the brew basket is usually too small to accommodate enough fresh coffee, which tends to expand much more when wet than older coffee. Plus, they brew too quickly to extract the most delicious flavors from the coffee. Then the coffee sits and cooks on a hot plate or gets stale in a thermal carafe, destroying any flavor the machine managed to obtain.

It makes me sad to think about how many millions of people start their day this way, especially because the craft of making really good brewed coffee with simple tools is immensely satisfying. Although the equipment is simple, you'll still need to invest in a few tools. You need good data, so you need tools that measure: a gram scale (see Why You Need a Gram Scale, page 62) and an accurate thermometer or thermocouple. Available at some hardware stores, a thermocouple is an electronic temperature sensor that's used in science and industry for testing the temperature of ovens and air conditioning. You need to have control over your water supply, and a pouring kettle with a fine spout (also called a swan-necked kettle) is the perfect tool for the job. You need to control the particle size of your ground coffee and therefore must

have a good grinder (discussed in detail on page 74). You also need a ceramic dripper and good-quality filters for basic pour-over coffee. Should you choose to explore other brewing methods (French press, nel drip, siphon, or Turkish), you'll also need the devices specific to those methods. And, of course, you need a supply of clean, fresh, good-tasting water.

Depending on where you live, you may be able to find most of these tools locally. If not, thanks to the wonders of the Internet, you can purchase even the most arcane coffee tools online (and some of the tools we recommend most highly are available at Blue Bottle's online shop). If you'd like some guidance on brands, here are some we recommend:

thermocouple

- **GRAM SCALE:** American Weigh, Escali, Oxo
- **THERMOCOUPLE THERMOMETERS:** Extech, Honeywell, Taylor, Cole-Parmer
- **SWAN-NECK KETTLES:** Hario, Takahiro, Kono, Kalitta
- **DRIPPERS:** Bonmac, Melitta, Kono, Hario
- **FILTERS:** Bonmac, Hario, Kono, Filtropa
- **FRENCH PRESSES:** Bodom, Freiling, Espro
- **NEL DRIP SETUPS:** Hario, Kono
- **SIPHON COFFEE DEVICES:** Hario (also branded Bonmac), Yama

POUR OVER

Sometimes I teach classes where I demonstrate Blue Bottle's pour-over method, allowing people to see how simple it is and how the coffee tastes so much better than what comes out of a plug-in machine. When you use this method regularly, every day you get slightly better at the pour, and eventually you get to the point where you can smell the subtle differences from one cup to the next.

Over the years, Blue Bottle's pour-over method has changed. A bit later, I'll give you a recipe based on experiments I did starting in 2007, after watching the method of Jay Egami, a coffee expert with UCC Ueshima Coffee Co., headquartered in Kobe, Japan (see page 91 for more on Jay). When I first saw Jay pouring so slowly, using exact amounts of coffee weighed to the gram and water heated to an exact temperature, I admit to thinking it would be too hard, even ridiculous, to use those methods in Blue Bottle's kiosk. Of course, my skepticism didn't stop me from drinking his coffee, and when I did, I became an instant convert. I think you will too.

Although the pour-over recipe on page 79 covers the basics, like many recipes it raises more questions than it answers. This actually shouldn't come as a surprise, given that even the simplest method of making coffee can yield seemingly infinite variations in taste depending on how various factors are manipulated. That might sound a little overwhelming, but as with so many things in life, the important thing is just to dive in and do it. Make coffee simply, taste it, enjoy it, and see how you'd like to improve it. You can take notes if you're feeling geeky, or you can just remember. Your intuition will eventually lead you to discover what you find most delicious. All of that said, let's take a look at some of the questions the pour-over recipe may raise.

HOW MUCH COFFEE? I like to express the amount of coffee used as a ratio. For example, 350 milliliters (about 12 fl oz) of water to 35 grams (1.2 oz) of coffee would be a brewing ratio of 10 to 1. The correct ratio, like many questions in the coffee world, is the subject of considerable debate. Although it's hotly contested, it is ultimately decided on purely subjective grounds. The real question is, what brewing ratio will you enjoy most? The truth is, considering brewing ratio in isolation doesn't make sense because the relationships among brewing ratio, water temperature, extraction speed, and particle size combine to influence the flavors in the cup. But I can offer a couple of guidelines on brew ratio.

GRINDERS FOR EVERYTHING BUT ESPRESSO

Purchasing only whole bean coffee and grinding it at home is one of the surest ways to improve your coffee experience. So if you don't already have a grinder, I highly recommend that you buy one. Now.

At Blue Bottle, we only sell whole beans, even though we take some heat for the decision. There are several reasons for this, but the most compelling is the incredible fragility of ground coffee. As mentioned in the Roast chapter, there's a clear decline in the taste and performance of espresso just ninety seconds after grinding. More coarsely ground coffee isn't as fragile, but there is a substantial difference after an hour or even twenty minutes.

So let's assume you are going to grind your coffee at home, and (for now) that you are brewing coffee, not making espresso. (For information on espresso grinders, see page 105.) When brewing coffee, you have some leeway in the type of grinder you use, especially if you are using a dripper and paper filters. Grinders in the style of a spice mill, with whirly blades, are the cheapest. The primary virtue of these grinders is that, for a very modest investment, you can break free from buying preground coffee. However, you will never be able to get a consistent grind. Never. The particles will range in size from powder to chunks, and your coffee will not be ground the same from one day to the next. You can get a slightly more even grind by employing the "pulse and shake" method: pulsing for 2 to 3 seconds while shaking the grinder, then pausing briefly so the coffee doesn't heat up too much, then pulsing again, and so on, until you achieve roughly the desired grind.

However, if you're brewing coffee in a French press, nel drip, or siphon, or making Turkish coffee, a whirly blade grinder will be a source of frustration. Because these grinders don't produce a consistent particle size, the smaller particles will overextract and the larger particles will underextract. This inconsistent extraction makes for an unreliable and often unpleasant result. Therefore, for these styles of coffee, you need an adjustable grinder that will reliably produce particles of approximately equal size—a burr grinder. This style of grinder crushes the beans between two metal disks (called burrs) with sharp ridges that spin at speeds of 500 to 1,500 rpm, with the distance between the burrs being adjustable to a very fine degree.

All burr grinders are not created equal. There are both electric and hand-cranked models, and the hand-cranked grinders often have very high-quality ceramic burrs instead of metal. This has upsides and downsides. Ceramic burrs stay sharp much longer than metal burrs and are easier to clean, but they are more fragile. Hand-cranked models are great for traveling but often require more than 250 turns to grind enough coffee for one serving. Manufacturers such as Porlex, Hario, and Zassenhaus have good hand-cranked burr grinders for less than $100, so you can also save money by agreeing to be the motor.

Good-quality electric burr grinders typically cost from $100 to $300. Select a grinder with larger grinding burrs, heavier overall weight, and a lower rpm motor. The higher the rpm of the motor, the greater the tendency to heat the coffee, which causes inconsistencies in grind size and also runs the risk of losing some flavor. Also look for larger numbers of grind settings or, for the most flexibility, a stepless grinder, which allows you to adjust the grind size without being locked into specific settings.

Darker-roasted coffees generally benefit from narrower, or tighter, brewing ratios (meaning smaller amounts of water per a given amount of coffee). They also benefit from larger particle size, more recent roasting, and lower-temperature water. For two of the most popular blends Blue Bottle serves, which are on the darker side, we like a 10-to-1 brewing ratio on the second through fifth day after roasting, with 188°F (87°C) water. In contrast, with dense, very high-altitude, meticulously harvested and processed single-origin coffees roasted very lightly, we've found that a wider brewing ratio, hotter water, and a longer rest time draws out the most enjoyable flavors. How have we discovered this? Trial and error, and a lot of meticulous note taking in our lab. In Japan, a 10-to-1 brewing ratio is pretty standard, but I've seen ratios anywhere from 4 to 1 to 15 to 1, with the combination of brewing ratio, pouring technique, brewing temperature, and contact time coming together to create the sought-after taste and texture.

WHICH DRIPPER IS BEST? There are a few options in drippers: the single-hole dripper, the three-hole dripper, and the big-hole dripper. We like the ceramic single-hole drippers made by Bonmac. This lets the coffee spend the optimal amount of time in contact with the water. In all of my travels in Japan, the cafés that I've been the most consistently inspired by have used this type of dripper. It is simple, inexpensive, old-fashioned, and has been tested by decades of use. The drippers with a large hole (often made by Hario and referred to by the model name V60) are experiencing an uptick in popularity in the United States, primarily (in my opinion) because they produce a cup of coffee more quickly. The downside is that it's very difficult, though not impossible, to control the pour so the water spends enough time in contact with the coffee. I haven't been to a single café in Japan that uses V60s. Kono drippers are superficially similar to the Hario V60s in that they have a large hole at the bottom, but they have a different interior geometry that tends to make extracting excellent coffee easier and more repeatable.

HOW FAST SHOULD THE EXTRACTION BE? I generally like a total brewing time of 3 to 3 1/2 minutes, which works out to about 1.5 seconds per milliliter. While it's fairly obvious that you can vary the extraction rate by the speed at which you pour, grind size is also a factor. A finer grind will extract more slowly, regardless of the rate at which you pour. Extraction will also be slower if you're using a grinder that produces a lot of fines, powdery particles that can clog the pores of the filter.

SHOULD YOU POUR CLOCKWISE OR COUNTERCLOCKWISE? In regard to the direction in which water should be poured, at the Ueshima Coffee Co. Academy in Japan, the adamant answer is clockwise. Always clockwise. In your own kitchen, this rule is flexible. For home coffee-making classes, I don't get too hung up on clockwise or counterclockwise. But when the subject comes up, some guy—and it's always a guy—wryly chuckles about pouring counterclockwise in Australia. Don't be that guy.

WHAT TEMPERATURE OF WATER SHOULD BE USED? Generally, the lighter the roast, the hotter water you want to pour, up to a max of about 205°F (96°C). A wider water-to-coffee ratio and a finer grind may also indicate that a higher temperature will yield more delicious results. But some of the most memorable coffees I've ever tasted in Japan have been darker-roast coffees made using small brewing ratios, large particle size, and extremely low brewing temperatures—175°F (79°C). Generally, water that is between 190°F and 205°F (88°C and 96°C) yields the best results, but experimenting is a fun part of the process. As a rule, the longer the extraction period, the lower the water temperature should be. Otherwise you risk heat damaging the coffee.

CONDIMENTS: THE LOVE THAT DARE NOT SPEAK ITS NAME?

A lot of you may be in the habit of adding cream or sugar, or both, to your coffee. I am going to ask you to do a simple but radical thing: Taste your coffee before you add anything to it. Just taste it. Every time. Notice what flavors are there, then notice how the flavors change after you add your condiments. Then you have my permission to add anything you want.

If you usually drink a caffe latte, every so often ask for a latte with an espresso on the side. Taste the espresso first, then try your latte. How does the milk mediate your experience? What does it add? What does it take away? The more you familiarize yourself with what a well-crafted drink made from well-roasted coffee tastes like, the more you might be interested in drinking an entire cup of black coffee. Is it somehow morally superior to drink coffee black? I'm not going to touch that one. But black coffee has a lot going for it: it's simpler, it's purer, and it's less caloric. It's all coffee.

Pour-Over Coffee

The two indispensable tools for making better pour-over coffee are a gram scale and a swan-necked kettle. Using a swan-necked kettle will help the accuracy of your pour and, hence, improve the consistency of your extraction. Some people might rebel at paying $50 for a kettle, but how many people have paid for a pizza stone they never use or an ice cream maker that lives in the back of a kitchen cabinet? If you buy a gram scale and kettle, you'll use them every day, and you'll drink better coffee almost immediately. Every morning your first thoughts will coalesce around making something wonderful. Your friends will beg you to make them coffee and share your mastery. It's money well spent.

A coffee mug usually holds around 10 fluid ounces. We're going to call that 300 milliliters. Conveniently, 1 milliliter of water (a measurement of volume) equals 1 gram (a measurement of weight). So, armed with this secret knowledge, you can proceed knowing that pouring on a tared (zeroed) gram scale tells you not only the weight of the water, but the volume of water you've poured. If you employ a timer as well, you'll have relevant information about flow rate and extraction time. And if you add a thermometer, you can also collect data about temperature of extraction. Data points, before breakfast!

WHAT YOU'LL NEED
About 20 fluid ounces (2½ cups / 590 ml) good-quality water
Swan-necked kettle
Gram scale
20 to 35 grams (0.7 to 1.2 oz) coffee beans
Coffee grinder
Thermocouple or other thermometer
Ceramic coffee dripper
Coffee cup
Paper filter (kenaf or bamboo-based paper is best)

You will need 10 fluid ounces (300 ml) of good-quality water for your coffee, so put double that amount in a kettle or other vessel used only for heating water. Why double? Because you'll use some of the water to preheat the dripper and cup. Put the kettle over high heat.

While the water is heating, weigh out the coffee; the amount depends on the brewing ratio you'll use, from 20 grams for a 15-to-1 ratio to 30 grams for a 10-to-1 ratio. Grind the coffee finely enough that it forms a clump when pressed between your thumb and forefinger; it should feel soft but still a bit gritty. Grind size and evenness is one of the few immeasurable factors—at least at home. At the roastery, we measure particle size and distribution of the powdery particles called fines when evaluating grinders, but at home intuition rules. Change it up and try different settings to find one you like.

When the water comes to a boil, pour it into the swan-necked kettle, then let it sit until the temperature is between 185°F and 205°F (85°C and 96°C). (Your choice of water temperature should be based on the type of coffee and roast level that you're serving; see page 75.) Warm the ceramic dripper and cup with some of the remaining hot water.

Put the filter in the dripper and pour in the ground coffee. The coffee should naturally take the shape of a gentle mound. Place your now-empty but warm cup on your gram scale, set the coffee-filled ceramic dripper on top, and tare the scale.

Gently and slowly drizzle a small amount of hot water in the center of the mound of coffee, away from the sides of the filter and making a circle about the size of a quarter. The goal is to pour in just enough water that the coffee will absorb all of it without any liquid dripping into your cup. Coffee generally holds double its weight in water. This is easy to check if your cup, dripper, and coffee assemblage is set up on your gram scale. For example, if you have 35 grams (1.2 oz) of ground coffee in the filter and have tared the scale, add water until the scale reads 70 grams (2.5 oz). Voilà! Pouring in water in such a way that none comes out is a skill. The better you are at soaking the coffee mass evenly, then the more water it will absorb. Can you pour twice the weight of the ground coffee amount without any dripping? 1.75 times? 2.25 times?

You can take satisfaction from doing this well, but it isn't just a geeky fine point; it has an impact on the coffee you brew. It facilitates blooming, the process in which hot water causes the coffee to expand outward in a fascinating way. Allow it to bloom for 30 to 45 seconds, or up to 60 seconds for coffee roasted over 1 week previously. A slightly longer blooming time can add a lot of depth and vitality to older coffee.

Pour in more water, once again pouring slowly in a small circular pattern in the middle of the filter. A light-brown cap should rise; at Blue Bottle we call it "the mushroom." The pace of your pour should be approximately equivalent to the speed at which coffee is flowing out of the filter into your cup; in other words, the level of the mixture of coffee and water in the filter should neither rise or fall. Furthermore, the level of the mushroom should be maintained at just about two-thirds up the sides of the cone. Aim for somewhere between 1 and 2 milliliters (1/4 to 1/2 teaspoon) of water per second. There are 15 milliliters in 1 tablespoon, so that's about 1 tablespoon per 7 to 15 seconds.

Remember, extraction rate is determined by many variables beyond how fast you pour: amount of coffee, grind size, percentage of fines, and water temperature. So the pour contributes to the speed of the extraction but doesn't define it. Don't be frustrated if you can't pour slowly and steadily right away. It's a skill. Just keep practicing.

Once you've poured the desired amount of water, remove the dripper. The coffee will taste better if you don't let all the water flow through the filter into the cup. At the end of the brewing cycle, you are starting to extract some undesirable compounds from the coffee; keeping those away from the coffee you are drinking will produce a more delicious product.

Drink your coffee, and marvel at your dedication and skill. Repeat as needed.

FRENCH PRESS COFFEE

Because a French press yields coffee that isn't filtered through paper, it has the hearty "that's rich coffee" quality that French press enthusiasts so admire. For that reason, the French press tends to produce coffee well suited to the addition of condiments. Adding cream actually smoothes out the sedimentary feel. Condiments aside, if you value thick body above all else in coffee, the French press is going to remain your brewing method of choice.

One caution with the French press is that the lack of a paper filter makes this method particularly vulnerable to overextraction. There are many more particles in solution, and compounds in those particles continue to be extracted over the life of the cup. Therefore, you should pour French press coffee out of the pot immediately after plunging and drink it as soon as possible. It's never a good idea to hold any coffee on a hot plate or in a carafe, but holding French press coffee for any length of time has particularly horrible results. This continual extraction keeps French-press coffee from cooling as delightfully as siphon or pour-over coffee in general. Overall, the fewer particles in suspension, the better the coffee will taste as it cools. However, removing some of the grounds before plunging, an option I outline on the following page, can help alleviate, but not eliminate, that problem.

French Press Coffee

For each 355 milliliters (12 fl oz) of water, use 20 to 35 grams (0.7 to 1.2 oz) of ground coffee, using more coffee if brewing a darker-roast coffee or adding condiments. For denser, lighter-roasted coffee or serving without condiments, I recommend the slotted-spoon method for removing grounds prior to plunging, with a brewing ratio of about 12 to 1, which translates to about 28 grams (1 oz) of coffee per 355 ml (12 fl oz) of water.

WHAT YOU'LL NEED

Good-quality water

Gram scale

Coffee beans

Coffee grinder, preferably a burr grinder

Thermocouple or other thermometer

French press

Chopstick or wooden spoon

Timer

Medium-size slotted spoon
 (optional)

However much finished coffee you wish to brew, put double that amount of good-quality water in a kettle or other vessel used only for heating water. (You'll use some of the water to preheat the empty French press and cup.)

While the water is heating, weigh out the coffee; the amount depends on the brewing ratio you'll use, for each 355-milliliter (12 fl oz) serving, use from 20 grams for a 15-to-1 ratio to 35 grams for a 10-to-1 ratio. Grind the coffee—not too finely. The grind should be gritty, resembling beach sand that's pleasant to walk on, but not too powdery.

When the water is hot but not quite boiling, at about 198°F (92°C), remove it from the heat. Pour some of the hot water into the empty French press to warm it up. After a few seconds, pour the water from the French press into your cup to warm it as well.

Put the ground coffee in the press pot and pour the amount of water desired in a thin stream over the grounds. Gently stir the coffee with the chopstick. Place the stem on the pot with the filter about 1/2 inch (1.3 cm) above the grounds. Let the coffee steep for 3 minutes.

Remove the stem, and for a full-bodied final result, briefly and gently stir with a chopstick. For a finer-bodied coffee, don't stir; instead, use a medium-size slotted spoon to remove the coffee grounds from the top of the pot.

Replace the stem and gently push the grounds down to the bottom of the pot. If the plunger thunks to the bottom with almost no resistance, your grind is too coarse. If you have to strain to get the plunger to the bottom of the pot, your grind is too fine. Using too fine a grind can be dangerous. If the stem torques as you're wrestling with it, near-boiling water and coffee grounds could spray all over you. Ideally, the plunger will lower smoothly and gradually with 15 to 20 pounds (6.8 to 9.1 kg) of pressure. If you're not sure what that feels like, press down on your bathroom scale with the flat of your hand until the scale reads 20 pounds (9.1 kg). It should take 15 to 20 seconds to push the plunger to the bottom.

When you have pushed the plunger down as far down as it will go, serve immediately.

COFFEE IN JAPAN, CHATEI HATOU, AND NEL DRIP

Japan's coffee culture is one of the most refined in the world, and it has had a huge influence on what we do at Blue Bottle.

Japan has a long tradition of manual brewing, especially siphon and pour-over coffee. The country's history with coffee started in the mid-1800s, during the late Edo period. Contact with all Westerners except the Dutch was forbidden, and among the Japanese, only merchants (and prostitutes) could meet with the Dutch, and only in the city of Nagasaki. The Dutch introduced the Japanese to coffee from their holdings in Java, and the love of artisanship that took root in Japan during the extended peace of the Edo period made its way to the new culture surrounding coffee.

During the rapid industrialization that occurred in the Meiji period (1868 to 1912), coffee assumed greater prominence in Japanese society. To protect Japan's sovereignty, which was threatened by unfavorable treaties forced upon it by the West, Japanese society entered an intense period of industrialization and militarization and began embracing Western values as a way to be more competitive. Wearing European attire and adopting other Western practices, like drinking coffee and building battleships, became societal imperatives.

Japan's café culture first blossomed in the 1920s, but was cut short during World War II due to an eight-year coffee embargo. It got going again in the late 1940s and early 1950s. Even today, Japan has some of the most meticulous and elegant cafés in the world. I have never been to so many cafés as dedicated to complete mastery over all the relevant details of coffee preparation and service than in Tokyo, Kyoto, and Kobe. There are terrible cafés in Japan, like anywhere else, but the great cafés demonstrate their greatness in such modest, perfect ways.

The best cafés in Japan, unlike the best cafés in the United States, are old, fusty, and unfashionable. They have no espresso machines and, for that matter, very little equipment beyond a few induction burners to heat water in big kettles. The clientele is primarily people in their fifties and sixties. The men wear jackets, or if they wear cardigans, they wear them unironically. Classical music is on the stereo, and the volume is hushed. The furniture, like the clientele, is usually dark, gloomy, quiet, and dignified. Many of the best cafés are hard for a Westerner to find, located down side streets and on upper floors, and they can also be difficult for Westerners to navigate, with signs and menus in Japanese only.

One of my favorite cafés in all the world, Chatei Hatou, is like this. It's near Shibuya Station in Tokyo, not a promising location for such unexpected excellence and beauty. The area around the train station is packed with fashionable young people, electronics stores, pachinko parlors, ramen shops, and what is rumored to be the world's highest-grossing Starbucks. But just a few blocks away, the din dies down a little. If you can find it, and if it's open (these types of cafés generally keep hours that we in the West think are a little strange, between around

11 a.m. and 11 p.m.), it's possible to enter a tiny corner of calm perfection. I've been there less than a dozen times, but it occupies an immensely significant place in my approach to making and drinking coffee. I'm sure I think about Chatei Hatou every single working day.

Every time I go to Chatei Hatou, I'm filled with an exhausting combination of elation and despondency: elation because I am participating in extraordinary, matchless, unnecessary excellence, and despondency because, although I aspire to produce an experience of such rarified perfection, I may never be smart enough or hardworking enough to figure out how to do it myself.

The first step is to enter.

The experience of entering is ambiguous. Sit, or wait to be told to sit? I think the employees tend to assume that Westerners will realize they are lost or be disappointed to find that they aren't in the right place. So they tend to give Westerners a few moments to figure it out. When they seem satisfied that Caitlin and I have indeed decided that we are not, in fact, lost, and that, furthermore, this is the café perhaps above all others in the entire world where we would want to drink coffee, they usually motion for us to sit. There are tables, and there is a long bar that seats twelve. We beg with our eyes to be seated at the bar.

On the wall behind the bar are dozens and dozens of delicate mismatched china cups and saucers. It's a bewildering array: Royal Doulton, Wedgwood, Japanese brands, in a wide variety of colors and patterns, some commemorating the wedding of Princess Di, or the Beatles' last concert in Tokyo, in sizes ranging from 60 to 240 milliliters ($1/4$ to 1 cup).

We are handed a menu in Japanese, so the best we can do is call out the name of a varietal or coffee-growing region: Mandheling? Ethiopia? Tanzania? Then we attempt to communicate a style: Paper drip? Demitasse? At Chatei Hatou, demitasse-style coffee means nel drip, and that means coffee filtered through a flannel sack suspended from a wire hoop. This method produces a coffee of extraordinary density and the most lapidary sweetness due to a tight brewing ratio, extremely low brewing temperature, and a very, very ponderous extraction regimen. (Read more about nel drip on page 88.)

There might be prices on the menu, but it's better not to think about them. A coffee here could run upward of $15. Tokyo is an expensive town, and it's possible to buy a bad cappuccino at a Doutor Café for the equivalent of $4 or canned coffee from a vending machine for $1. In that light, life-changing perfection for $15 is a bargain. And we must have cake! Tokyo is packed with patisseries and cafés that serve cake and coffee to enthusiastic crowds every day around 2 p.m. Chatei Hatou is known for its chiffon cake, so we point and hope.

Once our order is communicated, the barista takes a long, hard look at us, then turns his back and studies his wall of china cups. His body language seems to be saying, "Which one? Out of these hundred cups, which cups are precisely correct for these customers, at this time, and the coffees to be served?" It can take a moment. At last, he settles on the correct cups; we all seem to breathe a sigh of relief.

Apparently satisfied by his choice of china, the barista gets to work. The grinder and coffee are on the back bar, and the coffee pouring tools are on the front bar. The barista spends a moment grooming his nel filter with a bamboo rod: plumping it out and giving it exactly the correct shape for receiving the coffee. He takes a scoop of coffee and grinds it with an ancient Fuji Royal grinder. In these grinders, the motor is separated from the grinding burrs by an auger so the coffee won't be heated by the friction of the motor while it grinds.

The coffee is very coarsely ground and emptied into the nel, which is placed on an oddly provisional-looking wire stand. So much coffee! The brewing ratio must be 4 to 1. The barista decants water from a large kettle simmering on an induction burner. transferring it into a smaller pouring kettle. Even though there are no measuring instruments in sight, it seems evident that the barista has spent many an hour with a gram scale and thermometer, internalizing the correct measurements before ever serving a customer professionally.

The barista starts pouring water. The pouring kettle is the tool that lets him express his technique and desires on the coffee. He drizzles the water slowly and methodically, circumscribing a quarter-size circle on top of the coffee mass. The pour is so slow that, instead of a steady stream of water, we see what looks like the tiniest pearl necklace slipping from the kettle into the filter, comprised of connected droplets, plump and spherical. The speed of the pour is so rigorously controlled that the water never ceases to come out or splashes into the nel; it just continues to emerge as this perfect strand of connected droplets, making a slight tearing sound as it contacts the ground coffee. This goes on for a minute or two before we notice something odd: There's no cup under the nel! Coffee will start leaking out onto the counter at any second! But of course the barista knows precisely how long he can pour before the coffee loses its ability to absorb the water entering the filter. Seconds before the coffee starts to drip from the bottom of the nel, the barista slides the cup under the filter, suavely, as though this irresistible yet modest display of showmanship is all the quiet satisfaction he needs in his working day.

He pours, uninterrupted, for several more minutes, until enough coffee emerges to fill a demitasse—about 3 fluid ounces (90 ml). He places the cup in front of me, handle always turned to my right, and to my left he places a doll's-size pitcher of heavy cream, two tiny, individually wrapped containers of glucose syrup, and the daintiest teaspoon, all arranged on a small saucer. But, of course, using condiments would never cross my mind. The cake, which was sliced several minutes ago and placed in a refrigerator to firm up, is placed to my right. Every time I go to Chatei Hatou, I worry, "Is this the time when the coffee is not as glorious as I remember? Has time and my natural inclination to mythologize Japanese-style coffee made it impossible for this actual drink to equal the my expectations of it?" And every time I take the first sip, I relax. The answer, of course, is no.

After a few sips, I look around. On one side of the bar, the junior barista has poured roasted coffee beans in a single layer on a sheet pan. He scrutinizes every bean, giving the coffee a very skeptical look and pulling out beans he disapproves of. Each pan looks like it holds about 1¹/₂ pounds (680 g) of coffee. Chatei Hatou doesn't roast its own coffee; it uses beans from several suppliers. Depending upon the coffee, that junior barista might discard about fifty beans from the pan—or he might discard half. This counts as side work at Hatou.

On the other side of the bar, a young woman is frosting a chiffon cake with what looks like chocolate ganache—frosting it perfectly. My lovely wife is incomparably talented with an offset spatula, but even she is spellbound the first time we see the chiffon cake being frosted. The cake is made in tube pan, so it has a small hole going through the center. There is a moment of expectation as the process of frosting comes to completion: Is she going to frost the interior? The young woman puts down the offset spatula, picks up a smaller one, and—yes!—frosts the inside of the small hole. This is what having a coffee at Chatei Hatou is like: every bean is scrutinized, every cake is immaculately frosted, and every coffee is understood as an experience that can be as perfect as it needs to be.

Nel Drip Coffee

Dripping coffee through a flannel filter (shortened to "nel") has a long history in Japan dating back to the 1920s. Although now considered fusty and perhaps somewhat unfashionable in Japan, nel drip is happily experiencing a resurgent popularity in the United States.

There are dozens of styles of preparing nel drip in Japan and the United States; at Blue Bottle our favorite method has been adapted from notes taken and conversations held during my many visits to Chatei Hatou in Tokyo (see page 84), one of the most meticulous, inspiring, and refined cafes in all the world.

The first time I tried coffee prepared this way was at Café l'Ambre in the Ginza neighborhood of Tokyo. The coffee was so diligently prepared that I was perplexed at the ratio of showmanship per milliliters of coffee. But once I tried it, I was baffled and then furious that I never had coffee this stunning and complex—with such a bewildering viscosity—in my whole life. Why had this been kept from me?!?

The hallmarks of this style of nel drip are characterized by low brewing temperatures (approximately 175°F or 79°C), slow extraction, older coffee (post-roast), course grind, and very tight brewing ratios. For me the magic of nel drip is the texture. A beautifully made nel drip is radiant and plump—substantial like espresso without the same intensity, and thicker than a French press without the graininess. It is syrupy yet not heavy. The aftertaste, while shorter in duration than an espresso, is more intense. Many U.S. coffee experts consider the extraction "incorrect" because the brewing temperature is too low, the brewing ratio is too small, and the grind is much too coarse. However, this selective underextraction can produce an amazing range of flavors not present in more traditionally accepted methods of brewing coffee. The correct pour can coax out flavors of a coffee—copper pennies, cacao nibs, canned sliced mandarins in heavy syrup, tomato confit—that are unobtainable through any other means of extraction, so that even modest coffees properly prepared with a nel drip can seem like the rarest treasures. We have noticed that lighter, brighter coffees are best enjoyed on the nel quite a few days post-roast. We love Indonesian and Brazilian coffees roasted at a medium or deeper roast level from 3 to 4 days out, all the way up to 3 to 4 weeks after roast; lightly roasted Central American and African coffees will benefit from 10 days or more of rest after roasting. Using this method, we've made memorable cups with six-week-old coffees—unthinkable with any other extraction method we've tried.

We love the saturated sweetness and Madeira-like mouth feel of the nel. The Apollonian nel is solid, densely structured, and deeply rational compared with our other favorite—the Dionysian siphon: kaleidoscopic, wild, and ethereal. (See page 95 for more on siphon coffee.) The technique of nel drip is one of the most ineffable, so lots of practice and a few disappointing cups await a beginning nel coffee practitioner.

WHAT YOU'LL NEED
Nel drip filter
Soft-bristle brush
Coffee beans, ideally 1 to 3 weeks after roasting
Gram scale
Coffee grinder
Thin bamboo paddle, offset spatula, or butter knife
About 200 ml (6.8 fl oz) good-quality water
Thermocouple
Swan-necked kettle
Timer
Carafe

When new, remove the flannel filter from the wire frame, and submerge it in boiling water for 5 to 10 minutes. Carefully remove it from the hot water and brush lightly with a clean soft-bristle brush that you will only use for this purpose. If you have an already-used nel, remove it from its storage container.

Bring the water to a boil and grind 40 to 50 grams (1.4 to 1.8 oz) of coffee. The grind should be quite coarse—coarser than a French press grind—and the coffee should feel gritty and sharp. Individual particles of coffee should be easily discernable even if you are not wearing your reading glasses.

Take the still-damp nel, pinch the bottom between two fingers, and gently rotate it 360 to 540 degrees to wring more water out. Place the nel and frame between a clean dishtowel and spank both sides to coax even more water out of the nel. At the end of this, you should have a slightly damp, slightly warm nel. The seams should be on the outside.

Add the coffee to the nel in a loose mound. Don't compress it.

Take a thin bamboo paddle or offset spatula or butter knife and "groom" the coffee by gently sliding the paddle between the mass of coffee and the nel.

Push the paddle to the bottom of the nel and make a gentle sawing motion completely around the circumference of the nel. Then use your paddle to make an indentation on the top of the mass of coffee that is approximately the circumference of a nickel and the depth of a thumbtack.

Set the nel over a carafe that does not contact the sides of the nel. Place nel and carafe on a gram scale and tare. Place a timer next to your nel.

Pour the hot water into a swan-necked kettle. Let the water cool to approximately 175°F (79°C). Yes, this is a very low temperature.

Start the timer and begin drizzling water around the circumference of the nickel-sized indentation you made in the mass of coffee. Clockwise, of course. Don't worry about saturating all of the coffee. Time and the principle of capillarity will take care of that. Pour over approximately 45 ml (1.5 fl oz) of water over 45 to 60 seconds. Pause for 45 seconds. The coffee should look active and be churning upward.

After your pause, pour 80 ml (2.7 fl oz) of water in the same pattern but slightly faster, over 60 to 80 seconds. A cap should form over the coffee that is the approximate size, shape, and color of a button mushroom cap. Keep the mushroom in the center of the nel! Pause for 20 seconds.

Next, add 60 ml (2 fl oz) of water at an even faster pace—about 30 seconds.

The end result is 185 ml (6.2 fl oz) of water poured over 3 minutes, 20 seconds. About 100 ml (3.4 fl oz) will be in the carafe, the rest will be captured by the coffee grounds. Remove the nel from the carafe before all the liquid has dripped out.

There is a chance that the coffee will be not quite hot enough to drink with all necessary appreciation. Our friends at Café Hatou reheat the coffee before serving by pouring it into a small copper sugar melter and briefly setting it on an induction burner set to low. At Blue Bottle, we can't bring ourselves to reheat coffee so we compensate by heating our cups with very hot water before the coffee goes in. Serve.

After each use of the nel drip, rinse the nel in hot water and brush both sides again. Then place in a jar, pour in cold water to submerge, and store uncovered in the refrigerator. The damp nel can also be held in a sealed zip-top bag with the same results.

TROUBLESHOOTING If you are having problems making delicious coffees with this preparation method, these are often the culprits:

- Too high brewing temperature

- Too fine a grind

- Too long a brew cycle

- Coffee that is too close to its roast date

- Inadequately cared-for nel (i.e., dirty, dry, moldy)

JAPAN'S COFFEE TOOLS

There's a temptation to see new developments in coffee in the United States as being original, but using manual techniques to express the intricacies of flavor from single-origin coffees is something the Japanese have been great at for the last sixty years. Those of us in the States who are trying to put our own stamp on these techniques have one person to thank: a canned coffee salesman from the UCC Ueshima Coffee Co. named Jay Egami.

I met Jay in the winter of 2003. I was making coffee at the Blue Bottle cart at San Francisco's Ferry Plaza Farmers Market. Jay waited in line like everyone else, and then after I made him a cappuccino, he handed me his card showing his credentials as a San Francisco–based U.S. representative of UCC. He asked if he could see my roaster, which at the time was still in the potting shed in Oakland. Jay is a salesman, so in a sense he was just doing his job by meeting me, but I got the idea that he appreciated what I was trying to achieve, and we soon became friends.

Getting to know Jay over the years has been like taking a correspondence course in Japanese-style coffee. I had been doing pour-over coffee from Blue Bottle's beginnings in 2002, but I've always been interested in continually improving and refining my processes. To that end, over the years I asked Jay questions, and he came back with numbers from the UCC Coffee Academy for brewing ratios and extraction times. I realized that, given his travel schedule and enthusiasm for coffee and cafés, he had been to more cafés than anyone I knew. Jay's worldly attitude toward cafés and his opinions were a great touchstone for me, keeping me from getting too parochial.

After opening Blue Bottle's first permanent location in January of 2005, my priority was espresso, both from the roasting side and from the barista side. We made pour overs like we had been making at the farmers' markets—huge dose, a faster pour, agitation, and a lot of water. It was tasty and popular, but unsubtle, and as usual, I was interested how we might improve our pour over.

Jay first handed me a Bonmac catalog in 2006. Bonmac, a subsidiary of UCC, distributes equipment to cafés all around Japan—and what equipment it is! A dozen kinds of drippers, swan-necked kettles, siphons, siphon bars, kenaf-paper filters, bamboo-paper filters, nel drip kits, and mysterious drippers for iced coffee that resemble grandfather clocks, not to mention the siphons and siphon lights that I noticed in Tokyo during my first trip to Japan when I was nineteen years old. Back then Jay was one of the only people in the States who could import that beautiful gear, and in 2007 we started switching to more Japanese equipment and techniques, culminating with the siphon bar when we opened the Mint Plaza café in 2008.

Jay started getting calls from all over the country. Anytime I heard about a café with a pour-over bar opening or a shop with Hario gear for sale, I knew that Jay had helped them out. Now there are several importers of Japanese coffee gear, but none more influential and knowledgeable than Jay Egami.

THE ROAD TO SIPHON COFFEE AND THE MINT PLAZA CAFÉ

Siphon coffee was invented in the 1840s more or less simultaneously by a French housewife and a Scottish marine engineer. Over the decades, various refinements have been made to the process of preparing siphon coffee, but the basic principle, based on the physics of expanding water vapor, has not changed: when heated sufficiently, water boils.

Siphon coffee is the most theatrical of all brewing methods. When brewing siphon coffee with a beam heater, Japanese style, it's the closest we baristas get to being in the Rockettes. Blue Bottle opened the first Japanese-style siphon bar in the United States in our Mint Plaza location in San Francisco in 2008. There we serve a menu of three single-origin coffees, changing seasonally, prepared by dedicated siphon baristas. I dubbed the siphons bar's opening crew "siphonistas" as a joke during our initial training, but the name stuck (which is to say: I didn't learn a thing from the Gibraltar episode, discussed on page 125), and quite a few places around the world now use the term.

As I've mentioned, we opened our first permanent location, the kiosk on Linden Street, in January of 2005. Nestled in a garage on a dead-end alleyway in San Francisco's edgy but rapidly gentrifying Hayes Valley, it started out seeming like a goof, a performance art installation, a curiosity that would barely make $200 a day. But we were dead serious about making coffee, and people in the neighborhood started finding us—then people from other neighborhoods, then coffee-starved out-of-towners, and pretty soon the lines were as long as the lines at Blue Bottle's cart at the farmers' markets.

In mid-2006, when I started scouting around for a café that, unlike the Linden Street kiosk, actually offered customers protection from the rain, I came across the Provident Loan Building in downtown San Francisco. It's directly behind the glorious and empty pre–1906 earthquake Old Mint building. Constructed in 1912, the Provident Loan Building has been in continual use as a "collateral loan" institution. Don't say pawn shop. Our shop is located in the back of this building, on yet another pee-smelling alley. But the building! With 17-foot (5.2-m) ceilings, intact original details, and diffuse light from the north-facing windows, the proportions are harmonious and expansive. Its elegance and verticality combine to make it feel like a place where siphon coffee should be made.

So in spite of the fact that it was located a block away from San Francisco's diciest street, had essentially zero foot traffic, and almost no visibility from the nearest major streets, I blithely signed a lease based on my naive faith that great architecture, siphon coffee, and toast could overcome obstacles that far more astute businesspeople would run from. Once I secured a location that would harmonize beautifully with the preparation and service of siphon coffee, I needed Jay Egami's assistance. I didn't want to take him to the site, since it was so sketchy, but I showed him pictures of the building and told him about my plan for a full-service café complete with a siphon bar, single-origin espresso on a vintage espresso machine, and simple, house-made breakfasts and lunches.

To my surprise, he agreed with me and said he would order the siphon bar at once. We needed maximum time to practice. I didn't want to tell many people about the plan because

I wasn't sure how it was going to work out. The only way to find out was to write a big check and wait.

At last, the moment arrived. Jay pulled up with some big boxes in his truck, and we set up the equipment on a counter at the roastery. The machine itself looked as though it had been plucked from the *Nautilus*: five brass burners that looked like portholes and flashed an intense red-amber light strong enough to boil 300 milliliters (10 fl oz) of water in 90 seconds, a Fuji touchpad with a dozen buttons labeled only in Japanese, countdown timers, and the meticulous craftsmanship that I've come to expect from all of the gear I get from Jay. I was going to be the Captain Nemo of Mint Plaza, but instead of playing the organ, I would make coffee on my siphon bar!

We kept the siphon brewer at the roaster, and tucked it under a cloth during roasting days so it wouldn't get dusty. On Sunday afternoon (when we weren't roasting coffee and no one was around), I went in so I could have a little peace and quiet with the new siphon equipment. I imagined the serenity of preparing exquisite coffees one after the other—tasting one, sighing deeply with pleasure, and moving on to the next incredible coffee. I started on my first coffee. I fumbled a little with the paddle used to stir the coffee in the glass siphon bowl and the brew cycle was a little slow. But the lights! The pageantry!

After I finished brewing the coffee, I took a deep sniff of this incredible washed Ethiopian coffee I had been saving expressly for the purpose of enjoying my virgin siphon attempt. I inhaled the aroma of . . . diner coffee. Puzzled, I took a sip. It tasted like . . . diner coffee. I tried brewing it again. Diner coffee. I chose a different wonderful coffee, this one from Brazil. The result? Diner coffee. I tried a dry-processed Ethiopian. Diner coffee.

I had a lot to learn about making siphon coffee. The coffee can get very hot if you're not careful, and I was burning each and every pot beyond recognition.

The Japanese method of preparing siphon coffee can be maddeningly elusive. Siphonistas in Japan stay at their jobs for years and serve lengthy apprenticeships where they learn to delicately manipulate the water in the siphon with the bamboo paddle so it doesn't burn the coffee. There are competitions in Japan where siphonistas from all over the country vie to be the best at making siphon coffee. We had a competition winner brew siphon coffee at our shop once, and it was a humbling and inspiring experience.

I finally learned to make a good pot by practicing stirring water only in the upper bowl. I ended up spending hours doing that before the café opened. I realized that the baristas working at the Mint Plaza café needed to be able to make a good siphon coffee without several years of training and an apprenticeship. So eventually we gravitated to a method that's a little less poetic but more repeatable. In the recipe that follows, I offer you, the budding siphonista, that method, as well as a more traditional Japanese method.

Siphon Coffee

FOR HARIO TCA 2: MAKES 1 SERVING , ABOUT 8 FLUID OUNCES (240 ML);
FOR HARIO TCA 3: MAKES ABOUT 1.5 SERVINGS, ABOUT 12 FLUID OUNCES (360 ML)

There are many different makes of siphons; the recipe below is based on using the Hario TCA 2 or TCA 3. While the general principles can be adapted to other makes of siphons, our experience is greater with the Hario, and your results with non-Hario siphons may vary. For that matter, results on Hario siphons are not guaranteed to be consistent given the subtle nature of siphon coffee preparation.

Some siphons, including the Hario, come with a burner that uses denatured alcohol for fuel, which, in my opinion, is inadequate to the task of making excellent coffee. Seek out a Bunsen-style butane-fueled burner for best results, such as Yama brand. Butane is available at most hardware stores.

WHAT YOU'LL NEED
Siphon filter
Siphon upper bowl
Siphon holder
Gram scale
20 to 31 grams (0.7 to 1.1 oz) coffee beans
Coffee grinder
Siphon lower bowl with stand
8 fluid ounces (1 cup / 240 ml) good-quality hot water
Butane burner
Thermocouple or other thermometer
Bamboo stirring paddle

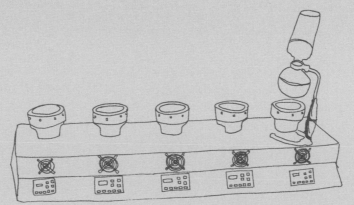

TO USE THE AMERICAN METHOD, soak the filter in warm water for 5 minutes. Drop the filter into the center of the upper bowl, then pull the chain to secure the filter and set the upper bowl into the holder.

Weigh out the coffee; the amount depends on the brewing ratio you'll use (see page 73). Grind the coffee to a medium coarseness, a little finer than you would for French press (see page 83).

Pour the hot water into the lower bowl in its stand.

Ignite the burner. Place the lower bowl over the flame and wait for all the water to rise to the upper bowl. Measure the water temperature in the upper bowl and adjust the flame until it stabilizes at 188°F (87°C).

Add the ground coffee to the upper bowl. Gently incorporate the ground coffee into the top layer of hot water by rubbing the paddle along the top of the coffee mass for no longer than 30 seconds. The motion is like trying to spread cold butter on a piece of particularly delicate toast. Within 30 seconds, all the coffee should be moistened by the hot water.

Let the coffee brew for 20 to 40 seconds.

Stir the coffee with the paddle for no more than 12 rotations. The goal is to create the fastest and deepest whirlpool with the minimum of rotations.

Physically separate the siphon pot from the heat source and remember to turn off your burner. The coffee should descend into the lower bowl in 30 to 45 seconds. If it takes longer, the coffee is ground too finely.

To remove the upper bowl, gently rock it back and forth as you twist and pull it out of the lower bowl. Rinse the filter (don't use soap) and dry it with a dish towel. You can store the clean, damp siphon filter in a resealable plastic bag in your refrigerator. If you make siphon coffee sporadically, keep the filter in a covered bowl filled with water and a quarter-teaspoon of espresso cleaning detergent. If you are storing your filter this way, you will need to make one pot and throw it away before making a pot to drink. Hand wash the upper and lower bowls. There's no need to take the lower bowl off the stand during cleaning.

TO USE THE JAPANESE METHOD, soak the filter in warm water for 5 minutes. Drop the filter into the center of the upper bowl, then pull the chain to secure the filter and set the top into the holder.

Weigh out the coffee; the amount depends on the brewing ratio you'll use (see page 73). Grind the coffee to a medium coarseness, a little finer than you would for French press (see page 83). Transfer the ground coffee into the siphon top.

Pour the hot water into the lower bowl in its stand.

Ignite the burner. Place the lower bowl over the flame and wait for the water to boil. Test the heat of the water by inserting the upper bowl so the chain touches the water. You want to see a reaction (bubbles), but if the reaction is too wild, remove the lower bowl from the heat and swirl it in a counterclockwise direction to release bubbles.

With the lower bowl over the heat, insert the upper bowl into the pot firmly but gently, as you will soon need to remove the top.

Once 1 inch (2.5 cm) of water has risen into the upper bowl, use the stirring paddle to immerse the coffee into the water. Scrape the edge and plunge the grounds into the water. Resist the temptation to stir.

Keep the siphon on the heat, undisturbed, for 30 seconds, then start stirring in a counterclockwise direction, with the burner still on. Stir for no more than 12 rotations. The goal is to create the fastest and deepest whirlpool with the minimum of rotations. (This skill is best acquired by practicing stirring without the coffee grounds.) Think of the coffee grounds as a school of fish that want to stay together. Don't cut into the mass of coffee with the paddle.

Physically separate the siphon pot from the heat source and remember to turn off your burner. The coffee should descend into the lower bowl in 30 to 90 seconds. If it takes longer, your grind is too fine.

To remove the upper bowl, gently rock it back and forth as you twist and pull it out of the lower bowl. Rinse the filter (don't use soap) and store it following the instructions, opposite. Hand wash the upper and lower bowls. There's no need to take the lower bowl off the stand during cleaning.

TURKISH COFFEE

Turkish coffee is a method of brewing that's popular across North Africa, Arabia, and the Middle East. It's not called Turkish coffee in every country it's made in, so don't ask for it in Armenia or Greece. However, for the purposes of this book, I'll call it Turkish coffee, and I'll refer to the pot as an *ibrik*, which is what they call it in Arabic-speaking countries, although it is more commonly called a *cezve* in Turkey. Sadly out of favor in coffee geek circles, Turkish coffee, when well made, can be a delightful change from an afternoon espresso, especially if you can't get to your favorite café and don't want to trust an unfamiliar café for something as important as an espresso. Turkish coffee is easy to make at home or when traveling, and at work, if you have access to a stove.

It starts with the ibrik, a long-handled, thin-necked copper or brass pot. The thin neck is important because it pressurizes the expanding water vapor, creating a foam without actually boiling the coffee. Traditionally, Turkish coffee is heavily sweetened and spiced with cardamom, but depending on the coffee you choose, a well-made pot can show a lot of varietal characteristics, and neither sugar nor cardamom is necessary to enjoy it. Turkish coffee is a concentrated and potent drink, so the recommended serving should be approximately 3 fluid ounces (92 ml).

Like espresso, Turkish coffee isn't a type of coffee, it is a preparation method. You can use any type of coffee as long as it's freshly roasted, isn't roasted too darkly, and is ground very finely, to a powder, just prior to brewing. At Blue Bottle, we like dense, dry-processed coffees for this style. When this style of coffee was first prepared in Arabia, the beans were probably wild, dry-processed coffees from the mountains of what is now Yemen. Originally, the ibriks were placed on a tray filled with sand and set over hot coals. The sand supposedly helps provide very even heat, but a modern electric or gas stove will work just fine.

Turkish Coffee

Different ibriks have different capacities. You need to fill yours with water to just below where the neck is narrowest. Then measure that amount of water and base the amount of coffee you use on an 8-to-1 ratio. One important note: you need a good burr grinder (see page 74) to achieve the powdery consistency necessary for Turkish coffee.

WHAT YOU'LL NEED
Good-quality cold water
Ibrik
Gram scale
Coffee beans
Burr grinder

Pour the correct amount of cold water into the ibrik (up to just below where the neck is narrowest). Weigh out the coffee, then grind it very finely; the texture should be similar to cornstarch.

Add the dry coffee on top of the water. Don't stir.

Place the ibrik on the smallest burner on the stove over medium heat. The coffee should foam up after 2 to 3 minutes, depending upon the size of the ibrik. As it approaches this point, you'll see some churning and seething as the water vapor pressurizes under the cap of ground coffee. Then it will start to foam and look like it's boiling. Immediately pull the ibrik off the heat.

Let the bubbles subside, then place the ibrik back on the heat and repeat. The coffee will foam up much more quickly the second time. When it does, remove the ibrik from the heat.

Repeat a third time. At this point, there will hopefully be a fairly persistent layer of foam on top of the coffee. Carefully pour the foam equally into the number of cups you're serving (dividing the foam equally is important for ensuring that all your guests have foam, as that is a traditional indicator of good hospitality). Slide the rest of the coffee down the side of each cup, being careful not to dissipate the foam. Serve immediately.

The silty powdered coffee will settle to the bottom of each cup, so be careful not to drink the last few sips.

Espresso

Like Turkish coffee, espresso is not a type of roast or a type of coffee bean. Espresso is a method. It's a way of extracting about 30 to 40 milliliters (6 to 8 teaspoons) of aromatic coffee essence, made with a brewing ratio of about 1.5 to 1 under about 9 bars of pressure. You can grind coffee from any origin and at any roast level and use it to make an espresso. However, making consistently delicious, well-crafted espresso is an art, and not an easy one to master. So before you go out and buy an espresso machine, you should ask yourself one simple question: are you sure you want to make espresso at home?

THE INS AND OUTS OF HOME ESPRESSO MACHINES

Suze Orman is wrong. You will not save money if you buy a home espresso machine. You will spend money. Making espresso at home also won't save time, compared to going out to your favorite crowded café. Unless you live far from a decent café, you probably won't make better drinks at home.

Various studies in the social sciences have shown that humans have evolved a capacity for self-deception. From an evolutionary perspective, the adaptive benefits of self-deception apparently allowed our species to survive when knowing our true motivations or desires might harm us or our ability to procreate. Optimism, confidence, exuberance—these are the delightful by-products of our evolved ability to deceive ourselves. So we buy things like espresso machines. Optimistically.

Perhaps you have thoughts like these:

> "I'll save $832 a year if I stop going to Starbucks!"
> "I can learn to make drinks better than that!"
> "I wouldn't have missed my train if the line wasn't so long!"

Let's be real: making espresso at home is expensive, difficult, and time-consuming. Struggling to be better at something makes us better people. Parenting, graduating from college, running a marathon, building a house with your own hands—these are all difficult activities, activities that no one should talk us out of just because they're difficult. And perhaps making a really great espresso, although a modest endeavor, belongs on the list of things that we probably will never do perfectly but will benefit from in the attempt to do so. In other words, perhaps it's worthy of our time, resources, and attention.

One of the reasons espresso machines hold such allure for a certain aspirationally geeky type of personality is that they are relatively simple devices that give the impression of being much more complicated. Your microwave is much more complex. Your wristwatch is much more intricate. But an espresso machine is sexy and mysterious—and it makes coffee.

UNDERSTANDING THE PROCESS AND THE EQUIPMENT If you're new to making espresso, a lot of the following discussion of espresso machines and their parts may not be clear. In that case, here's an outline of the basic steps to help you understand what we are discussing in such avid detail:

- Warm up the machine.
- Grind the coffee into the portafilter while rotating the portafilter slowly.
- Distribute and tamp the coffee.
- Lock the portafilter in place in the group head.
- Place the cup under the portafilter.
- Pull the shot by activating the pump.

An espresso machine has four basic parts: the boiler, the pump, the group head, and the portafilter assembly.

THE BOILER. The heating element, which heats water and keeps it at a consistent temperature, resides inside the boiler. As the water temperature increases, the pressure inside the boiler increases proportionally (you remember Gay-Lussac's law, of course) to approximately 5 bars. The happy result is that water at less than boiling temperatures can produce vaporized water (aka steam) to foam the milk for your cappuccino.

THE PUMP. The pump takes the pressurized hot water from the boiler and increases the pressure to approximately 9 bars. This can be accomplished mechanically, via either a rotary or vibratory pump, or with a lever.

THE GROUP HEAD. The group head receives hot water pushed by the pump from the boiler and distributes the water as evenly as possible through a system of fine holes to the portafilter.

THE PORTAFILTER AND FILTER BASKET. The portafilter is the assembly that holds the ground coffee on most espresso machines. A bottomless portafilter is one without the spouts or metal base on the bottom of the basket. At Blue Bottle, we use the bottomless version (as shown opposite) for training because it allows visual feedback on how well the coffee was distributed, based on how the espresso looks when it flows out of the machine. We also like the bottomless version when making espresso for service; because the espresso doesn't come in contact with so much metal (the spouts), the resulting espresso is palpably thicker.

The heating element, boiler, and pump are hidden inside a beautiful stainless steel box, and what is visible are the steam wand, the portafilter, the group head, and a few nice switches.

BEING REALISTIC ABOUT COSTS Think about how much you want to spend to make espresso drinks at home. Now double it—and be prepared to double it again. Why? The best espresso machines are made in Europe, and they are expensive (page 109 includes a

THE ANATOMY OF AN ESPRESSO MACHINE

The finely tuned parts of an espresso machine fit together so beautifully that the various components can be hard to identify when looking at a composed machine. In this exploded view, you can see the portafilter—we use a bottomless style, which is a "chopped" version that enables baristas to see the accuracy of the dose and distribution—which holds the perforated metal portafilter basket with the grounds against the group head. Espresso machines typically come with a single basket, which is usually sized to hold 7 grams (0.25 oz) of ground coffee, and a double basket, which can hold up to 22 grams (0.78 oz); we never use single baskets at Blue Bottle. The group head is the terminus of the valve in which hot, pressurized water emerges from the boiler and contacts the ground espresso.

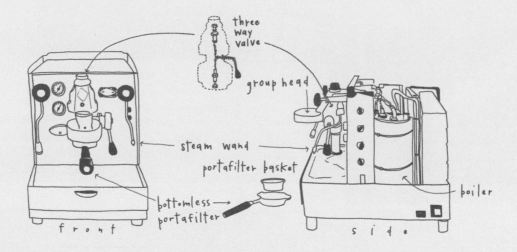

THE ANATOMY OF AN ESPRESSO GRINDER

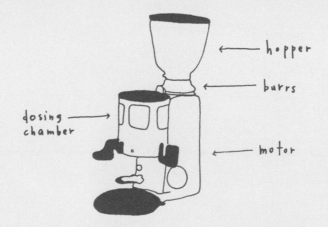

discussion of prices, but keep in mind that there are many other associated costs). Decide if you want to purchase something inexpensive that will be difficult and frustrating to operate and produce inferior results. And be aware that you can also purchase something expensive that will be difficult and frustrating to operate and produce inferior results. So be careful. Keep reading.

BUY A GRINDER FIRST

Any barista will tell you that the single most important piece of gear in the espresso-making chain is the grinder. So buy your grinder first.

Earlier, I discussed how grinding exposes more of the coffee's surface area to hot water, which acts as a solvent and dissolves particles and compounds from the exposed area. The shorter the time the coffee is exposed to hot water, the more important it is that it be ground to the correct size for optimal extraction. If it isn't ground correctly, the hot water will under-extract some parts of the coffee and overextract others. Since espresso is the method of brewing that uses hot water at the highest pressure and has the shortest extraction time, grinding—and hence an appropriate grinder—figures much more prominently than in other methods of making coffee.

People usually think that producing an even grind, with all coffee particles the same size, is the most important virtue of an espresso grinder. But that's not the case. Most of the better

A SPECIAL PLACE IN HELL: POD COFFEE

As I've pointed out elsewhere, taste is subjective. That different people will have different preferences in coffee is not only possible but likely, and reasonable people can disagree about many things, coffee included. But I'm going to issue one categorical opinion: pod coffee is bad and wrong—bad because it's impossible to use pod brewers to produce a delicious beverage, and wrong because it teases people into buying into an industrially produced product masquerading as handcrafted—and that involves almost 70 percent waste.

Let's first look at roasting for the pod. Good roasters tell you what type of coffee is in the bag. If it's a blend, they tell you what the constituent coffees are, and if it's a single-origin, they'll get a lot more specific than merely the country of origin. Good roasters tell you where the coffee was roasted and put the roast date, not a "best by" date, on the bag. With pod coffee, you don't get any of those details. Nominal information about country of origin is available on some pods, but that's rare. You don't know when the coffee was roasted, where it was roasted, or even when it was ground.

Pod coffee brands like K-Cup and Nespresso have appropriated the language and symbolism of exclusivity without any corresponding craft or deliciousness. Each K-Cup pod contains about 8 grams (0.28 oz) of coffee, and Nespresso capsules have about 5.5 grams (0.2 oz). Using 8 grams (0.28 oz) of coffee for a 355-milliliter (12 fl oz) serving translates to a brewing ratio of 44 to 1! Add an extraction time of less than 60 seconds and a brewing temperature and pouring pattern that is entirely out of your control, and the decisive, emphatic result to pod brewing is this: deliciousness is impossible.

Some people argue that K-Cups are less wasteful than brewing a pot of coffee because you only make what you'll drink. But for every 1 pound (455 g) of coffee purchased, approximately 83 aluminum Nespresso capsules or 57 plastic K-Cup capsules are wasted. Each empty capsule weighs approximately two-thirds the weight of the coffee, creating about 10 ounces (285 g) of waste for every 1 pound (455 g) of coffee brewed. Contrast that with buying coffee from a responsible roaster, who packs it in recyclable or compostable packaging, and who often pays significant premiums above the commodity-level prices that the pod manufacturers usually pay.

The seduction of pod coffee, then, centers around convenience, lack of mess, and the manufacturing of desire by creating beautiful boutiques in which to enjoy the terrible pod coffee, or beautiful advertisements to make us wish we were in the beautiful boutiques enjoying the terrible pod coffee. The manufacturers of pod coffee are telling us, in effect, something we know not to be true: that you can have something great without working for it, that craft can come at a push of a button, and that a shiny piece of plastic on the countertop is an adequate replacement for the experience of gathering with friends over handcrafted coffee at a good café.

espresso grinders have burrs that are carefully designed and constructed to create a mix of small powdery particles (fines) and larger particles. The fines act somewhat like mortar, filling the spaces between the "bricks" of the larger particles to offer the correct resistance to the hot, pressurized water. Most home grinders have flat burrs, but some have conical burrs.

Conical burrs are generally more expensive to replace but prized for how they produce a grind that gives espresso a "fluffy" mouthfeel and purer expression of the layers of the coffee's flavors. Grinders with conical burrs tend to be more expensive and slower than those with flat burrs. Either type is capable of grinding well for espresso. Generally, you want your grinder to be heavy (which implies a larger motor and more metal parts than plastic), have burrs that are 50 millimeters (about 2 in) or greater in diameter if flat or 36 millimeters (about 1³⁄₈ in) or greater if conical, and have the ability adjust the grind size in very fine increments. As mentioned previously, stepless grinders offer the greatest flexibility in grind size.

Do you have limited counter space? Too bad! Good grinders are big, and espresso machines are even bigger, so you're going to have to chop your onions somewhere else.

It's unlikely that you can get a decent espresso grinder for less than $200 or $300, and many home models cost $700 or more. Quality brands include Mazzer, Compak, Rancilio, and Baratza. The great thing about getting a good grinder is that it's a joyfully instantaneous way to improve the quality of your espresso. Plus, good grinders should work well for years and need only minimal maintenance. Just keep your grinder clean and change the burrs after grinding 300 to 400 pounds (135 to 180 kg) of coffee. That's it.

Don't imagine that you can use your espresso grinder to grind coffee for other brewing methods. Your espresso grinder should be used for making espresso—period. It's tricky to dial in a grinder just so for extracting espresso. If you are constantly making the huge grinder adjustments required to go from espresso to French press, for example, you will probably waste upward of a dozen shots as you get your grinder back in the ballpark for espresso. One option is to get a relatively inexpensive hand-crank grinder (see page 74) for other coffee-making needs.

TYPES OF ESPRESSO MACHINES

Assuming that you've selected a good espresso grinder, you're probably wondering if you can now buy an espresso machine. The answer is no.

There are a few different types of espresso machines, and you need to learn about them first:

- Super-automatic
- Automatic
- Semiautomatic
- Manual
- Professional

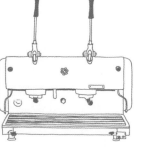

SUPER-AUTOMATIC Super-automatic machines take all of the craft out of the project of making espresso. They grind, tamp, dose, and extract coffee. Sometimes they can even steam and pour milk automatically. It sounds seductive, doesn't it? Imagine, your own robot barista, sans tip jar, willing to dispense macchiato after macchiato at the touch of a button, in your own home. Super-automatic machines manufactured for home use tend to be made with cheap components and therefore break down more often. But they do allow you to make really bad drinks effortlessly.

AUTOMATIC OR SINGLE-SERVE MACHINES On page 106, I dealt with the issue of pod coffee, hopefully once and for all.

SEMIAUTOMATIC MACHINES Semiautomatic machines are where good espresso becomes possible. Consumer semiautomatic machines have portafilters that must be dosed with ground coffee and inserted into the group head. They have steam wands that require using the correct amount of milk in a steam pitcher and the correct technique.

A subcategory of semiautomatic machine is the "prosumer" machine. An ungainly portmanteau word, *prosumer* in this context means that these machines have many of the virtues of the professional espresso machine: larger copper or brass boilers, a 58-millimeter portafilter, a rotary pump, and an articulated steam wand, with a 360-degree range of motion rather than a wand that can only go back and forth. In these machines, heavy components, mostly of metal construction, have been wedded to the needs of the consumer, such as standard (110-volt) electricity and no need for a plumbed-in water connection. These are often the most expensive espresso machines, but they are also the ones that perform best when used well, and they last the longest.

MANUAL MACHINES Also known as lever machines, these machines use a lever for applying pressure, rather than a pump. They look cool, oh yes they do. Many a newcomer to espresso looks longingly at the lever-handled La Pavoni and sees it in his kitchen as the indelible marker of Ian Fleming–style bachelor-pad cache. However, they can be impractical and very tricky to use. Unlike super-automatic machines, which are designed so that good drinks are impossible, it isn't impossible to make a good drink on a manual machine—it's just very, very difficult. Since you are, in effect, acting as the machine's pump, factors such as grind size, dosing, and distribution are even more critical. Most manual machines built for the consumer don't have a three-way valve, which releases built-up pressure, so if your machine doesn't have one, you need to wait to remove the portafilter until the machine has depressurized, or you risk being sprayed by hot, wet coffee grounds.

We do use lever machines at some Blue Bottle locations for single-origin espressi, but commercial lever machines have a spring that produces the brewing pressure on the upstroke of the lever, rather than the barista producing the brewing pressure on the downstroke, as in many home models of lever machines. This creates a little more excitement, owing to the fact that if the portafilter isn't seated correctly, the lever can spring upward with hundreds of pounds of force, possibly breaking jaws or causing concussions if the unfortunate and poorly trained barista happens to have his or her head where it shouldn't be.

PROFESSIONAL MACHINES The professional machines we use at Blue Bottle—usually made by La Marzocco (see page 111)—are monsters: huge, heavy creatures of brass and stainless steel built for artfully making espressi with speed and consistency. They draw 40 to 50 amps of power at 220 volts, and the electricity bill just to keep them running can be several hundred dollars a month. They are usually three-group machines (three portafilters capable of pulling three espressi at a time) and have a dedicated steam boiler, and either one brew boiler or a separate, tunable brew boiler for each group.

CHOOSING AN ESPRESSO MACHINE

It sounds simplistic, but the single best predictor of the adequacy of an espresso machine is weight. Heavy machines usually perform better than lighter machines. Weight implies metal rather than plastic parts, copper or brass boilers rather than steel, larger group heads rather than smaller, commercial-grade rather than consumer-grade.

So when choosing a machine, you can spend countless hours on the Internet, or you can keep a simple guideline in mind: if you spend around two grand on a semiautomatic machine that weighs more than 40 pounds (18.1 kg), you probably made as good a decision as you would have after lurking around boring chatrooms for months.

If you want to consider the important specs in more detail, here are some key features to look for: a commercial-size 58 millimeter portafilter, a rotary pump, an articulated steam wand, a three-way valve, a copper or brass boiler with a volume greater than 12 fluid ounces (355 ml), and a boiler pressure gauge, which lets you know what your brewing temperature is and lets you see the change if you make adjustments, since temperature is proportional to pressure. The same lever or button should turn the pump on and off; you don't need an automatic doser. The only automatic feature should be a sensor that cuts the power to the heating element if the boiler or reservoir runs dry.

If two grand seems like a lot of money, think of all the status symbols that sit lonely and unused day after day: the Steinway pianos, the Viking ranges, the KitchenAid mixers, the Vita-mix blenders. An espresso machine and grinder that are put to use frequently are objects that transform time and money into pleasure and deliciousness—and that, if you have the money, are nothing to be ashamed of.

Of course you don't have to spend $2,000 on an espresso machine to get something serviceable. There are a couple of reasonably priced (around $700) models by Rancilio and Gaggia that are heavy and simple, with larger boilers and commercial portafilters. One of those, paired with a good grinder, will work just fine.

YOU NEED A FEW MORE THINGS

So now you have a grinder and an espresso machine. You're probably wondering if you can start making espresso. Not yet.

There are a few tools that you simply must have. Some people cut corners here, but that's like buying yourself a nice car and then trying to save money by getting only three tires. You are so close. Finish the job. In addition to cleaning supplies (discussed in the next section), here are the accessories you need:

- A gram scale (see page 52). This will also come in handy for baking and cooking.
- A bottomless portafilter that is the appropriate size for your espresso machine.
- A double portafilter basket in your portafilter.
- A stopwatch (or use your phone's timer).
- A stainless steel steaming pitcher that is no more than double the size of the drink you're making. For example, if you typically make 6-ounce (180 ml) cappuccinos, get a 12-ounce (355 ml) pitcher. The sides should be straight, and there should be a pronounced taper on the spout.
- A heavy, metal-based tamper that fits exactly inside your portafilter basket. It can be flat or slightly tapered, but either way, it should fit snugly inside the basket without binding.
- The right cups. Espresso cups should be no more than 3 fluid ounces (90 ml) in capacity and should have thick walls to hold heat. Cappuccino cups should be 6 to 7 fluid ounces (180 to 210 ml). Latte cups should be no more than 12 fluid ounces (355 ml).

Don't forget the other things you'll have to spend a fair bit of money on: coffee and milk. When you're first learning to make espresso and steam milk, you'll probably have to toss most of what you make. Each morning, you may dump a shot or two while dialing in your grind. This adds up, but it's a necessary part of the process.

LA MARZOCCO AND ESPRESSO IN ITALY

We always like to get to know the people who make the products we use, from coffee growers and brokers to dairy companies to equipment manufacturers. While we haven't actually gone to the factory in Taiwan to see where our compostable paper cups and lids are made, we know the people who design them and produce them. The same is true of the people at La Marzocco, the espresso machine manufacturer 17 miles (30 km) outside of Florence, Italy.

We've purchased several dozen La Marzocco machines for our own shops as well as on the behalf of wholesale accounts over the years, so not too long ago Caitlin and I decided to visit the factory. La Marzocco produces about 3,500 espresso machines a year, so it is akin to visiting the Ferrari factory; as soon as you walk in, you can feel that something sleek, expensive, functional, beautiful, and extraordinary is made there. When we made it to the R&D lab, Piero Bambi, the seventy-eight-year-old son of the founder, was scrubbing the sink. He and a few others had been working on some machines and everyone was busy cleaning. Piero made us an espresso on a Strada MP, which turned out to be one of the better coffees we had in Italy.

This image of Piero bent over the sink definitely fits in with the company's gestalt. Piero's father, Giuseppe, started out as an apprentice in his grandfather's tinsmith shop. Always seeing himself as a craftsman at heart, Giuseppe and his brother, Bruno, went on to create a company that has always been on the leading edge of design and technology. They founded La Marzocco in 1927, naming it for the lion symbolic of Florence, where the company was first located. Aligning itself with the city's artisan traditions, the company made (and still makes) its machines by hand.

The first espresso machines were introduced earlier, at the turn of the nineteenth century, but drinking coffee at a bar didn't take off in Italy until a few decades later. The earliest machines were vertical boilers with taps that were used for heating milk and making espresso. Some ran on electricity, some on gas, and some even on coal, with a coal drawer beneath the boiler. The barista's responsibility extended to managing the temperature of the boiler by adding coals at judicious moments. Those early machines must have been incredibly hard to control.

In 1939, the Bambis patented the first horizontal boiler, the Marus, enabling baristas to make several drinks at a time and forever changing the design of espresso machines. The company says that all examples of the Marus were lost during the war, when many espresso machines were melted down for their steel or iron, but it still has a copy of the original patent.

La Marzocco machines being assembled by hand at the factory headquarters near Florence

The postwar period was really espresso's heyday, and La Marzocco continued its design innovations, creating sleek wonders that fit into the midcentury aesthetic. In 1970, the company came out with the GS series, which was groundbreaking for having a dual boiler, one for steaming milk and the other—exclusively for coffee—that could be maintained at a more constant temperature.

More recently, La Marzocco developed one of the first PID-controlled brew boilers to make espresso brewing more accurate. PID stands for proportional-integral-derivative, which is a very mathy way of describing a temperature control routine that makes the brewing boiler on these machines accurate to within 0.1°F (0.06°C). Espresso boilers generally are controlled with a mechanical thermostat that can have a "dead band," in which they don't respond to temperature changes of up to 4°F (2.2°C). Blue Bottle was the second roaster in the United States, after Espresso Vivace in Seattle, to modify our La Marzocco with a PID.

Though La Marzocco, which moved into its bigger and better headquarters outside of Florence in 2009, is still advancing the technology of espresso making, the majority of its machines, strangely, are exported to the United States, Japan, and other parts of Europe. In the high-end coffee world, and even within the walls of the La Marzocco factory, you often hear complaints about the quality of coffee in Italy.

The decline in the quality of Italian coffee quality is generally attributed to two factors: Because the cost of a cup of espresso is regulated by the government at around 1 euro, there's not a lot of incentive to seek out high-quality green coffee or to dose more than 7 grams (0.25 oz) for a single shot. Also, at the majority of coffee bars, the espresso machines are provided and serviced by the large coffee roasters, and as a result, the overall coffee culture has become entrenched and commodified. Because so many customers order a single espresso rather than a more expensive drink, running a profitable café hinges on making large numbers of espressi during the day and selling a lot of cocktails at night. On our trip, Caitlin and I sought out cafés in Florence, Bologna, and Venice that serve single-origin coffee or that use quality machines and found a handful. But there are far fewer than you'd expect.

What critics of the current state of Italian coffee often ignore is what the country has achieved, which is near-universal adequacy. At almost any café in Italy, you can rest assured that the coffee will be at worst not bad, and at best pretty darn good. This isn't faint praise; this is actually a glorious achievement—one that's hard to imagine occurring anywhere else on the planet. When we were leaving Italy, I ordered an espresso in the Florence airport and then another at the Frankfurt airport. Both used Illy coffee, and both were made on identical Cimbali machines. The one in Florence was a fine, pleasant drink, distinguished by an absence of negative qualities, while the one in Frankfurt was terrible. A forty-five-minute flight, and a world apart.

It's thrilling to see how professionally and smoothly the cafés are run in Italy—seeing old ladies putting their shopping bags down and having espressi for here. The customers know what to order and know how to behave. It's a deep tradition. We can't duplicate it in the United States, but we can learn from it, even if most Italian cafés aren't aspiring to hit the transcendent highs some U.S. establishments are shooting for.

La Marzocco's responsiveness to what the worldwide high-end coffee markets want is remarkable. They want to figure out where technology can take coffee, even if there's a lack of interest in Italy. Part of that can be explained by their partial American ownership and deep ties to the high-end coffee community in the United States, but much of it rests on the tradition of creativity and artisanship that is still embodied by Piero Bambi.

CLEANING YOUR ESPRESSO MACHINE

Old coffee smells and tastes bad. Therefore, you must get rid of old coffee that has accumulated in your machine. All of it. You'll need espresso machine detergent and an espresso machine brush. If your espresso machine has a three-way valve, after every twenty-five to thirty-five drinks made, you need to back flush the machine. This forces espresso detergent up through the group head and tubing and into other places a brush can't get to. Each manufacturer provides instructions on how to back flush. The important thing is to do it.

After back flushing, take your brush and some espresso detergent mixed with hot water and methodically scrub the group head, concentrating on the areas where coffee can accumulate. If the shower screen can be easily removed, take it off and soak it in a solution of hot water and detergent according to the instructions on the detergent bottle. Then scrub with your brush. Pop the portafilter basket out of your portafilter. Soak both in a solution of espresso machine detergent and hot water, and after a few minutes of soaking, scrub well. Wipe everything off. Espresso detergent doesn't taste good, so after cleaning everything, you need to make an espresso, dump it, and then rinse everything with hot water and no detergent. Now you're ready to make twenty-five more drinks.

UNDERSTANDING THERMAL STABILITY

Espresso machines are built to be left on. Thermal stability is paramount in extracting good espresso consistently, and the thermal mass of an espresso machine acts as a heat sink that helps to regulate the brewing temperature. However, keeping the machine preheated is hard to do at home. You probably want to make espresso first thing in the morning, and you probably tend to be concerned about using electricity unnecessarily and therefore don't want to leave your machine on all night. Given that you probably don't want to get up two hours early just to preheat your machine, the easiest way to ensure thermal stability is to use a simple appliance timer, which you can purchase at a hardware store. Set it to turn on your espresso machine an hour or two before you wake up.

Manufacturers usually include a recommended warm-up time of about 20 minutes. Some machines even have an indicator light that signals when the boiler is at adequate temperature and pressure. But usually the light turns on much sooner than optimal thermal stability would suggest. The difference in performance is striking between an inadequately warmed-up machine and one that is completely warmed up.

Making Espresso

Describing how to make espresso in a book is an endeavor that's both foolish and optimistic. This is a guide only in the sense that you may be a little closer to feeling confident about making espresso after you've read it. Read this, then go out and buy 5 pounds (2.3 kg) of coffee, then turn off your phone, and make one hundred espressi. This will take four to five hours. Do the same next week, and the week after that. Smell each espresso you make, and try sips of maybe one out of ten. Espresso is a physical act: a manifestation of will, effort, and desire exerted upon a machine and an agricultural product. Every espresso you make will be slightly different.

Familiarity is an essential part of the process. You and your espresso machine will evolve together—the various parts will feel strange in your hands when you're first learning to make espresso. The physical uncertainty of locking a portafilter into the group head or steaming some milk will vanish after a few hundred times, but probably no sooner than that. Familiarity and confidence are, ultimately, a simple matter of repetition. Think about what you will know with your body and your palate after you've made a thousand drinks—and after ten thousand drinks.

GETTING READY Warm up your espresso machine for at least an hour, and preferably two (see Understanding Thermal Stability, opposite). The portafilter and basket should stay in the machine as it warms up.

Get rid of any ground coffee that is in your grinder. You want all the coffee that ends up in your portafilter to be freshly ground.

The following instructions for dosing the portafilter involve lengthy descriptions. However, the process should be as brief and efficient as possible. For optimal extraction, the portafilter needs to stay warm, so minimize the amount of time it's out of the group head. Because bottomless portafilters have even less mass than stock portafilters, be even more assiduous about the amount of time they spend out of the group head.

DOSE THE PORTAFILTER Remove the portafilter from the machine and briefly wipe the portafilter basket with a dry cloth.

While you're learning to dose espresso, tare your portafilter on your gram scale so you can be sure that you're dosing the same amount of coffee every time. If you have a commercial-size portafilter, dose between 16 and 20 grams (0.6 and 0.7 oz) into the double basket. (Don't use the single basket—ever. Throw it away or let your two-year-old play with it.) Keep your

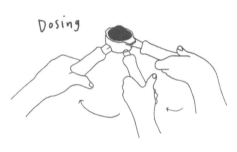

Dosing

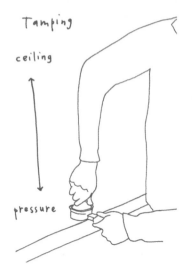

Tamping

ceiling

pressure

dose constant. Choose a number, say 18.5 grams (0.65 oz), and stick with it until you're making satisfactory extractions. It's best to change only one variable at a time.

Grind the coffee into the tared portafilter while slowly rotating the portafilter, holding it under the grinder with the handle starting at three o'clock and moving it slowly to nine o'clock, so the coffee disperses somewhat evenly into the portafilter basket.

Check the weight to confirm you have the correct dose. The coffee should form a mound that extends above the rim of the portafilter.

Sharply tap the portafilter on the countertop three times to reduce the size of the mound. This is called settling.

DISTRIBUTE THE GROUNDS AND TAMP The next step is generally considered the trickiest and most subtle step in the extraction process. Unfortunately, it's also the most difficult to describe. You want distribute those 18.5 grams of coffee equally within the portafilter basket. The level and density of the coffee need to be as even as possible; otherwise the hot, pressurized water will crash through the less-dense regions more quickly and overextract the coffee. The result will not be delicious.

If you're right-handed, take your right hand and form a backward L with your thumb and index finger. Place your right hand over the portafilter so the meaty flesh between your thumb and index finger is up against the remaining mound of espresso. Rotate the portafilter with your left hand (from five o'clock to nine o'clock) with your right hand up against the mound. Do this three times. The mound should diminish in size each time you rotate. If all goes well, the surface of the coffee will be roughly level.

Take the tamper and place it gently on the surface of the ground coffee, making sure it's level. Place the portafilter on a flat surface, such as kitchen counter, and press down firmly with the tamper, keeping your arm and wrist straight and your elbow pointing toward the ceiling. Apply about 30 to 40 pounds (13.5 to 18 kg) of pressure. You can check whether you're applying enough pressure by putting the portafilter on a bathroom scale and tamping, but I've always thought there's something unsavory about seeing a bathroom scale on a kitchen counter. It's your call.

To finish tamping, ease up and rotate the tamper 180 degrees, in effect, polishing the surface of the coffee. You have now created a dense, level, tidy puck of coffee in your portafilter. If you were to turn the portafilter upside down, the puck would stay in the portafilter because you've compressed and sealed it in the basket.

Pull 2 fluid ounces (60 ml) of water through the boiler to stabilize the brewing temperature. Lock the portafilter back into the espresso machine. Tare your espresso cup on the gram scale, then put the cup under the portafilter.

EXTRACTION This is the moment you've been waiting for. Now you get to extract the espresso.

Start a timer, actuate the pump, and then kneel down so you can see the hot, pressurized water coalesce into the first drops of espresso. If you have dosed, distributed, and tamped correctly, you will see all of the regions at the bottom of the portafilter basket start to ooze the same color of brown at the same time (see photo, page 103). If the process went awry somewhere, you'll see regions of much lighter brown and regions of very dark brown. The espresso will pour from the lighter regions first because those are regions of lesser density.

You're aiming for a flow rate of approximately 0.75 ml per second (or 1 teaspoon every 7 seconds). If everything goes according to plan, the espresso will gather at the bottom of the basket for several seconds, then fall from the basket drop by drop until a thin stream forms. Hopefully this stream is a beautiful reddish brown. After 20 to 30 seconds, the stream will lighten in color. This is your cue to shut off the pump, stop the timer, and remove the cup. Weigh the tared cup on the gram scale to measure the amount of espresso you extracted. The weight should be about 35 grams (1.25 oz), corresponding to 35 milliliters (0.8 fl oz) of espresso.

If the espresso looks beautiful, with a cap of reddish brown crema (see page 118), and smells like really good coffee, take a sip.

TROUBLESHOOTING If the espresso came out too fast—35 milliliters (1.2 fl oz) in 10 to 15 seconds—your grind is too coarse. Adjust your grinder and try again.

If the espresso came out too slowly—35 milliliters (1.2 fl oz) in 40 to 50 seconds, or not at all—your grind is too fine. Adjust your grinder in the opposite direction and try again.

That's really all there is to it. Extracting espresso isn't mysterious, it's just very difficult. If you use fresh high-quality coffee, grind it at the time, measure the dose, distribute the coffee in the portafilter basket accurately, time your extraction, and measure your output, the only variables are the coarseness or fineness of the grind and the brewing temperature of your machine. Since different machines have different protocols for adjusting the brewing temperature, the only variable that falls within the scope of this guide is the grinder adjustment. So to improve your results, keep everything else the same and adjust the coarseness or fineness.

However, once you find that perfect spot for the grinder, there's no guarantee that it will stay perfect as other factors change. For example, as the coffee ages, you'll need to loosen up the grind a little. If the weather changes, you'll have to change the grind. As the weather gets more humid—for example, if you have a crowd in the kitchen at a party—you need to loosen the grind. The important part is to pay attention—and to practice, practice, practice.

A NOTE ABOUT CREMA

The color, density, texture, and aroma of crema gives us an insight to what the espresso might possibly taste like. This diagnostic component of crema is often the most remarked about characteristic of the espresso. If the crema on an espresso is a thick, luxuriant blanket of dark mahogany foam (in which the constituent bubbles are so tiny they are hard to see with the unaided human eye) mottled with darker brown "tiger stripes," we anticipate something delicious and well-made; it's akin to the way char marks on a grilled steak signal something wonderful coming our way. The crema on top of an espresso is made of emulsified oils, sugars, and proteins that form a network of tiny spheres. Each of those holds a precious bit of sensory information—much more information per cubic milliliter than the coffee alone. However, crema has three very important functions, and serving as a diagnostic is only one. Crema also acts as a "cap" in much the same way that, when we cup, the cap of ground coffee sits on top of the liquid coffee and traps important gases. Because crema itself holds so much gas, it traps more

sensory information within it than espresso minus the crema—an espresso that has the crema scooped off the surface has less to say than the espresso with the crema left on.

ESPRESSO AT BLUE BOTTLE

At Blue Bottle, we have two sets of goals for our espresso, one for blends and one for single-origins. We don't think of these goals as being objectively correct, but we do think of them as having certain virtues that can be objectively described. Our goals are personal and have evolved over the years we've been making espresso. They have more in common with the style of one of the pioneers of modern American espresso, David Schomer of Espresso Vivace in Seattle, than traditional Italian-style espresso. Schomer, who founded his business in 1988 with a sidewalk coffee cart in Seattle, became well-known for his sweet, well-calibrated ristretto shots, and for introducing the country to latte art.

Ristretto, or restricted espresso, is a shot that uses a heavier brewing ratio than the classic Italian brewing ratio of 7 grams of ground coffee to produce 30 ml of espresso. Anywhere from a 1:1 to 1:1.5 brewing ratio is usually considered a ristretto extraction. Over the years, Schomer became increasingly obsessed with measuring and controlling the variables involved with making espresso, and in the process changed the way Americans think about coffee. All of us in the U.S. coffee trade who measure variables, take good notes, and strive to make beautiful drinks owe him a substantial debt of gratitude.

We usually offer four espresso blends at Blue Bottle. Each was developed for a specific location and machine, but all have several common threads, in both preparation and outcome. Generally, what we are looking for with our blends is an espresso that is thick, sweet, caramelly, and complex, with a subtle brightness that never crosses the line to strident but also isn't overly delicate. We want our blends to be likable. Avuncular. Sturdy. Buttery. We usually have one central idea for each blend and strive to maintain it from day to day and year to year, fine-tuning blending, roasting, and preparation to achieve that idea.

For example, the idea for the Hayes Valley Espresso is chocolate-dipped orange peel. During roasting, the beans for the Hayes Valley Espresso are never taken to second crack, but two of the components are usually taken pretty close to that point. Because it is so darkly roasted, we like to serve it three to six days after roasting. If we roasted it lighter, we would need to let it rest up to a week longer. We use a double basket and a bottomless portafilter to emphasize the thickness of the espresso. We serve it between 198°F and 200.5°F (92°C and 93.6°C) as measured by the PID (see page 111) on the La Marzocco espresso machines at our shops. We usually dose 18.5 to 21 grams (0.65 to 0.75 oz) of coffee, based on the particular machine, the season, the intuition of the barista, the weather, and the roast date. We pull lengthy extractions of about 34 seconds for a short 30 milliliters (slightly over 1 fl oz) of espresso, a double ristretto. The result, oftentimes, is a realization of our idea of this espresso blend. Ultimately, it's a collaboration among our green buyer, our roasters, our training department, our shop managers, our baristas, and, finally, our customers.

For single-origin espressi, we are less inclined to exert our will on the coffee and more inclined to let the coffee express itself more naturally. Modern pump-driven espresso machines produce admirably even amounts of pressure for the duration of the extraction of the espresso. If you were to plot the pressure on a graph, you would see a quick spike up to 9 bars of pressure, a flat line over the 30 or so seconds of the extraction, and a quick fall off as the pump was turned off. A lever machine produces a far more "inaccurate" pressure profile. But, oddly enough, the lazy ascent to 9 bars, and the equally unhurried descent, can do lovely things to the taste of a single-origin coffee, which is why we usually like to make single-origin espressi on lever machines. We've found that the bell-shaped pressure curve (as opposed to the more linear pressure curve of the modern pump-driven machine) extracts a sweeter, more rounded, espresso. Plus, vintage lever espresso machines are about the coolest thing ever, and it's wonderful to have these amazing objects, dating from as far back as the 1950s, restored and working perfectly in our shops. Generally, our approach for extracting single-origin espressi is to dose slightly lower, extract slightly faster, and draw more water through the group head—up to 40 milliliters (1.4 fl oz)—to bring out the qualities we liked best on the cupping table.

When you've made a few hundred drinks and your basic technique has been solidified by hours of practice, then you too will be able to draw out certain virtues from particular coffees. Varying the dose, the temperature, the length of extraction, and the volume of extraction will allow you to create a flavor tailored to your own desires. Each coffee, whether a blend or a single-origin, will have different attributes. By working on your technique, you can learn to bring out a manifestation of the coffee that is delicious and interesting to you.

STEAMING MILK

As with learning to make espresso, learning to steam milk is going to take some practice. Go out and buy about 3 gallons of good-quality, fresh, local whole milk, homogenized and pasteurized but not ultra-pasteurized. When you bring it home, refrigerate it immediately until well chilled, as cold milk steams more easily than warm milk. It's time to turn your phone off again and engage in an extended practice session. When you do, make sure you've eaten only lightly, because you're going to have to taste a lot of milk.

A good steaming pitcher should have straight sides, be made of stainless steel, and have a handle and a tight, pronounced spout. It should hold no more than double the amount of milk you're steaming. For example, if you're making a 12-ounce (355 ml) caffe latte, you should use a 20-ounce (590 ml) pitcher. If you're making 6-ounce (180 ml) cappuccinos, use a 12-ounce (355 ml) pitcher.

Pour milk into your steaming pitcher to a point about 1/2 inch (1.3 cm) below the base of the indentation of the spout. In order to develop a consistent technique, aim to fill the pitcher to this level every time.

Open and close the steam valve to let out a spurt of hot water. This is called purging. You should purge the steam wand before and after steaming, each and every time. After steaming, wipe the steam wand with a damp cloth so that no milk gets baked on, each and every time. A crusty steam wand is the single most depressing thing about going into a mediocre café. A crusty steam wand says, "I could care. It would be easy for me to care, but I'm choosing not to." A crusty steam wand makes me wonder what else that café doesn't care about. So wipe your steam wand.

When steaming milk, you need to think of one thing and one thing only: spinning the milk. Hold the steaming pitcher by the handle with one hand so you can touch the side with a finger to test the temperature. Bury the tip of your steam wand about 1/4 inch (6 mm) deep in the cold milk. Open the steam valve all the way with your other hand. Keep the tip buried and the bottom of the pitcher parallel to the counter. Let the steam push the milk so that a vortex forms. The milk is spinning! Tiny bubbles—ideally so small that they aren't visible—are being injected into the spinning milk. The bubbles are what make correctly steamed milk so much more pleasant to drink and perceptibly sweeter than milk that's simply warmed. Touch the pitcher with a finger. When it is a little hotter than is comfortable to touch, about 144°F (62°C), turn off the steam valve—and then purge! Then wipe the steam wand.

That's it. You want the milk to spin around as fast as possible inside the steaming pitcher. The goal is to create dense, sweet, shiny, elegant milk. It should be as shiny as chocolate pudding and pour like white paint. It should be sweet, not hot, and in the spring, after the rains let up, you should be able to taste when the cows get to go outside and eat grass.

It takes practice. If you get bubbles that are too big, the steam wand isn't deep enough in the milk. If there is no vortex or the final product isn't shiny—in other words, if you just end up with a pitcher of hot milk—your steam wand is too deep. So steam one hundred pitchers of milk. Smell each one. If it smells like overcooked custard, it's too hot. Rinse the pitcher with cold water before steaming again. When you get a pitcher that looks shiny, pour a little into a demitasse and take a sip. It should be pleasantly sweet, with a rich texture. After steaming a few gallons of milk, you might be ready to combine steamed milk with espresso, but not before.

THE BASIC POUR The pour is where a lot of home baristas get off track. They see the hearts, tulips, and rosettas made by baristas in their favorite cafés, and they get frustrated that they can't pour like that. They want to impress their buddies and let every pour become a referendum on their skills as a barista. In this way, latte art becomes an impediment to enjoyment of an otherwise delicious and well-made drink. You did not pay two or three grand to be made angry; you bought your espresso gear to make you happy. So be patient. Concentrate on making expertly extracted espresso and steaming silky, sweet, delicious milk. Work on the spin and taste the milk often. Leave embellishments to the professionals and work on deliciousness.

If the milk is a little foamy or has a harsh texture, give your steaming pitcher a few sharp taps on the counter. I used to end my shifts at the farmers' markets with dozens of fine flecks of milk on my eyeglasses from pounding my pitcher on the cart. After you have broken any larger bubbles by tapping, swirl the milk in the pitcher as though you were swirling a fine Bordeaux prior to drinking it. This polishes the surface of the milk more finely.

When you're ready to pour, place the spout of your steaming pitcher as close to the surface of the espresso as possible. Hold the cup with the espresso in your left hand if you're right-handed and in your right hand if you're left-handed and hold the pitcher in your more dexterous hand. Imagining the cup as a clock, start pouring at three o'clock if you're right-handed, and nine o'clock if you're left-handed. Pour quickly, otherwise the lighter-density foam on the surface of the pitcher will pour first, ruining your chances of a perfectly amalgamated liquid. Work your way quickly through the center to nine o'clock if you're right-handed, and three o'clock if you're left-handed.

The milk should be poured quickly enough so that it breaks through the surface of the crema and floats beneath it, raising the crema to the top of the cup. When you've moved from the starting position to the center of the clock face, imagine you're slapping a rival in the cheeks with buttery soft kid gloves, all wrist motion and no arms. If you've measured the amount of milk correctly and steamed it correctly, you'll be getting to the end of your milk supply as you approaching the opposite side of the cup. It's possible you will see a shape emerge in the crema. If you do, great. If you don't, it's not something to worry about. Again, focus on deliciousness; the pretty pour will eventually follow.

ESPRESSO-BASED DRINKS

So what is a macchiato, a cappuccino, or a caffe latte? At Blue Bottle, we instruct our baristas that the differences are mostly a matter of proportion: A macchiato is served in a 2.7-ounce (80 ml) demitasse and the ratio is 1 part milk (prior to steaming) to 1 part espresso. A cappuccino is served in a 6-ounce (180 ml) cup and is 4 parts milk to 1 part espresso. And a caffe latte is served in a 12-ounce (355 ml) cup and is 8 parts milk to 1 part espresso. The important

thing to realize is that there are as many conceptions of what constitutes a "proper" macchiato, cappuccino, or caffe latte as there are definitions of a "proper" martini. At Blue Bottle, what's important to us that we all agree on an internal standard for steaming, extracting, and pouring these drinks, and that our customers recognize and appreciate this consistency from barista to barista and from shop to shop. We use full-fat milk; these are not titanic proportions, and, face it, fat is delicious. If you insist on being put off by the fat content, choose a more compact macchiato or cappuccino, and enjoy a delicious drink.

THE GIBRALTAR At Blue Bottle, we serve a drink in a 4.5-ounce (135 ml) rocks glass with an octagonal beveled base made by the Libbey Glass company. The proportion is usually 1.25 fluid ounces (37 ml) of espresso to 2.5 fluid ounces (75 ml) of steamed milk, which fits nicely between the macchiato and the cappuccino. The milk is steamed thinly and elegantly and isn't very hot—it's a drink built for immediate quaffing. Even customers who are in a rush don't mind sticking around at the bar to have a quick exchange of pleasantries with the barista and polish it off in less than sixty seconds. It's in a cute glass, too, and people look great holding it. That never hurts.

We had these glasses around when we were getting ready to open the kiosk on Linden Street. An employee had bought them, mistakenly thinking that they would be big enough for cupping. They weren't, so we put them aside, in their cardboard box printed with the name Gibraltar in big capital letters. We pulled them off the shelf again when the espresso machine at the kiosk was ready for testing. We needed to see what the crema looked like, and the transparency and small size of the glasses made them perfect for evaluating shots—something that was crucial, as our espresso machine was a bit of a Frankenstein. It was the first PID-controlled La Marzocco in California (see page 111), and that plus our unfamiliarity with pump-driven machines—as opposed to lever-operated machines—at that time made the R&D process lengthy and often painful.

Linden Street was pretty seedy when we opened the kiosk, but there were some corset makers working at a store called Dark Garden next door. It didn't take long before they started wandering out of the store to see what was going on at the kiosk. If we were having a good day at the La Marzocco, we would offer them an espresso. But many of the Gardeners, as we came to call them, were dainty, so even an espresso that was up to our standards resulted in cutely wrinkled noses and the exclamation, "That's too strong!" We started pouring a little steamed milk on top of the espresso for them, like a baby latte. Eventually, after we opened a random passerby asked what that drink was called, and a quick-witted barista (who has since gone on to a distinguished career in coffee) said with a smirk, "Oh, that's our Gibraltar."

And just like that, people started ordering it. The kiosk's vinyl menu had already been printed, so we had inadvertently created an off-menu item with cachet. It's really a cortado—a beverage popular at Spanish espresso bars, where the relatively small amount of milk, suavely steamed (and served in a cute glass), takes the sting out of the punishingly dark-roasted Spanish espresso. But we didn't know that at the time.

Much to my puzzlement, other coffee bars soon began to offer the drink on their menus, and now you can order Gibraltars across the United States, in Europe, and even in Japan. I don't think the beverage we invented for the Gardeners was absolutely necessary in the uptick in popularity of a 4.5-ounce (135 ml) espresso drink. I do like to think, however, that we recognized and accelerated the unarticulated desire for a short, concentrated espresso drink that is consumed where it's made.

MOCHAS AND HOT CHOCOLATE

While the vast majority of our espresso drinks are the big four (espresso, macchiato, cappuccino, and caffe latte), we also take pride in serving a high-quality hot chocolate. Even at the farmers' markets, we make a ganache with drinking chocolate from TCHO, a San Francisco bean-to-bar chocolatier, and add steamed milk to make hot chocolate. It's delicious, and great for kids and people who don't drink coffee. Since we have chocolate ganache and espresso available at all times, it would be bad manners to refuse customers a mocha, which is basically a shot of espresso in hot chocolate. Besides, the tradition of combining coffee, chocolate, and milk or cream dates back to eighteenth-century Turin's Caffè al Bicerin. So even though it's not a purist's drink, we feel that a well-crafted mocha can be made and served with integrity and pride. In addition, we've noticed that the mocha often serves as a "gateway drug," offering those who aren't accustomed to stronger coffee and more austere drinks an entrée into our other offerings.

Ganache For Hot Chocolate and Mochas

This is the water-based ganache that we use as the foundation for our hot chocolates and mochas. After extensive tests by our training department, we found that using water (rather than milk or cream) to melt the chocolate yielded the most rich and delicious drinks. We're lucky to have neighbors on both coasts who make chocolate for us; in San Francisco, we use a drinking chocolate made by TCHO, and in New York, we use a single origin dark chocolate made by the Mast Brothers. The type of chocolate you use will affect the strength of the ganache, so you may need to adjust the amount to taste.

3 ounces (85 g) coarsely chopped dark
  chocolate

¼ cup (2 fl oz / 60 ml) boiling water

Put the chocolate in a small bowl or 2-cup glass measuring cup. Pour the boiling water over the chocolate and stir until smooth and the chocolate is melted. If you have an immersion blender, use it to fully emulsify the mixture.

The ganache can be stored in an airtight container in the refrigerator for up to 1 week. Reheat gently in a microwave before using.

Mocha

Sure, the mocha is often a gateway to other coffee drinks (see previous page)—it just takes some customers longer to move along than others. One of our very first regulars at the Hayes Valley kiosk became so addicted to mochas that, at the apex of his habit, he consumed five mochas in one day, earning the nickname Five Mocha David. Eventually, David moved on to drinking straight black coffee, but he hasn't been able to shake his chocolatey moniker. Since the ganache is extra-thick and is used warm, we have to respectfully deny requests for iced mochas; we've found the chocolate will seize up into unsightly globs in a cold and icy environment.

Note: omit the espresso and, voilà, you've got a hot chocolate.

3 tablespoons Ganache for Hot Chocolate
  and Mochas (above)
8 fluid ounces (1 cup / 240 ml) steamed milk
  or steamed soy milk

1 double ristretto shot of espresso
  (see page 119)

Put the ganache in a 10-ounce ceramic cup. Pull the espresso directly over the ganache, then pour the steamed milk over the top from 12 to 20 inches above the cup. The force of gravity will be all the agitation that is required to mix the ganache with the milk. No stirring will be required. Serve immediately.

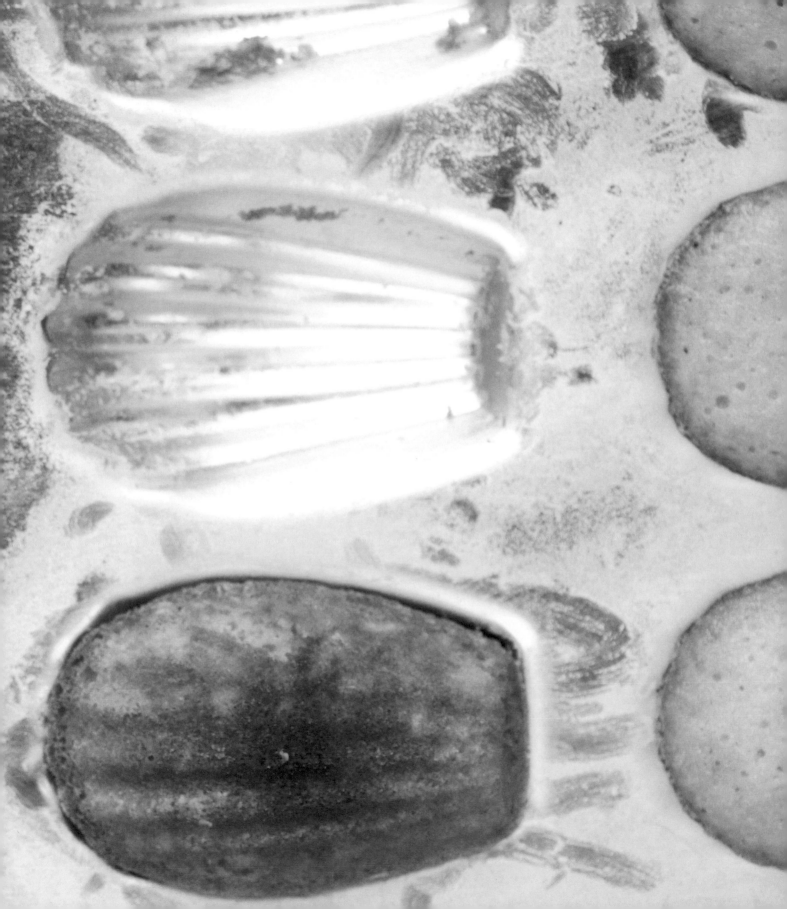

EAT

When James and I met in 2002, he had just started Blue Bottle, and at that time Miette, the cake shop I co-owned with Meg Ray and Liz Dunn, was only about a year old. James and I were both getting our start in business as outdoor vendors at Bay Area farmers' markets, he at the Old Oakland market on Fridays, selling coffee beans, and me at the Downtown Berkeley market on Saturdays, selling cakes. At Miette, we had a coffee cart, complete with a cute pink awning, that I precariously hauled to the Berkeley farmers' market every week to set up next to my table of cakes. We were James's second wholesale account, and though he may be pained by this admission, we chose his coffee based entirely on the fact that his bags were adorable. And I have to confess that I was a complete disaster at making coffee drinks. Fortunately, a cute dress, a bashful smile, and a perky "Would you like a cookie with that?" could usually remedy the situation. And luckily, since Blue Bottle was so new, very few people knew how delicious the coffee *could* be.

To try to improve the situation, I asked James to come help make coffee drinks on Saturdays in Berkeley, which soon turned into begging him to buy the cart from us. Luckily he finally did, and he was able to keep the spot next to me at the Downtown Berkeley market, becoming my in-house tasting panel (see the story of my Chocolate Parisian Macarons, page 175), and the new darling of the market. We were great friends and, long before we became a couple in 2004, we understood and admired each other's work ethic, determination, aesthetic sensibilities, and commitment to making the best possible product.

On October 29, 2008, James and I were married. I was still in my wedding dress after a quiet ceremony at San Francisco City Hall and a quick coffee with friends at our Hayes Valley kiosk, when we took a cab to the lawyer's office to sign the paperwork finalizing the sale of my interest in Miette. And, just like that, I started a new life. I was lucky to have a three-month sabbatical, after which I had planned to start a small pastry department for Blue Bottle and then move on to open a pie shop on my own. I spent the final month of this sabbatical gathering family recipes from friends, playing with flavors that would pair well with coffee, and developing the first set of pastries for our two retail locations, the kiosk in Hayes Valley and the Mint Plaza café.

What started as a short-term project to help my beloved turned into a job I never wanted to leave when we opened our café in the rooftop sculpture garden at the San Francisco Museum of Modern Art. Years earlier, when I was an art student, Wayne Thiebaud's cake paintings captured my imagination and led me down the path to becoming a pastry chef. At our new café, I could turn my art background into a ever-rotating line of desserts inspired by the art on display in the museum, including, of course, cakes inspired by the paintings of Wayne Thiebaud. Blue Bottle has grown by leaps and bounds since I started working for the company in 2009, and I now oversee three pastry departments, one at our Oakland roastery, which produces cookies and cakes for four of our retail shops, a tiny kitchen at the SFMOMA, and an even smaller kitchen in our Brooklyn roastery. We have different menus for each and a delightful crew of bakers who make beautiful things, but the one common thread is that every pastry we make is designed to pair deliciously with a cup of coffee.

You'll find recipes for a lot of those pastries, from breakfast treats to a version of the *macarons* that once gave James goose bumps, in the following pages. You will also see a selection of the savory breakfast and lunch dishes we serve at the Mint Plaza café, as well as a few recipes from friends who have come up with inventive ways to cook with our coffee.

Just as in making coffee, there are an infinite number of small variables in cooking that can affect your results, from techniques to equipment to ingredients, and how they're measured. Before you get started, here are a few pointers to keep in mind. —C.F.

Equipment

All of our recipes are written with the assumption that you have a stand mixer. Most have been tested with a hand mixer and, in some cases, with just a wooden spoon and a bowl, and in all cases they came out quite well. If you aren't using a stand mixer, let your intuition and experience with your equipment guide you.

Ovens are all so different that it would be impossible for me to give perfectly accurate baking times that would work in every home kitchen. Thanks to my group of home recipe testers, these recipes were made in a variety of ovens: my old Wedgewood stove at home, new ovens with spot-on temperatures, convection ovens, and even toaster ovens. As expected, baking time varied for each, so using the visual cues to assess when baked goods are done is the most fail-safe way to go.

One of the most exciting developments for me as a home baker was when 1 realized that I didn't have to follow instructions about what type of pan to put my cake in or what size to make my cookies. What I've specified in these recipes is either how we make them at Blue Bottle or how I think they would be easiest for you to make at home. So you have an understanding of how to successfully execute each recipe, I suggest you first make it as I specify. But let's say, for example, you have some friends coming over for Sunday brunch in the garden, and you don't want to be bothered with cutting and serving a cake; go ahead and make the Fruit Buckle as small cupcake-size individual cakes. Of course, you'll have to adjust the baking time to account for the smaller cakes, but having previously made the cake in a large pan, you can easily use visual and other cues to check for doneness in the smaller cakes. As long as you're watching and paying attention to the cues, you can vary the size of cookies or baking pans and handle the peculiarities of your oven with grace.

One of the greatest kitchen gadgets you can have is a thermocouple (shown at right). A thermocouple is an electronic temperature sensor that can be purchased at the hardware store, and is typically used in science and industry for testing the temperature of ovens and air conditioning. They're fairly inexpensive, absolutely accurate, and very easy to use and clean. I use mine for verifying my oven temperature and for taking temperature readings on sugar syrups and other temperature-sensitive recipes, such as Homemade Yogurt (page 141). It's an invaluable and extremely accurate tool that is worth investing in for both baking and coffee preparation.

Weight Measurements

While I love my thermocouple for temperature measurements to a tenth of a degree, I love my partial gram scale even more because it measures to a hundredth of a gram. All three Blue Bottle pastry kitchens are equipped with three types of digital scales: one that weighs up to 5,000 full grams (5 kg, or 11 lb), one that weighs up to 2,000 grams (2 kg, or 4.4 lb) to the hundredth of a gram, and one measures only up to 140 grams (4.9 oz) but is the most accurate for small measurements, such as for spices. As Rose Levy Beranbaum, the legendary author of *The Cake Bible*, said in reference to whether 1 gram really makes a difference in the end result, "If one starts becoming lax, the concept of 'will it really make a difference' soon would be transferred to other things where it might indeed make a difference. Being exact in measuring is a good approach to life."

All of that said, I haven't included the weights for small amounts in this book. For home-size recipes, these small quantities can be measured more accurately in teaspoons and tablespoons than on most scales. But I have included weights for everything else, and using weight measurements will help ensure that you to achieve the best results when baking. Rose's conversion chart in *The Cake Bible* has become a standard for weight-to-volume conversions, and her values are what I have used here.

A Note about Measuring Flour by Volume

Of all of the ingredients in these recipes, flour is the trickiest to measure accurately by volume, yet it is also often the most crucial for success in a pastry. For all-purpose flour, I use the conversion of 140 grams (4.9 oz) per cup—slightly more than Rose's 135 grams (4.8 oz). This is based on using the dip and sweep method of measuring a cup of flour. You scoop a 1-cup measure directly into the flour and then sweep with a knife to level. This fills the cup with up to 20 more grams of flour than if you spoon the flour into the cup.

If the fear of using wildly inaccurate amounts of flour isn't enough for you to go out and buy a digital gram scale, then consider the reduced number of dishes you will need to wash. When you weigh ingredients, all you need is a bowl or two and a scale; you won't need to dirty several dry measuring cups plus your liquid measuring cup, and never again will you question whether you need to chop nuts before measuring or leave them whole. As Gertrude Stein might have said, a gram is a gram is a gram.

Ingredients

Unless specifically stated in the recipe, all ingredients should be at room temperature, especially butter and eggs. To quickly get butter to room temperature, cut it into small pieces and let it sit in a warm spot in the kitchen for about 10 minutes. To quickly get eggs to room temperature, place the whole eggs (in their shells) in a small bowl, cover with lukewarm water, between 90°F and 100°F (32°C and 38°C), and let stand for about 10 minutes. For recipes where you first cream butter and sugar and then add eggs, using ingredients at room temperature will be what ensures a perfectly emulsified dough or batter.

Use standard large eggs, weighing approximately 50 grams (1.8 oz) per whole egg (out of its shell). When choosing chocolate, opt for something dark that you would love to eat on its own, with a cacao level of at least 60 percent. Regarding salt, I like my sweets on the saltier side, often with larger grains to give occasional unexpected hits of salt. Kosher salt is the default in these recipes, and I specify Maldon brand sea salt when larger grains are preferable. (See page 165 for more on the differences in between types of salt and how to substitute if you don't have the type called for in your cupboard.)

Beyond these considerations, the rest is entirely up to you. I choose to bake with organic dairy, eggs, and flours, and I try to support local purveyors whenever possible, both at home and in our production kitchens. Although these products are a bit more expensive, I think they yield a superior result. I encourage experimenting with spices and occasionally other ingredients, and I often offer suggestions in this regard. Please see page 163 for ideas for simple substitutions that will personalize these recipes to suit your tastes.

Go forth: bake, cook, and drink coffee! It is my highest hope that you enjoy the process almost as much as the final products.

With Your Morning Coffee

Brown Sugar and Winter Spice Granola

MAKES 12 TO 15 SERVINGS / HANDS-ON TIME: 25 MINUTES
FROM START TO FINISH: 2 HOURS, 30 MINUTES

It would be quite a stretch to call Blue Bottle's granola health food. Salty and sweet and broken into big slabs, it is sweetened with brown sugar syrup and delicately spiced with cinnamon and nutmeg. This recipe includes a somewhat generous measure of coarse sea salt to make it utterly crave-worthy. It's great served with milk, fantastic with yogurt (especially Homemade Yogurt, page 141), and stupendous with fruit. The long, slow baking at a low temperature gently cooks the oats and nuts and results in a texture that's both tender and crunchy. With the heavenly smell of toasting nuts, cinnamon, and nutmeg, you'll find it hard to leave the granola alone while it's in the oven. But be patient and bake it, without stirring, until crunchy and dry; this is the key to creating big chunks suitable for snacking.

This recipe makes a fairly large batch size. It can easily be halved, but between the two-plus hours of bake time and the long storage life, I think it's just as well to make a big batch.

1½ cups (11.5 oz / 325 g) packed light brown sugar
⅓ cup (80 ml / 80 g) water
4 cups (14 oz / 400 g) rolled oats
1½ cups (6 oz / 170 g) walnuts, coarsely chopped

1½ cups (6 oz / 170 g) pecans, coarsely chopped
1 teaspoon freshly ground cinnamon
1 teaspoon freshly ground nutmeg
¾ teaspoon Maldon sea salt (see page 165)
⅓ cup (80 ml / 71 g) canola oil
2½ teaspoons vanilla extract

Preheat the oven to 250°F (120°C).

In a small heavy saucepan, combine the brown sugar and water. Cook over medium-high heat, stirring constantly, until the sugar is completely dissolved and the mixture comes to a boil. Let cool to room temperature.

In a large bowl, combine the oats, walnuts, pecans, cinnamon, nutmeg, and salt and mix well.

Add the oil and vanilla extract to the brown sugar syrup and stir until thoroughly combined, then pour over the oat mixture. Mix well with your hands, until thoroughly combined and uniform in texture; it will be messy, but your hands are the best tool for the job.

Transfer to a rimmed 13 by 18-inch (33 by 46-cm) baking sheet and pat down in an even layer; it will be thick but shouldn't be higher than the rim of the pan.

Bake for 75 minutes. Remove from oven and use a large metal spatula to flip the granola, keeping it in as large of chunks as possible. Return the granola to the oven and bake for about 60 minutes, until completely dry and no longer at all soft if you take a bite. Let cool before serving.

Stored in a tightly sealed container at room temperature, the granola will keep for 2 weeks.

Homemade Yogurt

MAKES ABOUT 8 SERVINGS / HANDS-ON TIME: 30 MINUTES
FROM START TO FINISH: 10 HOURS, 30 MINUTES

James and I love tart homemade yogurt, and we make two quarts of it each week for our breakfasts at home. A typical morning at our house looks like this: the *New York Times* spread out over the table, James in his Blue Bottle pajamas, a cappuccino for him, a pot of tea for me, and a big bowl of yogurt for each of us, usually topped with homemade granola (see page 138), or with fresh fruit from the farmers' market and chopped almonds. Making yogurt is an easy weekly ritual, but be sure to start the process when your oven or another warm spot will be available for six hours.

Although the process requires very little equipment, accurate temperatures are crucial to a successful outcome, so you do need a kitchen thermometer. The microorganisms that turn liquid milk into creamy yogurt will die at temperatures above 120°F (49°C). So once you add your starter yogurt, make sure the temperature of the mixture never rises any higher than this.

Because there are no emulsifiers or gelling agents in homemade yogurt, it generally isn't as uniform in texture as store-bought. However, it is pure, simple, tangy, and more satisfying than any commercial yogurt I've ever tried.

4 cups (945 ml / 968 g) whole milk   2 tablespoons plain yogurt with live cultures

In a heavy medium saucepan, heat the milk over medium heat to just below boiling, between 180°F and 190°F (82°C and 88°C). Remove from the heat and let cool to 110°F (43°C).

Place the yogurt in a small bowl, then add ¼ cup of the 110°F (43°C) milk and whisk until smooth and thoroughly combined. Add this mixture into the remaining warm milk, and whisk thoroughly.

Pour the yogurt into a lidded heatproof container, such as a 1-quart (945 ml) Mason jar or multiple smaller jars, or the containers of a yogurt maker.

If using a yogurt maker, follow the manufacturer's instructions. Otherwise, put the yogurt in a warm place, such as the oven with only the pilot light lit or atop an electric heating pad set to medium and covered with a towel. The ideal temperature is between 100°F (38°C) and 105°F (41°C). If not using a yogurt maker, check the temperature of the mixture occasionally and make sure it doesn't exceed 120°F (49°C). Let sit for about 6 hours—less for a flavor that isn't as tart, and longer for a flavor that's more tart.

Refrigerate for at least 4 hours, until cool, or ideally overnight before serving. Stored in a sealed container in the refrigerator, the yogurt will keep for 1 week.

Liège Waffles

MAKES ABOUT 6 WAFFLES / HANDS-ON TIME: 30 MINUTES
FROM START TO FINISH: 2 HOURS

These Belgian-style waffles are made to order and served piping hot at our Ferry Building café. Because the Ferry Building is still an active transit center, as well as a quick stopover for Financial District lunches, shoppers are often in too much of a hurry to sit and enjoy a waffle breakfast. The Liège waffle, with its caramelized crust that makes syrup unnecessary, is the perfect portable breakfast or sweet snack. Stuart Brioza, our good friend and savory menu adviser, created this recipe when he found our dusty, unused waffle iron, which had been imported from Belgium and rewired by our espresso tech Arno Holschuh, sitting in storage. That formerly abandoned appliance has become an object of obsession for many Ferry Building customers.

SUBSTITUTIONS: 1 teaspoon vanilla extract can be substituted for the vanilla bean. All-purpose flour can be substituted for the pastry flour.

1¼ teaspoons active dry yeast,
  or 1½ teaspoons fresh yeast
¼ cup (60 ml / 60 g) lukewarm water,
  between 90°F and 100°F (32°C and 38°C)
½ cup (4 oz / 113 g) unsalted butter
¾ cup (3.7 oz / 105 g) pastry flour
⅔ cup (3.2 oz / 91 g) all-purpose flour

1 tablespoon granulated sugar, plus more for
  sprinkling
½ teaspoon Maldon sea salt (see page 165)
5 eggs (8.75 oz / 250 g), at room temperature
1 vanilla bean
3 tablespoons pearl sugar (see Note)

In a small bowl, combine the yeast and water and let sit for 5 minutes.

Melt the butter and let cool to about 115°F (46°C). Sift the flours and granulated sugar into a separate large bowl. Stir in the salt.

Crack the eggs into a medium bowl. Split the vanilla bean in half, scrape the pulp into the eggs, and whisk vigorously until well blended. Add the egg mixture to the flour mixture, along with the yeast and melted butter. Whisk until smooth.

Cover the batter with plastic wrap and let rest until doubled in size, 1 hour, or refrigerate overnight.

Gently mix the pearl sugar into the dough and let rest for 15 minutes. Preheat a Belgian-style waffle maker to medium-high heat.

Scoop ½ cup to ¾ cup (120 ml to 150 ml) of the batter into the waffle maker and sprinkle a bit of granulated sugar on top. (Amounts of batter can vary between waffle makers; err on the smaller side until you know how much makes the perfect waffle.) Cook until the indicator light goes off or until browned and crisp. Serve immediately.

NOTE: *Pearl sugar is compressed beet sugar that looks a bit like rock salt. It has a very high melting point, which makes it stay whole while baking, adding an extra crispness to the waffles.*

Zachte Waffles

MAKES 6 TO 7 WAFFLES / HANDS-ON TIME: 30 MINUTES
FROM START TO FINISH: 30 MINUTES

We serve these big buttery waffles at the Mint Plaza café. Unlike the Liège Waffles (page 142), which are designed to be eaten on-the-go, these soft and tender waffles are meant to be slathered with butter and maple syrup and enjoyed at the breakfast table, coffee in hand, on a slow weekend morning. The idea to serve waffles came from a trip to Tanaka Bar, an incredible twenty-four-hour siphon coffee café in Kyoto, where a photo-illustrated waffle menu is presented alongside the coffee menu. There is no drunk person more dignified than a young Japanese man in Tanaka Bar at 6 a.m., clad in a perfectly tailored blue suit and tie, eating a waffle and drinking a siphon coffee, trying to sober up in time for the train to work.

SUBSTITUTIONS: 1/2 teaspoon vanilla extract can be substituted for the vanilla bean.

2 1/2 cups (12.3 oz / 350 g) all-purpose flour
1/2 cup (3.5 oz / 100 g) sugar
2 teaspoons baking powder
1/2 teaspoon kosher salt
2 eggs (3.5 oz / 100 g), at room temperature
2 cups (475 ml / 484 g) half-and-half

1/2 vanilla bean
7 tablespoons (3.5 oz / 100 g) unsalted butter, melted, plus softened butter for serving
Maple syrup, for serving

In a large bowl, combine the flour, sugar, baking powder, and salt and mix well.

In a medium bowl, combine the eggs and half-and-half and whisk vigorously until well blended. Split the vanilla bean, scrape the pulp into the egg mixture, and whisk until the vanilla seeds are evenly distributed. Add to the flour mixture and stir just until evenly combined. Gently stir in the melted butter.

Preheat a waffle iron to medium-high heat. Cook each waffle until the indicator light goes off or until browned and crisp. Serve immediately with softened butter and maple syrup. Waffles are the most delicious, and have the crispiest exterior, when eaten hot from the iron. If eating with a group, the waffles can be held in a 200°F (93°C) oven until all of the waffles are finished, but the exterior won't be as perfectly crisp.

Any leftovers can be cooled completely, stored in a zippered freezer bag, and frozen for up to 1 month. Reheat them in the toaster for an easy weekday breakfast.

Strawberry Buckle with Lemon-Pistachio Streusel

MAKES ONE 9-INCH (23 CM) CAKE; SERVES 6 TO 8 / HANDS-ON TIME: 45 MINUTES
FROM START TO FINISH: 1 HOUR, 45 MINUTES

James is very proud to have a pastry department at Blue Bottle Coffee. He loves that making our own food gives us control over the customer's entire experience. He has made a big deal about not having what he calls a PBM (perfunctory bran muffin) on his shelves. Well, it turns out that many people really like to have a muffin for breakfast, and customers who came in expecting to find one in the pastry case were disappointed that we didn't have anything resembling a muffin. Knowing full well that "muffin" is a euphemism for "cake for breakfast," I decided not to hide it—I developed a buttery, fruit-based cake that we serve in an elegant paper cup.

A buckle is a traditional American cake, essentially a coffee cake with fruit, usually blueberries. Legend has it that you're supposed to pile so much streusel on top of the cake that it buckles during baking, creating a ravine of fruit and streusel goodness through the center of the cake. I've never actually seen a buckle buckle, but when making this recipe at home, I like to bake it as one large cake, which increases the surface area (and, therefore, chances of buckling) and reassures James that it is a coffee cake, not a muffin.

SUBSTITUTIONS: The buckle allows us to showcase seasonal fruit in our pastry cases; for example, a traditional blueberry buckle with vanilla-almond streusel in the spring; a raspberry and peach buckle with lemon-pistachio streusel in the summer; pumpkin buckle with spiced walnut streusel in the autumn; or a roasted mandarin buckle with pecan streusel in the winter. Substitute an equal amount of any fruit for the strawberries. Substitute any nut for the pistachios, and add any type of citrus zest to the streusel. For a pumpkin buckle, substitute 3/4 cup pureed roasted pumpkin or other winter squash (see Note) for the fruit, and add 1/4 teaspoon each of ground nutmeg and cinnamon to the flour mixture when making the cake.

STREUSEL

6 tablespoons (3 oz / 85 g) cold unsalted
   butter
1 cup (4.9 oz / 140 g) all-purpose flour
1/2 cup (3.5 oz / 100 g) sugar
3/4 teaspoon kosher salt
Finely grated zest of 1 lemon
1/2 cup (2.7 oz / 76 g) unsalted shelled
   pistachios, coarsely chopped

CAKE

1 cup (4.9 oz / 140 g) all-purpose flour
1 teaspoon baking powder
11 tablespoons (5.5 oz / 156 g) unsalted
   butter, at room temperature
3/4 cup (5.3 oz / 150 g) sugar
3/4 teaspoon kosher salt
2 eggs (3.5 oz / 100 g), at room temperature
1 teaspoon vanilla extract
1 cup (4.7 oz / 133 g) strawberries, cut into
   bite-sized pieces

CONTINUED

TO MAKE THE STREUSEL, cut the butter into small chunks and let sit at room temperature for 5 minutes.

In the bowl of a stand mixer fitted with the paddle attachment, combine the flour, sugar, salt, and zest. Add the butter and mix on low speed until the mixture resembles coarse beach sand, about 2 minutes. Add the pistachios and mix just until the streusel begins to clump together and look like gravel, being careful not to let it come together to form a dough. If not using the streusel right away, store it in an airtight container in the refrigerator for up to 3 days or in the freezer for up to 1 month.

TO MAKE THE CAKE, preheat the oven to 350°F (175°C). Butter and flour the bottom and sides of a 9-inch (23 cm) springform pan.

Sift the flour and baking powder into a small bowl.

In the bowl of a stand mixer fitted with the paddle attachment, beat the butter on low speed until smooth, 1 to 2 minutes. Add the sugar and salt and mix on low speed until well combined. Scrape down the sides of the bowl, then mix on medium speed until light and fluffy, 4 to 5 minutes.

In a small bowl, combine the eggs and the vanilla extract and whisk vigorously until well blended.

With the mixer on medium speed, add the egg mixture very slowly, in a steady stream, and mix until well-incorporated and very smooth, about 30 seconds. Scrape down the sides of the bowl, then mix on medium speed for 30 more seconds.

Scrape down the sides of the bowl, then add the flour mixture. Mix on low speed just until uniform in texture. Use a rubber spatula to gently fold in the fruit until evenly incorporated.

TO ASSEMBLE AND BAKE, pour the batter into the prepared pan, smooth it with an offset or rubber spatula, and sprinkle the streusel evenly over the top. Bake for 55 to 60 minutes, until the streusel is dry and golden and the buckle is firm and springs back when gently pressed in the center, rotating the pan midway through the baking time.

Let the cake cool in the pan on a wire rack for 30 minutes, then remove from the pan. Serve warm or at room temperature. Stored in a covered container at room temperature, it will keep for up to 3 days.

NOTE: *To make pumpkin puree, preheat the oven to 375°F (190°C). Halve an edible variety of pumpkin or an acorn, kabocha, curry, or butternut squash and scoop out the seeds. Put the halves face down on an oiled baking sheet and bake for about 45 minutes, until the squash collapses and is easily pierced with a knife. Let cool until it can be handled safely, then scrape out the pulp. Mash or process in a food processor until smooth. For a quicker, if less distinguished puree, it's fine to use unsweetened canned pumpkin puree.*

Stout Coffee Cake with Pecan-Caraway Streusel

MAKES ONE 9-INCH (23 CM) COFFEE CAKE; SERVES 6 TO 8 / HANDS-ON TIME: 45 MINUTES
FROM START TO FINISH: 3 HOURS, 45 MINUTES

For our 2009 Blue Bottle company holiday party, my friend Nicole Krasinski, pastry chef–owner of the incredible San Francisco restaurant State Bird Provisions, made us a wonderful cake with stout beer and oats. It could have been the fact that there was beer in the cake, and our staff can be almost as nerdy about beer as they are about coffee, but the room was more atwitter about that dessert than anything I had ever made for them. With a room full of coffee experts giving their thumbs-up, I realized that it might be an ideal pairing with coffee. I asked Nicole if she would share the recipe and allow me to modify it as a coffee cake to serve at our shops, and she graciously agreed.

I'm partial to putting streusel on just about anything, but I was stumped about what additional flavor I could add in the streusel to complement this already complex cake. I went to my drawer of spice inspiration and found a bag of beautiful caraway seeds that I had been hoping to use in a dessert. This was it! The pecans add a toasty richness that keeps the caraway from evoking the flavor of a pastrami sandwich, and the brown sugar is sweet and comforting. When this cake is on the menu, we use local stouts—either Magnolia Brewery Stout of Circumstance in San Francisco, or Brooklyn Brewery's Black Chocolate Stout in New York. I recommend a dark, rich stout or porter and encourage you to use a local beer if you can.

Keep in mind that the stout, oats, and currants need 2 hours of soaking time before making the cake, so you'll need to plan ahead.

STREUSEL

7 tablespoons (3.5 oz / 100 g) cold unsalted butter
1 cup (4.9 oz / 140 g) all-purpose flour
1/4 cup (1.8 oz / 50 g) granulated sugar
1/4 cup (1.9 oz / 54 g) packed light brown sugar
2 teaspoons caraway seeds
3/4 teaspoon kosher salt
1 1/4 cups (5 oz / 142 g) pecans, chopped

CAKE

1 cup (240 ml / 240 g) stout beer
1 cup (3.5 oz / 100 g) rolled oats
1/4 cup (2 oz / 57 g) currants
1 1/2 cups (7.4 oz / 210 g) all-purpose flour
1 teaspoon baking soda
1/2 cup (4 oz / 113 g) unsalted butter, at room temperature
1 cup (7.1 oz / 200 g) granulated sugar
1 cup (7.7 oz / 217 g) packed light brown sugar
1 1/4 teaspoons kosher salt
2 eggs (3.5 oz / 100 g), at room temperature

TO MAKE THE STREUSEL, cut the butter into small chunks and let sit at room temperature for about 5 minutes.

In the bowl of a stand mixer fitted with the paddle attachment, combine the flour, granulated sugar, brown sugar, caraway seeds, and salt. Add the butter and mix on low speed until mixture

CONTINUED

resembles coarse beach sand, about 2 minutes. Add the pecans and mix just until the streusel begins to clump together and look like gravel, being careful not to let it come together to form a dough. If not using the streusel right away, store in an airtight container in the refrigerator for up to 3 days or in the freezer for up to 1 month.

TO MAKE THE CAKE, 2 hours before you begin mixing the cake, combine the stout, oats, and currants in a bowl or lidded container and mix well. Cover and set aside at room temperature for 2 hours. Drain the mixture, reserving the liquid. (You can also do this step up to 1 day ahead; soak for 2 hours, then drain and store the stout and the soaked ingredients in separate covered containers in the refrigerator.)

Preheat the oven to 350°F (175°C). Butter and flour the bottom and sides of a 9-inch (23 cm) springform pan.

Sift the flour and baking soda into a small bowl.

In the bowl of a stand mixer fitted with the paddle attachment, beat the butter on low speed until smooth, 1 to 2 minutes. Add the granulated sugar, brown sugar, and salt, and mix on low speed until well combined. Scrape down the sides of the bowl, then mix on medium speed until light and fluffy, 4 to 5 minutes.

In a small bowl, whisk the eggs until the whites and yolks are completely combined.

With the mixer on medium speed, add the egg mixture very slowly, in a steady stream, and mix until well-incorporated and very smooth, about 30 seconds. Scrape down the sides of the bowl, then mix on medium speed for 30 more seconds.

Scrape down the sides of the bowl, then, with the mixer on low speed, alternate adding the flour in three additions and the reserved stout in two, beginning and ending with the flour. Mix just until combined. With a rubber spatula, gently fold in the oats and currants until evenly combined.

TO ASSEMBLE AND BAKE, pour the batter into the prepared pan, smooth with an offset or rubber spatula, and sprinkle the streusel evenly over the top. Bake for 55 to 60 minutes, until the streusel is dry and golden and the cake is firm and springs back when gently pressed in the center, rotating the pan midway through the baking time.

Let the cake cool in the pan on a wire rack for 30 minutes, then remove from the pan. Serve warm or at room temperature. Stored in a covered container at room temperature, the coffee cake will keep for up to 3 days.

Poached Eggs on Toast

MAKES 2 TO 4 SERVINGS / HANDS-ON TIME: 15 MINUTES
FROM START TO FINISH: 15 MINUTES

For Blue Bottle's first six years in business, coming to one of our retail locations meant standing outdoors while drinking your coffee, whether at the farmers' market or at the Hayes Valley kiosk. When planning his first café, located on a dicey street behind San Francisco's historic Mint building, James envisioned a civilized place with Japanese coffee-making equipment and a simple food program built around poached eggs on toast. And this turned out to be a wildly successful idea. The café's tiny kitchen, with its two induction burners and single convection oven, produces more poached eggs than we could have imagined. In our first three years there, we estimate that our cooks, brothers Angél and Enrique Argüello, made as many as sixty thousand poached eggs in this rudimentary kitchen, each one perfectly cooked. In their method, the eggs are poached in just-boiled water that's been removed from the heat, so you don't have to keep an eye on the simmering water. Be careful not to crowd the water with too many eggs, or the temperature will drop and they will be underdone.

POACHED EGGS
4 eggs
2 tablespoons white vinegar or wine vinegar
Kosher salt

Butter, at room temperature
2 to 4 thick slices of bread, toasted
   (see Note)
Freshly ground black pepper

Crack each egg into its own small bowl or ramekin.

Put 4 inches (10 cm) of water in a large, wide saucepan with a tight-fitting lid. Add the vinegar and a pinch of salt. Bring to a rolling boil, then turn off the heat. Immediately, carefully slip the eggs into the water, making sure there's about 2 inches (5 cm) of space between them. (If there isn't enough room, cook the eggs in batches, bringing the water back to a boil before adding new eggs.) Cover and let sit until the whites are cooked and the yolks are runny, 3 to 3 1/2 minutes. Gently lift the eggs out of the pan with a wide slotted spoon and drain well.

Butter the toast and top each slice with 1 or 2 eggs. Season with salt and pepper and serve immediately.

NOTE: *At the Mint Plaza café, we use Sweet Loaf bread from the Bay Area's Acme Bread Company. It's a simple white bread that, when cut thickly and toasted lightly, has a tender crispness and soft interior. I recommend using a fresh loaf or baguette from your local bakery, but this recipe is flexible and you can use any type of bread you like.*

Catalan Eggs with Braised Greens and Tomato Sauce

MAKES 4 SERVINGS / HANDS-ON TIME: 50 MINUTES
FROM START TO FINISH: 50 MINUTES

In addition to poached eggs on toast, the Mint Plaza café offers this seasonal breakfast dish, also featuring poached eggs. This is a wintertime favorite of our son, Dashiell, and we couldn't be more proud. The sight of an eight-year-old gobbling down dark leafy greens is surely every parent's dream.

TOMATO SAUCE
3 tablespoons extra-virgin olive oil
1 clove garlic, minced
1 (14 oz / 400 g) can tomato puree, or about
    1 1/2 cups (355 ml) pureed fresh tomatoes
Kosher salt
Freshly ground black pepper

GREENS
1/4 cup (60 ml / 54 g) extra-virgin olive oil
2 teaspoons unsalted butter, at room
    temperature
1 1/2 pounds (680 g) chard, chicory, kale,
    escarole, or a combination, cut into
    ribbons about 1 inch (2.5 cm) thick
Kosher salt
Freshly ground black pepper

4 poached eggs (see page 152)
Grated hard cheese, such as Parmesan,
    Pecorino Romano, or Idiazábal, for garnish

TO MAKE THE TOMATO SAUCE, heat the olive oil in a medium nonreactive skillet over medium-low heat. Add the garlic and sauté until aromatic, about 30 seconds, then add the tomato puree and cook, stirring occasionally, until the tomatoes taste and smell sweet and less acidic, about 20 minutes for canned tomatoes or 10 minutes for fresh. Season to taste with salt and pepper.

TO MAKE THE GREENS, heat the oil and butter in a large saucepan over medium-high heat. Carefully add the greens, watching out for popping oil. If using a mixture of greens, start with the sturdier greens, such as kale, and add more tender greens, such as chard, a minute or two later (escarole takes even less time). Stir to wilt the greens evenly and make more space for more greens. Cook until the greens are emerald green and wilted but still crunchy, 5 to 7 minutes. Season to taste with salt and pepper.

TO ASSEMBLE, divide the greens evenly among 4 plates, making a nest on each plate. Put a poached egg on top, season lightly with salt and pepper, then spoon the tomato sauce over the top of each. Sprinkle the cheese over the top and serve immediately.

Blue Bottle Benedict

MAKES 4 SERVINGS / HANDS-ON TIME: 45 MINUTES
FROM START TO FINISH: 45 MINUTES

In the tradition of modifying the Benedict to fit your locale (such as eggs Florentine, country Benedict, or even huevos Benedict), we've made our own version of this classic to serve at the Mint Plaza café. In place of the English muffin, we use thick slices of Acme Bread's Sweet Loaf, and instead of hollandaise, this recipe utilizes a béchamel sauce. Although I love the tangy richness of a hollandaise, a rich gravylike béchamel pairs perfectly with the maple-cured ham we use from Prather Ranch Meat Company. Falling somewhere between the classic eggs Benedict and a country Benedict, this breakfast is perfectly San Francisco. The sauce can be made a few hours ahead; keep it at room temperature until ready to use, then gently reheat it.

BÉCHAMEL
5 tablespoons (2.5 oz / 70 g) unsalted butter,
   at room temperature
1 cup (7 oz / 198 g) diced shallots
1 tablespoon white wine
1 cup (240 ml / 242 g) whole milk
1 cup (240 ml / 242 g) half-and-half
1 bay leaf
Kosher salt

Freshly ground pepper
1½ tablespoons all-purpose flour
4 large, thick slices country-style bread,
   about 1½ inches (4 cm) thick, toasted
4 slices cured ham
½ cup (2 oz / 57 g) grated Gruyère cheese,
   for garnish
8 poached eggs (see page 152)

TO MAKE THE BÉCHAMEL, melt 3 tablespoons of the butter in a heavy medium saucepan over medium-low heat. Add the shallots and sauté until fragrant and translucent, 3 to 5 minutes. Add the wine to deglaze the pan, then cook the alcohol off for 1 to 2 minutes. Add the milk, half-and-half, and bay leaf and season with salt and pepper. Cook, stirring frequently, until barely simmering; don't let the milk scald or boil. Decrease the heat to low and cook, stirring occasionally, for about 10 minutes to infuse the milk with the flavor of the shallots. Strain through a fine-mesh sieve, discarding the shallots and bay leaf, and set aside.

In the same pan, heat the remaining 2 tablespoons of butter over medium-low heat until all of the water in the butter is cooked off, about 5 minutes. Whisk in flour to form a smooth paste and cook, whisking often, until browned, 3 to 4 minutes. Be careful not to burn the mixture. Slowly add the milk mixture while whisking constantly; if you add the milk too quickly or don't whisk constantly, the sauce won't thicken. (If it doesn't thicken, briefly bring to a simmer, whisking, then remove from the heat.) Season with salt and pepper to taste.

TO ASSEMBLE, put the toast on serving plates, and top each with a slice of the ham and 2 eggs. Pour the béchamel over the top, distributing it evenly, then sprinkle 2 tablespoons of the Gruyère over each serving. Serve immediately.

Perfect for Dunking

Saffron-Vanilla Snickerdoodles

MAKES 9 LARGE COOKIES / HANDS-ON TIME: 30 MINUTES
FROM START TO FINISH: 4 HOURS

These definitely aren't traditional snickerdoodles, a relatively plain cookie made with cream of tartar that you would expect to see rolled in cinnamon and sugar. Instead, they have an unusual butterscotch flavor from the combination of saffron, brown sugar, and vanilla and are soft and chewy, with a golden exterior. I admit that I co-opted the name *snickerdoodle* in order to increase sales. I originally called them Vanilla-Saffron Cookies, and under that name we could hardly give the things away. I suspected that the idea of saffron in a sweet treat was turning people away, so I decided to choose a comforting and familiar name to offset the fear of saffron, and lure people into giving these a try. Sure enough, it worked. The only downside is that now I have the job of trying to explain myself whenever a snickerdoodle lover catches my little white lie!

SUBSTITUTIONS: Rather than use a vanilla bean, you can double the vanilla extract.

About 30 threads of saffron (to yield
⅛ teaspoon ground saffron; see Note)
½ vanilla bean
2 tablespoons milk
2 cups (9.9 oz / 280 g) all-purpose flour
1 teaspoon baking soda
½ cup (4 oz / 113 g) unsalted butter, at room
temperature

½ cup (3.5 oz / 100 g) granulated sugar
½ cup (3.8 oz / 109 g) packed light
brown sugar
1 teaspoon kosher salt
1 egg (1.8 oz / 50 g), at room temperature
½ teaspoon vanilla extract

Crush the saffron threads with a mortar and pestle until powdery or grind them in a clean spice grinder; alternatively, you can finely mince the saffron. The finer the powder, the more intense the saffron color and flavor in the cookies.

Split the vanilla bean in half and scrape the pulp into a small saucepan. Add the vanilla pod, milk, and saffron and cook over very low heat, just until bubbles begin to form at the edges, between 180°F and 190°F (82°C and 88°C). Alternatively, combine the vanilla pulp, pod, milk, and saffron in a small microwavable bowl, and microwave just until the milk is hot, 20 to 30 seconds. Cover and let steep for about 10 minutes; the milk should have a sunny yellow color.

Sift the flour and baking soda into a medium bowl.

In the bowl of a stand mixer fitted with the paddle attachment, beat the butter on low speed until smooth, 1 to 2 minutes. Add the granulated sugar, brown sugar, and salt and mix on low speed until well combined. Scrape down the sides of the bowl, then mix on medium speed until light and fluffy, 4 to 5 minutes.

CONTINUED

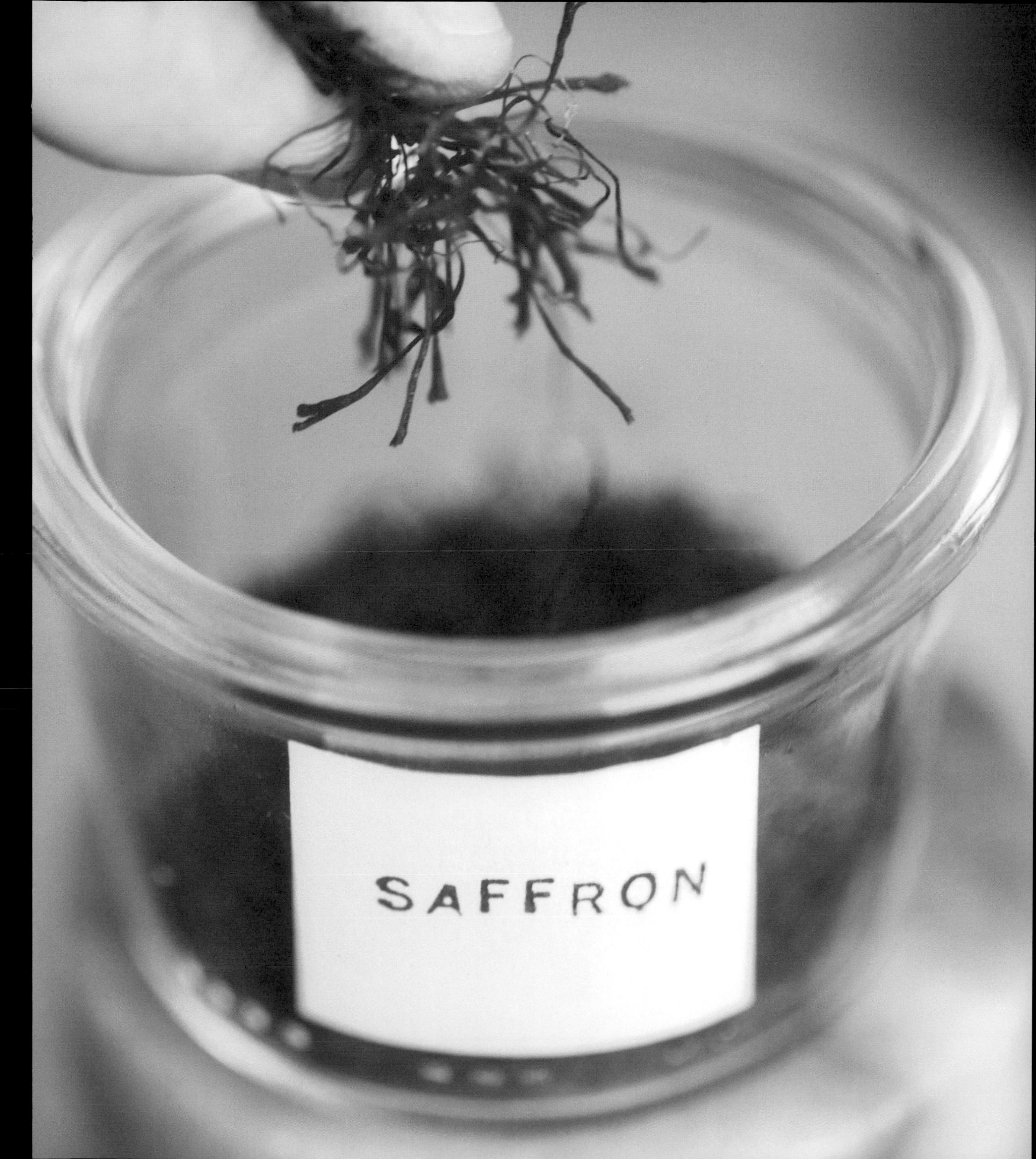
SAFFRON

Remove the vanilla pod from the milk, squeezing off any liquid or pulp clinging to it back into the milk. In a medium bowl, combine the milk mixture, egg, and vanilla extract and whisk vigorously until well blended.

With the mixer on medium speed, add the egg mixture very slowly, in a steady stream, and mix until well-incorporated and very smooth, about 30 seconds. Scrape down the sides of the bowl, then mix on medium speed for 30 more seconds.

Scrape down the sides of the bowl, then add the flour mixture. Mix on low speed just until uniform in texture.

Using a rubber spatula, scrape the dough out into an airtight container or onto a piece of plastic wrap. Cover the container, or, if using plastic wrap, shape the dough into a rough disk, wrap tightly, and refrigerate for at least 3 hours and up to 5 days.

Preheat the oven to 350°F (175°C). Line a baking sheet with parchment paper or a silicone mat.

Roll ¼-cup (60 ml) portions of the dough into balls, and place them on the baking sheet, spacing them at least 2 inches (5 cm) apart. (To make different sizes of cookies, see the sidebar on page 162.)

Bake for about 16 minutes, until golden but not too dark, rotating the pan midway through the baking time. Ideally, the baked cookies will be tall and slightly undercooked in the center, and will buckle shortly after coming out of the oven. (I've found that electric ovens produce the best buckle.) If the cookies don't buckle, don't worry; they'll still be delicious.

Let the cookies cool on the pan for 10 minutes before removing.

These cookies are best when eaten warm, shortly after they come out of the oven. However, they can be stored in an airtight container at room temperature for up to 2 days. Alternatively, the dough can stored in an airtight container in the refrigerator for up to 5 days, so consider baking only as many cookies as needed and saving the rest of the dough to bake another day.

NOTE: *Saffron is most commonly used in savory cuisine. To avoid having visions of paella haunting you as you eat these cookies, be sure to measure the saffron carefully—there's a fine line between just perfect and too much. When the amount of saffron is correct, the biscotti should be subtly yellow in color with a slight clean honey taste that doesn't necessarily come across as saffron.*

Ginger-Molasses Cookies

MAKES 9 LARGE COOKIES / HANDS-ON TIME: 30 MINUTES
FROM START TO FINISH: 4 HOURS

My dad, my mentor in how to best enjoy all things sweet, has long been known for having cookies squir-reled away in his bedroom for emergency witching-hour cravings. Of all of the cookies in his collection, Nabisco Ginger Snaps were the ones I considered the most grown-up, and, of course, the ones I wanted to like most as a five-year-old. I remember them as incredibly spicy and great for dunking in milk and, accu-rate or not, that thirty-year-old taste memory is lodged in my brain.

As much as I love ginger snaps, I wanted to create a chewy ginger cookie for our shops. To achieve the ideal chewy-without-being-cakey texture, I loaded up these cookies with molasses and left out the eggs. Bored of traditional Christmas spices, I decided to use black cardamom, a smoked relative of the more common green cardamom, for an earthy flavor evocative of a campfire. To round out and soften the hint of camphor from the black cardamom, I've added cocoa powder for richness, but just a small quantity so it doesn't create the impression of chocolate. These cookies are particularly spicy, with two types of ginger and good dose of black pepper. Complex and sophisticated with a definite kick, they make me feel just like my sneaky five-year-old self, breaking into my dad's secret stash of ginger cookies.

SUBSTITUTIONS: This is definitely a spicy cookie, but the flavors can be adjusted and toned down if you'd like something with a bit less heat. Decrease the amount of fresh ginger and black pepper by half for a less spicy but still delicious cookie. I highly recommend you track down black cardamom, but if you don't have it on hand and want to make these cookies anyway, substitute 1/2 teaspoon ground cloves and 1/4 tea-spoon ground green cardamom. If you're a big fan of ginger, you can go for an even bigger ginger punch by adding 1/4 cup of chopped candied ginger with the flour. Note that one ingredient that shouldn't be altered is the molasses—only use light molasses, also known as Barbados molasses. It has the mildest fla-vor of any type of molasses. If you substitute another type, it will overwhelm the other flavors in this cookie.

2 cups (9.9 oz / 280 g) all-purpose flour

1 tablespoon natural (not Dutch-processed) cocoa powder

1 tablespoon ground dried ginger

3/4 teaspoon baking soda

3/4 teaspoon ground black cardamom

1/2 teaspoon freshly ground black pepper

1/2 cup (4 oz / 113 g) unsalted butter, at room temperature

3 tablespoons (1.6 oz / 45 g) grated fresh ginger

1/2 cup (3.8 oz / 109 g) packed light brown sugar

1/4 cup (1.8 oz / 50 g) granulated sugar, plus extra for rolling the cookies

1/2 teaspoon kosher salt

1/2 cup (5.7 oz / 161 g) unsulfured light molasses

CONTINUED

Sift the flour, cocoa powder, powdered ginger, baking soda, cardamom, and pepper into a bowl.

In the bowl of a stand mixer fitted with the paddle attachment, beat the butter and grated ginger on low speed until smooth, 1 to 2 minutes. Add the brown sugar, granulated sugar, and salt and mix on low speed until well combined. Scrape down the sides of the bowl, then mix on medium speed until light and fluffy, 4 to 5 minutes.

Add the molasses and mix until well combined. Scrape down the sides of the bowl, then add the flour mixture. Mix on low speed just until uniform in texture.

Using a rubber spatula, scrape the dough out into an airtight container or onto a piece of plastic wrap. Cover the container, or, if using plastic wrap, shape the dough into a rough disk, wrap tightly, and refrigerate for at least 3 hours and up to 5 days.

Preheat the oven to 350°F (175°C). Line a baking sheet with parchment paper or a silicone mat. Fill a small plate with granulated sugar.

Roll 1/4-cup (60 ml) portions of the dough into balls, then roll the balls in the sugar. Place them on the baking sheet, spacing them at least 2 inches (5 cm) apart. (To make different sizes, see below.)

Bake for 11 to 13 minutes, until crackly on top but still be somewhat soft to the touch, rotating the pan midway through the baking time.

Let them cool on the pan for 10 minutes, then remove. The surface will get firmer as they cool.

These cookies are best when eaten the day they are baked. However, they can be stored in an airtight container at room temperature for 2 days. Alternatively, the dough can be stored in an airtight container in the refrigerator for 5 days, so consider baking only as many cookies as needed and saving the rest of the dough to bake another day.

COOKIE SIZES

We make our cookies on the large side at Blue Bottle. Our scooped cookies are slightly bigger than I've specified in these recipes, about 60 grams (2.1 oz) apiece. I did that for two reasons. First, when I was a one-person pastry department, I couldn't bear scooping more cookies than I needed to. But, second, and more significantly, with larger cookies you can really play with baking time to achieve two distinct textures in a single cookie: crisp on the outside and soft and gooey on the inside. Smaller cookies tend to be well-done and crisp throughout. You can choose to make smaller cookies; just be careful about baking time. It's usually best to test bake one or two cookies to dial in the timing before you bake the entire batch.

SPICES AND ALCOHOL

All pastry chefs have a bag of tricks they go to when developing a new recipe. Some look to architecture and make sky-high pastries, others take inspiration from the farmers' market to make fresh and seasonal treats, and still others raid the savory cupboards to teeter on the edge of what can be called dessert. Because my only goal at Blue Bottle is to make treats with flavors that pair well with coffee, my bag of tricks has become my spice rack and alcohol cabinet—or, to be more specific, Le Sanctuaire for spices and St. George Spirits for alcohol.

Le Sanctuaire, located in San Francisco, is a chef's haven, offering spices of the finest grade and specializing in the rare or unusual. Le Sanctuaire spices and other goods, previously available only in bulk to industry professionals, are now sold to the public in retail-size tins via their website. St. George Spirits is a distillery in Alameda, just across the marina from Blue Bottle's Oakland roastery. It was founded as an eau-de-vie distillery and is best known for Hangar One vodka but also makes incredible whiskeys, brandies, and gins, all produced in small batches with the finest ingredients. I've been lucky to be allowed into both of these establishments to sniff, taste, talk the ears off the staff and proprietors, and bring home samples of enticing ingredients.

The great thing about both spices and alcohol is that you don't have to make major adjustments to a recipe to entirely change the direction of the flavor. Bored with traditional gingerbread spices? Go ahead and use black cardamom. Tired of using vanilla extract? Grab that bottle of moonshine.

The recipes in this book are now yours, and I encourage you to change them as you please. I recommend trying them as written first, because they are the result of much experimentation and have proven popular among customers. Then, once you've experienced the original version, adjust at will according to your taste. I can try to come up with an objectively

delicious pastry, but chances are, you'll wish something about it was a bit different. It's possible that half a vanilla bean in a cookie recipe doesn't have the full vanilla flavor you're looking for, or maybe you really wish I had put cinnamon in the fruit buckle. As long as you're working with the same basic proportions, changing up spices and extracts is an easy way to personalize a recipe to your taste.

Some of the spices I use are a bit uncommon, and you won't find them at your supermarket, and perhaps not even at your natural food store. In some cases I've suggested a substitution, but I encourage you to look online or explore your local ethnic food shops to find these, and others, that you can add to your own bag of tricks.

Double-Chocolate Cookies

MAKES 9 LARGE COOKIES / HANDS-ON TIME: 30 MINUTES
FROM START TO FINISH: 4 HOURS

Okay, I'll admit that I'm not a huge fan of chocolate. In fact, when I was developing the first round of pastries for Blue Bottle, it didn't occur to me until just before we debuted the treats that I had completely overlooked including chocolate in anything. It was as a freshman at UC Santa Cruz at a grimy campus cafe that I discovered the one chocolate baked good I was excited about: stale brownies—sweet, buttery, and, most importantly, chewy. An unlikely of a source of inspiration, those stale brownies gave me the idea for our most popular cookie at Blue Bottle.

The most important thing when making this cookie is to use a high-quality chocolate. At Bay Area Blue Bottle cafés, we use large chips made for us by Michael Recchiuti, a San Francisco chocolatier who creates legendarily beautiful chocolates and candies; in Brooklyn, we use extraordinary chocolate made by the Mast Brothers. I encourage you to find a really delicious dark chocolate bar and chop it into chunks; the slightly bitter chocolate will offset the amount of sugar it takes to get these cookies to that perfect stale brownie texture I was after. A healthy dose of large-grained sea salt is really what puts this cookie over the top. The occasional crunch of a salt crystal within the deep, dark chocolate is stunning—and what keeps me craving this cookie. Indeed, these cookies made me realize that I might like chocolate a little more than I've been admitting to.

1 cup (4.9 oz / 140 g) all-purpose flour
1/3 cup (1.1 oz / 31 g) natural (not Dutch-
    processed) cocoa powder
1/2 teaspoon baking soda
5 tablespoons (2.5 oz / 70 g) unsalted butter,
    at room temperature

1 cup (7.1 oz / 200 g) sugar
1 teaspoon Maldon sea salt (see opposite)
1 egg (1.8 oz / 50 g), at room temperature
1 tablespoon vanilla extract
3.5 ounces (100 g) dark chocolate, 62% to
    70% cacao, coarsely chopped

Sift the flour, cocoa powder, and baking soda into a medium bowl.

In the bowl of a stand mixer fitted with the paddle attachment, beat the butter on low speed until smooth, 1 to 2 minutes. Add the sugar and salt and mix on low speed until well combined. Scrape down the sides of the bowl, then mix on medium speed until the mixture gets lighter in color and the texture becomes fluffier, 5 to 6 minutes. Because of the high ratio of sugar to butter, this mixture won't be as fluffy as similar mixtures for other cookie recipes in this book.

In a medium bowl, combine the egg and vanilla extract and whisk vigorously until well blended.

With the mixer on medium speed, add the egg mixture very slowly, in a steady stream, and mix until well-incorporated and very smooth, about 30 seconds. Scrape down the sides of the bowl, then mix on medium speed for 30 more seconds.

Scrape down the sides of the bowl, then add the flour mixture. Mix on low speed just until uniform in texture. Scrape down the sides of the bowl, then add the chocolate. Mix on low speed until the color is a uniform brown and no streaks of white remain.

Using a rubber spatula, scrape the dough out into an airtight container or onto a piece of plastic wrap. Cover the container, or, if using plastic wrap, shape the dough into a rough disk, wrap tightly, and refrigerate for at least 3 hours and up to 5 days.

Preheat the oven to 350°F (175°C). Line a baking sheet with parchment paper or a silicone mat.

Roll 1/4-cup (60 ml) portions of the dough into balls and place them on the baking sheet, spacing them at least 2 inches (5 cm) apart. (To make different sizes of cookies, see the sidebar on page 162.)

Bake for 11 to 12 minutes, until the cookies are slightly firm to the touch and the surface is no longer glossy, rotating the pan midway through the baking time.

Let the cookies cool on the pan for 10 minutes before removing.

These cookies are best when eaten warm, shortly after they come out of the oven. However, they can be stored in an airtight container at room temperature for up to 3 days. Alternatively, the dough can be stored in an airtight container in the refrigerator for up to 5 days, so consider baking only as many cookies as needed and saving the rest of the dough to bake another day.

SALT

I love finding that sweet spot in a dessert where there's just enough salt to taste, but not so much that it's overwhelming. I especially love getting a quick hit of salt, a surprise you wouldn't normally expect in a sweet treat. Of course, there are many cases where you just need the salt to play a supporting role, enhancing the flavor but staying silent and unassuming on the sidelines.

We use two types of salt in the Blue Bottle kitchens: kosher salt, which has larger grains than table salt and a mellow and not too salty flavor, and Maldon brand sea salt, beautiful crystalline flakes harvested in Essex, England since 1882. Kosher salt is, indeed, kosher, but the same is true of all salt; the name comes from its use in the meat koshering process. The large grain size is crucial because, rather than dissolving into the meat, it stays on the surface to do its job and then can be washed off to eliminate saltiness. These large and hard-to-dissolve grains are exactly why I love kosher salt. I like to be able to play with the amount of saltiness per bite, not necessarily bomb baked goods with an overall salty flavor. Whereas kosher salt does this on a smaller scale, Maldon does it on a larger scale, yet the large crystals have a surprisingly mild salt flavor because of their thin and delicate shape.

In these recipes, my distinction is based on grain size—Maldon is a large and flaky crystal, kosher salt has a medium grain size. Because there are many salts to choose from and sometimes you may not have exactly the form a recipe calls for, here's a quick and easy conversion: 1 teaspoon of a large-flake sea salt = 1/2 teaspoon kosher, or medium-grain, salt = 1/4 teaspoon fine-grained refined table salt.

Sesame-Absinthe Cigars

MAKES 24 COOKIES / HANDS-ON TIME: 40 MINUTES
FROM START TO FINISH: 1 HOUR

These cookies, which are more of a biscotti-style treat that are ideal for dunking in coffee, are easy to over-look when faced with the sweet and chocolaty options in Blue Bottle's pastry cases. Don't let their subtlety fool you; they are one of the most popular items among our staff, and my very favorite cookie to make.

This version is based on a beloved family recipe given to me by my friend Gina Roccanova. She was skeptical (at best) when I said that I wanted to modify her Sicilian grandmother's original recipe. Where the original recipe called for anise extract, I had visions of using absinthe by St. George Spirits. Absinthe, a distillate of many herbs, but primarily wormwood, anise, and fennel, was made legal in the United States in 2007 after a 92-year ban. Demonized as a dangerous psychoactive drug, absinthe addiction is said to have been the cause for some of history's most scandalous episodes, from Oscar Wilde's trysts to Van Gogh's missing ear. Possibly not a Sicilian grandmother's first choice for her cookies.

I was delighted with the results. The absinthe imparted an amazingly complex subtle sweetness with both earthy and herbal tones, and swapping out extra virgin olive oil for grandma's vegetable oil contrib-uted a slight grassiness that paired well with the toasted sesame seeds. The question was, would Gina agree? Absolutely! She might have even whispered to me that she prefers this version—but grandma must never know.

SUBSTITUTIONS: You can substitute Chartreuse, Sambuca, or any anise-flavored liqueur for the absinthe. To omit the liqueur altogether, use water for brushing; add 1 teaspoon anise seeds, crushed in a mortar, to the flour mixture; and add 1 tablespoon of whole anise seeds to the sesame seeds for rolling.

13/4 cups (8.6 oz / 245 g) all-purpose flour,
   plus more for kneading
1/2 cup (3.5 oz / 100 g) sugar
11/4 teaspoons kosher salt
3/4 teaspoon baking powder

1/3 cup (80 ml / 71 g) extra-virgin olive oil
2 eggs (3.5 oz / 100 g), at room temperature
1 tablespoon plus 1/4 cup absinthe
1 cup (5 oz / 142 g) sesame seeds

Preheat the oven to 350°F (175°C). Line a baking sheet with parchment paper.

Sift the flour, sugar, salt, and baking powder into a medium bowl.

Drizzle the olive oil over the top of the flour mixture, then pinch and rub the mixture between your hands until it has the texture of fluffy cornmeal; this should take about 5 minutes.

Make a well in the center of the mixture. Crack the eggs into the well. Add the 1 tablespoon of absinthe and, with a fork, immediately begin whisking the eggs vigorously to incorporate the absinthe before it curdles the eggs. Begin mixing the flour mixture into the eggs, working it in gradu-ally until fully incorporated.

CONTINUED

Generously flour a work surface, then turn the dough out on the floured area. Knead until the color lightens significantly, the oil is fully incorporated, and the dough is smooth, about 3 minutes, adding flour only as needed to prevent sticking. If the dough looks greasy or pockmarked, keep kneading.

Put the 1/4 cup of absinthe in a small bowl. Put the sesame seeds in a separate small, shallow bowl.

Divide the dough into 4 equal pieces. Still working on a floured surface, roll each piece into a long snakelike rope, about 18 inches (46 cm) long. Cut into 6 equal pieces, each about 3 inches (8 cm) long. Dip each piece in the absinthe, then gently roll in the sesame seeds until evenly covered.

Place the cookies on the prepared baking sheet, spacing them at least 1/2 inch (1.3 cm) apart.

Bake for about 12 minutes, until the sesame seeds are a very light golden brown but the cookies are still pale, rotating the pan midway through the baking time.

Let the cookies cool on the pan for 10 minutes before removing.

Serve either warm or at room temperature. Cooled completely and stored in an airtight container at room temperature, the cookies will keep for up to 2 days.

Biscotti Pizzetta

MAKES ABOUT 3 DOZEN BISCOTTI / HANDS-ON TIME: 45 MINUTES
FROM START TO FINISH: 2 HOURS, 30 MINUTES

Pizzetta 211 is a charming little twenty-four-seat pizza restaurant in San Francisco's Outer Richmond district. Without a doubt, it is our son Dashiell's very favorite place to eat—their cracker-thin pizzas and little ramekins of olives are some of his very first taste memories. It was also one of the earliest Blue Bottle wholesale accounts, and from the start, James has had a love affair with the restaurant's saffron biscotti. Eaten after pizza, accompanied by a little glass of vin santo, it's a perfectly civilized way to end a meal.

After we spent years trying to convince Pizzetta to make biscotti for Blue Bottle, they finally relented and, for a time, made a small batch for the Hayes Valley kiosk every week. Sadly for us, though happily for them, the demand for biscotti in their own restaurant became so great that they were no longer able to keep making a weekly batch for us. Proprietor Jack Murphy graciously invited me into his kitchen so he could teach me the art of these delicately flavored and tender biscotti. It was a funny scene: the laid-back *pizzaiolos*, just back from surfing in the Pacific, saying, "Oh, a pinch of this, a dash of that, and you'll just know when it's done," and me furiously scribbling notes and measuring everything with my tenth of a gram scale. My precisely calculated recipe is pretty close to their intuitive and freestyle biscotti, and delightfully, this treat is now available at all of our locations.

About 30 threads saffron (to yield
   1/8 teaspoon ground saffron; see Note,
   page 160)
1 egg (1.8 oz / 50 g), at room temperature
1/2 cup (3.5 oz / 100 g) sugar

1/4 cup (1.4 oz / 40 g) almonds
1 cup (4.9 oz / 140 g) all-purpose flour
1/2 teaspoon kosher salt
1/4 teaspoon baking soda
1 egg white (1.1 oz / 31 g)

Preheat the oven to 350°F (175°C). Line a baking sheet with parchment paper.

Crush the saffron threads with a mortar and pestle until powdery or grind them in a clean spice grinder; alternatively, you can finely mince the saffron. The finer the powder, the more intense the saffron color and flavor in the biscotti.

In a small bowl, combine the egg, saffron, and sugar and whisk until smooth. Let sit for 10 minutes.

Chop the almonds by hand or pulse in a food processor until about half are finely ground and half are roughly chopped.

Sift the flour, salt, and baking soda into the bowl of a stand mixer. Using the bread hook, mix on low speed until well incorporated. Add the egg mixture and mix on low speed until the flour is moistened. Increase to medium speed and mix until well combined, about 5 minutes, frequently scraping down the sides of the bowl. Gradually add the almonds and mix until incorporated.

Generously flour a work surface, then turn dough out onto the floured area. Knead until the dough no longer sticks to your palms, adding flour only as needed to prevent excessive sticking, about 2 minutes.

CONTINUED

Divide the dough into 2 equal pieces. Still working on a floured surface, roll each piece into a snakelike rope about 15 inches (38 cm) long. Transfer to the prepared pan, pressing down lightly to flatten slightly.

In a small bowl, whisk the egg white until frothy. Lightly brush the egg white over the dough, evenly covering the top and all sides.

Bake for 18 to 20 minutes, until firm to the touch and the egg wash has browned slightly.

Remove from the oven and let cool for 10 to 15 minutes. Lower the oven to 225°F (107°C) and leave door ajar briefly if necessary to bring the temperature down.

Transfer one biscotti log to a cutting board. Using a sharp serrated knife, carefully slice diagonally into pieces about 1/4 inch (6 mm) thick and about 4 inches (10 cm) long. Place the slices, cut side up, on a baking sheet; they can be packed in tight, with the edges touching. Repeat with the second log.

Bake for about 1 hour and 15 minutes, until completely dried out but without any darkening of color.

Let cool completely on the pan before serving. Serve at room temperature.

Stored in an airtight container at room temperature, the biscotti will keep for up to 2 weeks.

Madeleines

MAKES 16 TO 18 LARGE MADELEINES / HANDS-ON TIME: 45 MINUTES
FROM START TO FINISH: 5 HOURS

Every year James asks me to make madeleines on July 10, for the birthday of Marcel Proust, one of the most influential figures in his life—and every year I forget and let him down. Let this be my atonement to the memory of Proust! A love letter to my husband! And yet another madeleine recipe forever tied to those 486 words in *In Search of Lost Time: Volume 1—Swann's Way*.

The two keys to getting a madeleine's signature shape, with the flared edges and pronounced bump on top, are a very cold pan and well-rested batter. Madeleines can be tricky to get right, so I advise baking one or two at a time until you get a handle on how your oven and madeleine pan best work together. These can also be baked in mini madeleine pans. Use about 1/2 teaspoon of batter per madeleine and bake for about 8 minutes. Again, test one or two in your oven to gauge the batter quantity and time before committing the whole batch to the oven.

SUBSTITUTIONS: You can substitute any citrus zest for the lime. I choose lime to recreate, as faithfully as possible, the taste memory made famous in *Swann's Way*, when the narrator receives a madeleine dipped in his aunt's lime-blossom tea.

6 tablespoons (3 oz / 85 g) unsalted butter	1/4 teaspoon kosher salt
Finely grated zest of 1 lime	2 eggs (3.5 oz / 100 g)
3/4 cup (3.7 oz / 105 g) all-purpose flour	1/2 cup (3.5 oz / 100 g) sugar
1 teaspoon baking powder	2 tablespoons honey

Melt the butter, then pour it into a medium bowl. Stir in the lime zest and let cool.

Sift the flour, baking powder, and salt into a medium bowl.

In the top of a double boiler or a medium metal bowl set over a saucepan of simmering water, combine the eggs, sugar, and honey. (Make sure the bottom of the bowl doesn't touch the water in the saucepan.) Whisk vigorously until well blended, then cook, stirring constantly, until the sugar has dissolved and the mixture is slightly warm, about 130°F (54°C). Transfer to the bowl of a stand mixer fitted with the whisk attachment.

Whip the egg mixture on high speed until tripled in volume, about 10 minutes.

Remove the bowl from the stand mixer and sift in one-third of the flour mixture. Use a rubber spatula to gently fold in the flour. Repeat twice more to incorporate all of the flour.

Add 1/4 cup of the mixture to the cooled butter and whisk until thoroughly combined and there are no longer streaks of butter. Gently fold the butter mixture into the egg-flour mixture until the batter has a homogenous color and texture.

Press plastic wrap onto the surface of the batter and refrigerate for at least 4 hours and up to 3 days; the ideal is about 12 hours.

CONTINUED

for many never con
come into possession o
they call out to us, an
ell is broken. Delivered
turn to live with us.
s the same with our past. It
n it, all the exertions of our
outside the realm of our intel
aterial object (in the sensation t   object would

the drink, but on me. The
oes not know this truth, and can do
indefinitely, with less and less force, this same
least to be able to ask of it again and find again, intact, available to
me, soon, for a decisive clarification. I put down the cup and turn to
my mind. It is up to my mind to find the truth. But how? Such grave
uncertainty, whenever the mind feels overtaken by itself; when it, the

Butter and flour 2 madeleine pans (or enough to make 16 to 18 madeleines), then refrigerate. Preheat the oven to 400°F (205°C).

Portion the batter, using about 1 tablespoon for each madeleine mold, forming each portion into a ball and placing it in the center of the mold. Refrigerate while the oven heats.

Bake for about 9 minutes in a nonstick madeleine pan or 12 minutes in an aluminum pan, until the madeleines are golden brown and resist slightly when lightly pressed in the center of the bump, rotating the pan midway through the baking time.

Let the madeleines cool in the pan for 5 minutes, then turn them out onto a plate.

Madeleines are best when eaten warm, shortly after they come out of the oven. However, they can be wrapped tightly and stored at room temperature for up to 1 day. Alternatively, the batter can be stored in an airtight container in the refrigerator (with plastic wrap pressed against the surface) for up to 3 days, so consider baking only as many as needed and saving the rest of the batter to bake another day.

Chocolate Parisian Macarons

MAKES ABOUT 28 *MACARONS* / HANDS-ON TIME: 1 HOUR
FROM START TO FINISH: 2 HOURS, 20 MINUTES

Around the time James and I became neighbors at the Saturday Downtown Berkeley Farmers' Market, me selling cakes, him selling coffee, I was headlong into my obsession with developing a Parisian *macaron*, inspired by my first trip to Paris. I was determined to create a beautiful *macaron* with organic ingredients, free from the food coloring that makes them so famously colorful, and with a texture more suggestive of the almonds from which they are made. Instead of using processed almond flour, I used whole almonds from John Lagier, a local almond and grape farmer who had a market stall next to us. Every week I'd try another batch of *macarons*, some utter failures, some showing a glimmer of progress, and I'd bring my results to the farmers' market for James to try. This went on for months until, giddy with the revelation of a thirty-minute rest time for the perfect shape, I finally had what I thought was a successful batch to bring to him. I remember his reaction as clear as can be: he closed his eyes, let out a little sigh, and, rendered unable to speak, rolled up his sleeve to show me goose bumps on his arm. I had it right.

The Parisian *macaron* is one of the most difficult confections to conquer. It took me two years to develop and master my first recipe, a process that left me unable to enjoy eating *macarons* for the next five years. To this day, with each bite of a perfect *macaron*, I have a Proustian memory of each and every failed batch. I've made this a more fail-safe recipe than my original, using an Italian meringue rather than simply whipped egg whites; this allows a little more leeway when folding and increases the chance of success—which, hopefully, will result in your beloved being overcome with goose bumps as well.

SUBSTITUTIONS: Almond flour can be substituted for an equal *weight* of whole almonds, but you will still need to process the flour with the powdered sugar and cocoa powder for 3 to 4 minutes in the food processor, so you won't be saving much time. Plus, almond flour is expensive, so you won't save much money either. Regarding fillings, chocolate ganache is classic, but you can use any filling you like. Strawberry buttercream, cherry jam, and salted caramel are all incredible fillings, and each will add a different—and illuminating—taste and texture element.

GANACHE
4 ounces (113 g) dark chocolate, 62% to 70% cacao, finely chopped
1/2 cup (120 ml / 116 g) heavy cream

MACARONS
1 1/3 cups (5.4 oz / 153 g) powdered sugar
1 cup (5.6 oz / 160 g) almonds
1/2 cup (1.4 oz / 40 g) natural (not Dutch-processed) cocoa powder
3 egg whites (3.2 oz / 91 g), at room temperature
3/4 cup (5.3 oz / 150 g) granulated sugar
1/4 cup (60 ml / 60 g) water

CONTINUED

TO MAKE THE GANACHE, put the chocolate in a medium heatproof bowl. In a small saucepan over medium-low heat or in a microwave, heat the cream just until bubbles begin to form at the edges, between 180°F and 190°F (82°C and 88°C). Pour the hot cream over the chocolate and, using rubber spatula, mix until the chocolate is mostly melted.

Blend until smooth using an immersion blender or food processor, or transfer to a double boiler or a metal bowl set over a saucepan of simmering water and whisk until smooth. The ganache should be shiny. Set aside at room temperature until the ganache has cooled to the spreadable texture of slightly warm butter, about 2 hours.

TO MAKE THE MACARONS, put the powdered sugar, almonds, and cocoa in a food processor and process until powdery, about 5 minutes, stopping occasionally to scrape the sides and bottom with a rubber spatula. The mixture will start to look powdery fairly quickly, but give it the full 5 minutes so the almonds will be broken down to a combination of fine dust and small particles.

Pour the mixture into a large bowl and break up any large chunks with your fingers.

The sugar and egg whites need to be prepared at roughly the same time, so the next two steps will require some coordination. Put 2 egg whites (2.2 oz / 62 g) in the bowl of a stand mixer fitted with the whisk attachment (both the bowl and the whisk should be very clean) and whisk on medium speed for 1 to 2 minutes. Increase the mixer speed to high and continue whisking until firm peaks form, 3 to 4 minutes. If firm peaks form before the sugar is ready, decrease the mixer speed to low and continue whisking.

Meanwhile, combine the sugar and water in a very small saucepan; a milk steaming pitcher works well for this task because its small diameter gives the mixture sufficient depth to get a good temperature reading, and because it makes it easy to pour the sugar syrup into the egg whites. Cook over medium-low heat, swirling occasionally, until the sugar melts, then cook without stirring until the syrup reaches 238°F (114°C), about 5 minutes.

If using a small saucepan rather than a steaming pitcher, transfer the syrup to a glass measuring cup. With the mixer on medium-high speed, slowly add the sugar syrup to the eggs in a thin steady stream. Aim to pour the syrup into the small gap between the mixer bowl and the whisk; the splatter of hot sugar syrup onto the rotating whisk will result in stringy particles in your *macaron* batter.

Increase the mixer speed to high and whip until stiff, shiny peaks form and the mixture holds its shape at the end of the whisk, 4 to 5 minutes.

Pour the remaining egg white (1.1 oz / 31 g) over the almond mixture, then top with the whipped egg white mixture. With a rubber spatula, fold the whipped mixture into the almond mixture until no dry spots remain. Continue folding carefully but thoroughly for about 35 folds, until the mixture

is very dark and shiny and no dry lumps remain. This is the most critical step because it's all too easy to undermix or overmix the batter. I've found that taking the time to count the number of folds, and watching carefully for the a change in color and texture is the best way to achieve perfect *macaron* results.

Fit a pastry bag with an Ateco 804 tip or a similar plain ½-inch (1.3 cm) tip. Fill the pastry bag about halfway with the batter. (If there's too much batter in the bag, you might struggle more with the bag than with the piping.)

Line 2 heavy baking sheets with parchment paper.

Position the piping tip about ¼ inch (6 mm) above the baking sheet and, holding it still, pipe batter until it forms a circle 1 inch (2.5 cm) in diameter and about ¼ inch (6 mm) thick. Release pressure on the bag and make a quick, slight circular motion, almost wiping the pastry tip on the top of the *macaron*, to remove the tip without creating a big peak. Continue piping circles, spacing them ½ to 1 inch (1.3 to 2.5 cm) apart until the tray is filled. (When first starting to make *macarons*, you may want guidance to create the correct size and shape. Try dipping a 1-inch, or 2.5 cm, round cookie cutter in powdered sugar or cornstarch, then tap it on the parchment paper to make a perfect little circle.)

With a folded towel on the countertop to soften the blow, very firmly rap the baking sheet on the counter three times to release any air bubbles from the batter. Rotate the pan 180 degrees and repeat. Continue until all of the batter has been used.

CONTINUED

Set the baking sheets aside and let rest for 30 minutes. Meanwhile, preheat the oven to 350°F (175°C).

Bake 1 tray at a time, starting with the pan that has rested the longest, in the center of the oven for 10 minutes, rotating the pan midway through the baking time.

Let cool completely on the pan, about 30 minutes, before removing.

TO ASSEMBLE THE *MACARONS*, pair *macarons* of matching sizes. Using a pastry bag, pipe about 1 teaspoon of cooled chocolate ganache onto the bottom (flat side) of one cookie from each matched pair; alternatively, you can use a small offset spatula to spread the ganache.

Set the second cookie of each pair atop the ganache, bottom (flat side) down. Gently press together to evenly distribute the ganache, taking care not to crush the tops of the cookies. It works well to take one half in each hand, grasp the edges with your fingers and shimmy them together—a motion not unlike trying to separate the two halves of an Oreo cookie.

Macarons are best when eaten the day they are made. However, they can be wrapped tightly in plastic wrap and stored in an airtight container in the refrigerator for up to 3 days. Serve at room temperature.

MACARON TROUBLESHOOTING

An ideal *macaron* has a shiny round top centered atop a thin, ruffled base (called the foot). If your first attempts don't achieve this ideal shape and configuration, here are some troubleshooting tips.

- Wet top: the shaped batter didn't get a long enough rest.
- Dome not centered on foot: the piped batter rested too long.
- A big air gap between the surface of the dome and the interior: the batter had too much egg white; consider weighing them next time.
- A split dome due to explosion of batter: the batter was overworked.
- A fat dome with a pointy tip: the batter wasn't worked enough or wasn't rapped on the countertop hard enough.
- Sticking to the parchment paper: the *macarons* weren't baked long enough or were removed before completely cool.

Olive Oil and Rosemary Shortbread

MAKES 35 SHORTBREAD COOKIES / HANDS-ON TIME: 20 MINUTES
FROM START TO FINISH: 4 HOURS

My best friend's mother, Deborah Dunsworth Quinn, made piles of her legendary shortbread cookies every Christmas season while we were growing up. Their house was like a factory, with stacks of well-seasoned clay shortbread molds being filled and refilled with dough by her three daughters, Vanessa, Robin, and Zoe, and packages going out to eager friends and neighbors around our small hometown of Ojai, California. Just before Christmas 2007, Deborah unexpectedly and tragically passed away. It was a heart-wrenching time, and in the week after her passing, her daughters consoled themselves by grabbing the well-worn recipe, dusting off the shortbread molds, and making piles and piles of their mother's short-bread, this time for the hundreds of guests attending their mom's memorial service.

Our Mint Plaza café opened shortly after her passing, and in memory of Deborah, I modified her recipe into what has become one of our most popular cookies. The base recipe is very similar to the original—buttery, salty, and with the perfect shortbread texture—but varied by the addition of chopped fresh rosemary and a generous brush of olive oil straight out of the oven. The quantities we make at Blue Bottle necessitate that we cannot use shortbread molds, but I have a special clay mold I use when making these cookies at home—which, hopefully one day, will be as well worn as Deborah's are. This recipe details how we make the shortbread at Blue Bottle, without a mold. If you have a mold, see the Note below for details on baking the shortbread Deborah's way.

SUBSTITUTIONS: This is an incredibly flexible recipe that is perfect for modifications. Add 1/3 cup toasted pine nuts for a slightly more savory and even more rich shortbread, as photographed. Or for a delightful Turkish coffee shortbread, substitute 1 tablespoon coarsely ground coffee for the rosemary and add 1/4 teaspoon of ground green cardamom. These are just a couple of ideas, and I encourage you to experiment and come up with your own variations.

1 cup (8 oz / 227 g) unsalted butter, at room
   temperature
1 cup (4.1 oz / 115 g) powdered sugar, sifted
1 teaspoon finely minced fresh rosemary, or
   1/2 teaspoon dried

1 1/4 teaspoons kosher salt
2 cups (9.9 oz / 280 g) all-purpose flour, sifted
Extra-virgin olive oil, for brushing

In the bowl of a stand mixer fitted with the paddle attachment, beat the butter on low speed until smooth, 1 to 2 minutes. Add the sugar, rosemary, and salt and mix on low speed until well combined. Scrape down the sides of the bowl, then mix on medium speed until lighter in color and the texture resembles mayonnaise, 4 to 5 minutes.

Scrape down the sides of the bowl, then add the flour. Mix on low speed just until uniform in texture. Scrape down the sides of the bowl and mix on low speed for 1 minute.

CONTINUED

Gather the dough into a ball, transfer to a piece of plastic wrap, cover with a second piece of plastic wrap, and flatten to form a rectangle measuring 7 by 10 inches (18 by 25 cm) and about 1/2 inch (1.3 cm) thick. Wrap tightly and refrigerate for at least 3 hours and up to 5 days.

Preheat the oven to 350°F (175°C). Line a baking sheet with parchment paper.

Cut the dough into small rectangles measuring 1 by 2 inches (2.5 by 5 cm), and place the cookies on the lined baking sheet, spacing them at least 1 inch (2.5 cm) apart. Bake for about 18 minutes, until golden around the edges, rotating the pan midway through the baking time.

Brush the tops with olive oil as soon as the cookies come out of the oven. Let cool on the pan for at least 10 minutes before removing, then let cool completely before serving for optimal texture.

Cooled completely and stored in an airtight container, the cookies will keep for up to 3 days.

NOTE: *To use a shortbread mold instead of forming the dough into a rectangle, press the just-mixed dough into an 8-inch (20-cm) clay mold and flatten it into an even layer. Bake at 350°F (175°C) for about 12 minutes, until the edges begin to brown. Let cool for 10 minutes before inverting the shortbread onto a sheet pan, then immediately brush the tops with olive oil. Let cool completely before serving for optimal texture.*

Fennel-Parmesan Shortbread

MAKES 35 SHORTBREAD COOKIES / HANDS-ON TIME: 30 MINUTES
FROM START TO FINISH: 4 HOURS

This shortbread was intended to be a short-term product to use up extra ingredients in our kitchen. A few years back, I thought it would be nice to make a yeasted bread product our shops. I will readily admit that yeast scares me, and I've been less than successful as a bread baker, so when my good friend Nicole Krasinski offered to develop a recipe and train our staff to make brioche, I jumped at the chance. Nicole is both an accomplished bread baker and very talented pastry chef, and she really shines at making inventive sweets with a surprising savory element. The brioche she developed for us was absolutely lovely: a flaky, lightly sweetened and buttery bread with a hint of pepper and large flecks of Parmesan cheese studded throughout. Before baking, we sprinkled the tops with a mixture of crushed fennel and large-grained sea salt. It was delicious, and I ate one every day.

Sadly, the brioche never caught on with our customers, and eventually our accountants sat me down to talk about the brioche's limping profitability. With a huge wheel of leftover Parmesan cheese, a pound of fennel seeds, and staff unhappy with the bread baker's 3 a.m. start time, I needed to come up with a recipe that would use up the ingredients we had on hand and didn't require hours of early morning labor. I decided to modify our Olive Oil and Rosemary Shortbread recipe with Nicole's great flavor profile. The result was easy to make and surprisingly delicious, and has become a permanent and popular homage to the brioche that I loved so much.

SUBSTITUTIONS: Any salty hard cheese, such as an aged Manchego, Grana Padano, or Mimolette, would be a suitable replacement for the Parmesan.

1 cup (8 oz / 227 g) unsalted butter, at room temperature
1/2 cup (2 oz / 57 g) powdered sugar
1 1/4 teaspoons kosher salt
1 teaspoon freshly ground black pepper
2 cups (9.9 oz / 280 g) all-purpose flour, sifted

1 cup (3.5 oz / 100 g) finely grated Parmesan cheese
1 tablespoon fennel seeds
1 tablespoon Maldon sea salt (see page 165)
Extra-virgin olive oil, for brushing

In the bowl of a stand mixer fitted with the paddle attachment, beat the butter on low speed until smooth, 1 to 2 minutes. Add the sugar, kosher salt, and pepper and mix on low speed until well combined. Scrape down the sides of the bowl, then mix on medium speed until lighter in color and the texture resembles mayonnaise, 4 to 5 minutes.

Scrape down the sides of the bowl, then add the flour. Mix on low speed just until uniform in texture. Scrape down the sides of the bowl, add the Parmesan cheese, and mix on low speed for 1 minute.

Gather the dough into a ball, transfer to a piece of plastic wrap, and cover with another piece of plastic wrap. Flatten to form a rectangle measuring 7 by 10 inches (18 by 25 cm) and about 1/2 inch (1.3 cm) thick. Wrap tightly and refrigerate for at least 3 hours and up to 5 days.

Preheat the oven to 350°F (175°C). Line a baking sheet with parchment paper.

Coarsely crush the fennel seeds with a mortar and pestle or grind them in a clean spice grinder. Transfer to a small bowl, add the sea salt, and mix well.

Cut the dough into small rectangles measuring 1 by 2 inches (2.5 by 5 cm), and place the cookies on the lined baking sheet, spacing them at least 1 inch (2.5 cm) apart. Brush the tops liberally with olive oil and sprinkle the fennel mixture evenly over the tops.

Bake for about 18 minutes, until the cookies are golden brown and the flecks of cheese are medium brown, rotating the pan midway through the baking time.

Let cool on the pan for at least 10 minutes before removing, then let cool completely before serving for optimal texture.

Cooled completely and stored in an airtight container, the cookies will keep for up to 3 days.

NOTE: *Unlike Olive Oil and Rosemary Shortbread (page 181), this shortbread doesn't work in a clay shortbread mold.*

In the Afternoon

Brooklyn Bootleg S'mores

MAKES 20 SMALL S'MORES / HANDS-ON TIME: 2 HOURS
FROM START TO FINISH: 5 TO 6 HOURS

James and I have known Sarah Cox, a lovely and talented baker, since the early days at Blue Bottle in San Francisco. Nicknamed "Five-Cappuccino Sarah," she was a stalwart patron at the Ferry Plaza Farmers Market, buying cappuccinos for herself and her coworkers, who were at the market shopping for their restaurant, Rubicon. Fast-forward six years to 2010, with Blue Bottle planning a roastery and café in Brooklyn and my hunt for a baker I could trust to run the show on the other side of the country. Sarah, my top choice for the position, was totally up for it and packed her boyfriend and her beloved parakeet, Miss K, into a U-Haul trailer with quite a few pounds of Blue Bottle coffee to keep them going on their road trip.

Upon landing in Brooklyn, her first order of business was to find local products to use, either adapting Blue Bottle's existing recipes or creating new recipes to feature them. Mast Brothers Chocolate, Kings County Distillery Moonshine, Tremblay Apiary Fallflower Honey, and Daisy brand organic whole wheat pastry flour said one thing to me: s'mores! Only available at Blue Bottle's Brooklyn location, these s'mores have become the mascot of our East Coast pastry department.

SUBSTITUTIONS: Any alcohol will work in the marshmallows. I have made wonderful marshmallows with Lillet Blanc, champagne, and bourbon.

MARSHMALLOWS
5 gelatin sheets, or 2$\frac{1}{2}$ teaspoons
   powdered gelatin
$\frac{1}{4}$ cup (60 ml / 60 g) cold water, if using
   powdered gelatin
$\frac{1}{4}$ cup (1.1 oz / 31 g) cornstarch
$\frac{1}{4}$ cup (1 oz / 28 g) powdered sugar
3 tablespoons moonshine
$\frac{3}{4}$ cup (5.3 oz / 150 g) granulated sugar
6 tablespoons (2.9 oz / 85 g) agave nectar
2 tablespoons water
Pinch of kosher salt

GRAHAM CRACKERS
1 cup (4.9 oz / 140 g) all-purpose flour
$\frac{1}{2}$ cup (2.5 oz / 70 g) whole wheat flour
$\frac{1}{2}$ teaspoon baking soda
$\frac{1}{2}$ teaspoon freshly ground cinnamon
11 tablespoons (5.5 oz / 156 g) unsalted
   butter, at room temperature
3 tablespoons honey
$\frac{1}{4}$ cup (1.8 oz / 50 g) granulated sugar
$\frac{1}{4}$ cup (1.9 oz / 54 g) packed light brown
   sugar
$\frac{1}{2}$ teaspoon Maldon sea salt (see page 165)
1 recipe Ganache (see page 175)

TO MAKE THE MARSHMALLOWS, if using gelatin sheets, submerge them in a medium bowl filled with ice water until soft, 5 to 10 minutes. If using powdered gelatin, sprinkle it evenly over $\frac{1}{4}$ cup cold water; let sit for 5 to 10 minutes, then gently warm in a microwave or in a small saucepan over very low heat until all of the granules are dissolved.

CONTINUED

Sift the cornstarch and powdered sugar into a small bowl.

Line a 9 by 13-inch (23 by 33 cm) baking pan with two layers of parchment paper or waxed paper, arranged perpendicularly so that all sides of the pan are covered. (To get the paper to stay put, you can butter the pan first.) Dust generously with some of the powdered sugar mixture, evenly coating the entire bottom of the pan. Set aside the remaining powdered sugar mixture for coating the finished marshmallows.

If using sheet gelatin, squeeze out all excess water and put the gelatin in the bowl of a stand mixer fitted with the whisk attachment. If using powdered gelatin, pour the dissolved mixture into the bowl. Add 2 tablespoons of the moonshine.

In a small heavy saucepan, combine the granulated sugar, agave nectar, 2 tablespoons water, salt, and the remaining 1 tablespoon of moonshine. Stir until well combined, then cook without stirring over medium-high heat until a candy thermometer reads 238°F to 240°F (114°C to 116°C).

Pour the mixture over the gelatin and whip, first on low speed and gradually increasing the speed to high, until smooth and glossy and firm peaks form, 8 to 10 minutes. The mixture won't begin to resemble a marshmallow until around the 5-minute mark.

Using a rubber spatula, scrape the mixture into the prepared pan and smooth the top with an offset spatula. Let sit at room temperature for at least 3 to 4 hours, until set.

Sift a generous amount of the reserved powdered sugar mixture over the top of the marshmallows. Using a clean, hot knife or clean, hot scissors, cut into 2-inch (5 cm) squares and generously dust the edges with more of the powdered sugar mixture to prevent sticking.

The marshmallows can be stored in an airtight container at room temperature for up to 1 week.

NOTE: *To easily clean a pot or measuring cup that is sticky with the remnants of hot sugar syrup, fill it with warm water and let it sit until the sugar has dissolved, about 30 minutes.*

TO MAKE THE GRAHAM CRACKERS, sift the all-purpose flour, whole wheat flour, baking soda, and cinnamon into a medium bowl.

In the bowl of a stand mixer fitted with the paddle attachment, beat the butter and honey on low speed until smooth, 1 to 2 minutes. Add the granulated sugar, brown sugar, and salt and mix on low speed until well combined. Scrape down the sides of the bowl, then mix on medium speed until light and fluffy, 4 to 5 minutes.

Scrape down the sides of the bowl, then add the flour mixture. Mix on low speed just until uniform in texture.

Turn the dough out onto a piece of parchment paper. Press into an even, flat rectangle and put another piece of parchment paper on top. Roll out to about $1/8$ inch (3 mm) thick. With the dough still sandwiched between the sheets of parchment paper, transfer to a baking sheet and refrigerate until firm, about 1 hour and up to 1 week. This is a sticky dough, so don't try to remove the parchment paper until it is chilled; then it can be pulled off cleanly and easily.

Remove the top piece of parchment paper and score the dough into 2-inch (5 cm) squares.

Preheat the oven to 350°F (175°C). Line two baking sheets with parchment paper.

Poke each square with a fork, creating vent holes. Use a small metal spatula to transfer the cookies to the lined baking sheets, spacing them 1 inch (2.5 cm) apart. Bake for 12 to 15 minutes, until golden.

Let cool on the pan for 10 minutes before removing. Let cool completely before using to make s'mores. The graham crackers can be stored in an airtight container at room temperature for up to 2 days.

TO ASSEMBLE EACH S'MORE, smear about 1 teaspoon of ganache on the bottom (flat side) of two graham crackers. Place a marshmallow atop the ganache on one graham cracker, top with the second graham cracker, ganache side down, and gently squish.

S'mores are best eaten right away. However, they can be stored in an airtight container for up to 2 days. Note that the graham crackers will get increasingly soft the longer they're stored. Alternatively, all of the components can be stored for 1 week; the marshmallows at room temperature, and the ganache and unbaked graham crackers in the refrigerator, so consider baking only as many graham crackers as needed and saving the rest to bake for s'mores another day.

Salted Chocolate and Vanilla Bean Ice Cream Sandwiches

MAKES 10 TO 12 ICE CREAM SANDWICHES / HANDS-ON TIME: 1 HOUR, 30 MINUTES
FROM START TO FINISH: 9 HOURS

At the Blue Bottle café in the rooftop sculpture garden at the San Francisco Museum of Modern Art, one of my first art-inspired desserts, and still an all-time favorite, was based on the Katharina Fritsch sculpture *Kind mit Pudeln* (Baby with Poodles), a series of 224 black poodles packed into four concentric circles with a white sculpture of a baby in the center. An ice cream sandwich of salted, chocolate poodle-shaped cookies with vanilla-flecked poodle-shaped ice cream tucked inside was the perfect summertime treat for our first season at the museum, and an adorable homage to the sculpture. We only serve the themed pastries while the related art is displayed in the galleries, so, sadly, when the curators packed up the poodles to make way for new art, we had to pack up this ice cream sandwich.

Of course, we used a poodle-shaped cookie cutter when making this treat at the museum, but I like to use a scalloped circle when making these at home. Feel free to go with a square to reduce cookie and ice cream "waste" (not that no one will eat the scraps!), or use whatever shape makes you feel most happy.

SUBSTITUTIONS: $^1/_2$ teaspoon vanilla extract can be substituted for the vanilla bean.

ICE CREAM
2 cups (475 ml / 464 g) heavy cream
1 cup (240 ml / 242 g) half-and-half
$^2/_3$ cup (4.7 oz / 133 g) sugar
$^1/_2$ vanilla bean
6 egg yolks (3.9 oz / 114 g), at room temperature

CHOCOLATE SABLÉS
$1^1/_2$ cups (7.4 oz / 210 g) all-purpose flour
$^1/_4$ cup (0.8 oz / 23 g) natural (not Dutch-processed) cocoa powder
$^1/_2$ teaspoon baking soda
11 tablespoons (5.5 oz / 156 g) unsalted butter, at room temperature
$^3/_4$ cup (5.3 oz / 150 g) sugar
$^1/_2$ teaspoon Maldon sea salt (see page 165)
1 teaspoon vanilla extract

TO MAKE THE ICE CREAM, combine the cream, half-and-half, and sugar in a heavy medium saucepan. Split the vanilla bean in half, scrape the pulp into the saucepan, then throw in the pod. Cook over medium-low heat, stirring often, until bubbles begin to form at the edges, between 180°F and 190°F (82°C and 88°C). Remove from the heat, cover, and let sit for 10 minutes.

Put the egg yolks in a medium bowl. Add $^1/_4$ cup of the warm cream mixture and whisk until well blended. Repeat five more times, until $1^1/_2$ cups of the cream mixture have been added and the egg yolk mixture is as warm as the remaining cream mixture.

Slowly pour the egg yolk mixture into the saucepan in a steady stream while whisking continuously. Cook over low heat, whisking constantly, until the mixture thickens and coats the back of a spoon, about 10 minutes. Strain through a fine-mesh sieve into a bowl and return the vanilla pod to the mixture. Press plastic wrap onto the surface and refrigerate for at least 3 hours and up to 12 hours.

CONTINUED

Remove the vanilla pod and freeze in an ice cream maker according to the manufacturer's instructions.

Line a 9 by 13-inch (23 by 33 cm) baking pan with plastic wrap. Pour the soft ice cream into the pan, spread it in an even layer, and smooth the surface with an offset spatula. Cover with plastic wrap and freeze for at least 4 hours. The ice cream can be stored in the freezer for up to 2 weeks.

TO MAKE THE SABLÉS, sift the flour, cocoa powder, and baking soda into a medium bowl.

In the bowl of a stand mixer fitted with the paddle attachment, beat the butter on low speed until smooth, 1 to 2 minutes. Add the sugar and salt and mix on low speed until well combined. Add the vanilla extract and mix just until incorporated. Scrape down the sides of the bowl, then mix on medium speed until light and fluffy, 4 to 5 minutes.

Scrape down the sides of the bowl, then add the flour mixture. Mix on low speed just until uniform in texture.

Turn the dough out onto a piece of parchment paper. Press into an even, flat rectangle and put another piece of parchment paper on top. Roll out to about 1/4 inch (6 mm) thick. Remove the top piece of parchment paper and cut the dough into squares with a knife or use cookie cutters to cut shapes. Don't try to remove the cookies until the dough has been chilled. Slide the parchment paper and dough onto a cookie sheet, cover with plastic wrap, and refrigerate until firm, at least 30 minutes.

Preheat the oven to 325°F (165°C). Line a baking sheet with parchment paper.

Use a small metal spatula to transfer the cold cookies to the lined baking sheet, spacing them about 1 inch (2.5 cm) apart.

Bake for 12 to 14 minutes, until crisp, rotating the pan midway through the baking time.

Let cool on the pan for 10 minutes before removing. Let cool completely before using. The cookies can be stored in an airtight container at room temperature for up to 1 day.

TO ASSEMBLE THE ICE CREAM SANDWICHES, line up the cookies, all facing up. If you used a cookie cutter for the cookies, fill a small bowl with hot water and soak the cookie cutter to warm it for cutting the ice cream.

Remove the ice cream from the freezer and cut it into squares the same size as the cookies or cut into shapes using the hot cookie cutter.

Working quickly, place a portion of ice cream on a cookie and top with another cookie. Store the ice cream sandwiches on a tray in the freezer as you go. If the ice cream starts to melt, put it in the freezer until it's firm enough to work with.

The assembled ice cream sandwiches can be stored in an airtight container in the freezer for up to 1 week.

Affogato with Smoky Almond Ice Cream

MAKES 1 QUART (945 ML) ICE CREAM, ENOUGH FOR 5 AFFOGATOS
HANDS-ON TIME: 30 MINUTES / FROM START TO FINISH: 6 HOURS, 30 MINUTES

I think carob has a bad rap. Made from the pod of the Mediterranean tree *Ceratonia siliqua*, it is sold in powdered form or in chips, most often in the bulk bins at natural food stores. Although typically thought of as a substitute for chocolate, it most definitely is not chocolate, and most people who try it as such are horrified at the flavor. However, I'm convinced that if you let go of thinking of it as a replacement for something you love (but somehow don't want to eat), and focus on it as its own thing, carob is totally lovable. Nutty, sweet and malty, with a slight coffeelike bitterness, it's a fascinating flavor to play with when applied in small amounts.

Unfortunately, all of this big talk has never eased James's dislike of carob or made him happy about the carob peanut clusters I bring home from the natural food store. So suffice it to say he was skeptical, at best, at my plan to make a carob dessert for Blue Bottle. Determined to prove that he could like it, I came up with the idea of pairing carob with a smoky alcohol and toasted almonds in an ice cream, and then pouring espresso over the top for a classic affogato. Smoke, coffee, alcohol—if he didn't love it, at the very least it would appeal to his macho side. I'm not sure if eating an affogato is really that macho, but as it turns out, he really loves this dessert.

SUBSTITUTIONS: If you don't have an espresso machine, pour 1/4 cup strong coffee over each serving of ice cream. Tequila can replace the mezcal; for a smoky flavor, use an añejo or reposado tequila.

SMOKY ALMOND ICE CREAM
2 cups (475 ml / 464 g) heavy cream
1 cup (240 ml / 242 g) half-and-half
2/3 cup (4.7 oz / 133 g) sugar
3 tablespoons carob powder
2 tablespoons mezcal

6 egg yolks (3.9 oz / 114 g), at room
    temperature
1/2 cup (2.8 oz / 80 g) almonds

5 shots (125 to 175 ml) espresso

TO MAKE THE ICE CREAM, combine the cream, half-and-half, sugar, carob, and mezcal in a heavy medium saucepan. Cook over medium-low heat, stirring often, until bubbles begin to form at the edges, between 180°F and 190°F (82°C and 88°C).

Put the egg yolks in a medium bowl. Add 1/4 cup of the warm cream mixture and whisk until well blended. Repeat five more times, until 1 1/2 cups of the cream mixture have been added and the egg yolk mixture is as warm as the remaining cream mixture.

Slowly pour the egg yolk mixture into the saucepan in a steady stream while whisking constantly. Cook over low heat, whisking constantly, until the mixture thickens and coats the back of a spoon, about 10 minutes. Strain through a fine-mesh sieve into a bowl. Press plastic wrap onto the surface and refrigerate for at least 3 hours and up to 12 hours.

CONTINUED

In a heavy medium skillet, cook the almonds over medium heat, shaking often, until fragrant and slightly brown, about 5 minutes. Let cool completely, then coarsely chop.

Freeze the cream mixture in an ice cream maker according to the manufacturer's instructions, adding the almonds almost at the end of the churning time. Transfer to a container, cover, and freeze until firm, at least 3 hours. The ice cream can be stored in the freezer for up to 2 weeks.

TO ASSEMBLE THE AFFOGATOS, divide the ice cream evenly among five cups or bowls and pour a shot of espresso over each. Serve immediately.

Chocolate Pudding

MAKES 6 TO 8 SERVINGS / HANDS-ON TIME: 1 HOUR
FROM START TO FINISH: 5 HOURS, 15 MINUTES

Prior to opening of the Mint Plaza café, James and I devoted a lot of discussion to civilized desserts that could be enjoyed alongside the beautifully prepared siphon coffee. I came up with the idea of a pudding bar: many different types of beautiful silken puddings served in beakers and topped with freshly whipped cream. I imagined a texture similar to panna cotta, only more joyful, voluptuous, and peaked, like the pudding you see in commercials. Though the pudding bar was to remain a dream (at least for now), a luscious chocolate pudding did seem both appealing and practical, so I set about developing a recipe.

Unable to achieve the texture I was looking for using traditional methods involving cornstarch, I asked my friend (and algae enthusiast) chef Daniel Patterson his thoughts on pudding. Very opaquely, he said, "Dissolve agar into your liquid. Refrigerate. And then whip up in a blender." I've long been familiar with agar as a gelling agent made from algae that can be used as a vegetarian replacement for gelatin; Daniel, however, has been using it innovatively in other cooking applications for years. After some experimentation, I applied his gelling technique to a luxuriously rich and delicious chocolate crème anglaise. This pudding, which was briefly but gloriously served in delicate Hario beakers alongside siphon coffee at Mint Plaza, was the wonderful result.

6 ounces (170 g) dark chocolate, 62% to 70% cacao
1 teaspoon vanilla extract
1 cup (240 ml / 240 g) water
1/4 cup (0.5 oz / 14 g) agar flakes (see Note)
2 cups (475 ml / 464 g) heavy cream

1 cup (240 ml / 242 g) half-and-half
3/4 cup (5.3 oz / 150 g) sugar
6 egg yolks (3.9 oz / 114 g), at room temperature
Whipped cream, for serving

Finely chop the chocolate or process it in a food processor. Transfer to a large bowl and add the vanilla extract.

In a small saucepan, combine the water and agar. Cook over low heat, stirring constantly, until the agar is completely dissolved and a thick, clear gel forms, with no visible agar pieces, about 8 minutes.

In a heavy medium saucepan, combine the cream, half-and-half, and sugar. Cook over low heat, stirring often, until bubbles begin to form at the edges, between 180°F and 190°F (82°C and 88°C). Whisk in the agar mixture and remove from the heat.

Put the egg yolks in a medium bowl. Add 1/4 cup of the warm cream mixture and whisk until well blended. Repeat five more times, until 1 1/2 cups of the cream mixture have been added and the egg yolk mixture is as warm as the remaining cream mixture.

CONTINUED

Slowly pour the egg yolk mixture into the saucepan in a steady stream while whisking constantly. Cook over low heat, whisking constantly, until the mixture thickens and coats the back of a spoon, about 10 minutes.

Pour the mixture into the bowl with the chocolate and stir until the chocolate is completely melted. Strain through a fine-mesh sieve into a bowl or other container. Press plastic wrap onto the surface and refrigerate for at least 4 hours and up to 3 days; the pudding will become very firm.

Transfer the pudding to a food processor or blender and process until smooth, shiny, and lightened in color, 4 to 5 minutes. Spoon into cups and serve immediately, topped with whipped cream.

Whipped pudding is best eaten right away. However, it can be stored in an airtight container in the refrigerator for up to 1 day. Alternatively, the unwhipped pudding can be stored in an airtight container in the refrigerator for up to 3 days, so consider whipping only what you plan to serve and saving the rest for another day.

NOTE: *Agar flakes are available at Japanese markets or natural food stores, located near the seaweed. The key to working with agar flakes is to be sure they are completely dissolved before adding them to other mixtures. In this recipe, the final pudding is strained, so particles of agar aren't an issue. But to get maximum gelling and the smoothest possible texture, it's crucial to cook the agar and water until a thick, clear gel forms.*

Ellsworth Kelly Fudge Pops

MAKES 10 FUDGE POPS / HANDS-ON TIME: 15 MINUTES
FROM START TO FINISH: 2 TO 3 HOURS

At the Blue Bottle café in the rooftop sculpture garden at the San Francisco Museum of Modern Art, all of the pastries we make are inspired by works of art on display at the museum. Taking a cue from the Ellsworth Kelly sculpture *Stele 1*, a giant weathered oblong steel obelisk that once dominated the sculpture garden, I developed a fudge pop that, when frozen, has a surface texture and color similar to the giant original. We use silicone Popsicle molds shaped to look like the sculpture, but you can use any shape of mold for this recipe.

These fudge pops have a fairly low melting point, so you won't want to dawdle while eating one. In fact, before *Stele 1* returned to its permanent home with its owners, it was a delightful and daily sight to see adults and kids posing in front of the sculpture, melting fudge pop in hand, trying to manage the dripping while their companions attempted to fit the entire scene into the frame of a picture.

SUBSTITUTIONS: This recipe is also delicious—of course!—with a hint of coffee. For this purpose, I think it's best to infuse whole coffee beans in the milk in the recipe overnight. This gives the fudge pops a beautiful coffee flavor without marring their unctuous texture with coffee grounds. The night before making this recipe, combine 1/2 cup (120 ml) of whole coffee beans with the milk. Cover and refrigerate overnight. Omit the milk when warming the cream mixture and blend the cream mixture as directed. Strain the coffee-infused milk and stir it into the chocolate. Then pour into molds and freeze as directed.

8 ounces (227 g) dark chocolate, 62% to 70% cacao	1/4 cup (1.8 oz / 50 g) sugar
1 teaspoon vanilla extract	4 teaspoons natural (not Dutch-processed) cocoa powder
1 1/4 cups (300 ml / 290 g) heavy cream	1/2 teaspoon kosher salt
1 cup (240 ml / 242 g) whole milk	

Finely chop the chocolate or process it in a food processor. Transfer to a large bowl and add the vanilla extract.

In a heavy medium saucepan, combine the cream, milk, sugar, cocoa, and salt. Cook over medium-low heat, whisking often to break up the cocoa powder, until bubbles start to form around the edges, between 180°F and 190°F (82°C and 88°C).

Pour the cream mixture over the chocolate and stir until the chocolate is completely melted. Strain through a fine-mesh sieve into a liquid measuring cup.

Pour into ice-pop molds and freeze until firm. If you don't have ice-pop molds, use ice cube trays; freeze for 1 hour, then insert toothpicks or short skewers and continue freezing until firm.

When ready to serve, dip the molds into hot water to loosen the fudge pops.

The fudge pops can be stored in the freezer for up to 2 weeks.

Brandy Cake with Arborio Rice and Almonds

MAKES 1 LARGE LOAF; SERVES 8 TO 10 / HANDS-ON TIME: 2 HOURS, 45 MINUTES
FROM START TO FINISH: 2 TO 3 DAYS

This cake is based on a traditional Bolognese Easter treat that, like many Italian celebration cakes, has alcohol poured over the top right when the cake comes out of the oven. This cake is rich, dark, labor-intensive, and at its best three to four days after you begin the process of making it. Though conceptually similar to the much-maligned Christmas fruitcake, the result is an enticing cake that you'll find delightful and worthy of celebration. The dark crust conceals a golden, lemon-scented, and almond-studded interior. Its moist texture, similar to rice pudding, and brandy kick make this a really delicious alternative to the nightcap.

A traditionalist would use rum to soak the cake, but I thought it would be fun to experiment. I took the cake and two faithful tasters (James and our friend sommelier Paul Einbund) to St. George Spirits to explore their barrel-aged brandies and find the best fit. On the production floor of the distillery, we marveled at the hundreds of aging barrels filled with various whiskeys and brandies, and sniffed and tasted many samples that Dave Smith, one of the distillers, siphoned straight from the barrels for us. Hands down, of all the liquors we sniffed and the few I brought home to test, the aged Sauvignon Blanc brandy was the perfect pairing. Unfortunately, St. George doesn't bottle that brandy for retail sale, so when you make this at home, I encourage you to explore and try different spirits. After all, that's really what makes this cake so special. (For more on St. George Spirits, and spirits in general, see the sidebar on page 163.)

4 cups (945 ml / 968 g) whole milk
1½ cups (10.6 oz / 300 g) sugar
⅓ cup (2.3 oz / 65 g) Arborio rice
1 teaspoon kosher salt
Finely grated zest of ½ lemon
½ cup (2.8 oz / 80 g) almonds

4 eggs (7 oz / 200 g), at room temperature
1 egg yolk (0.6 oz / 19 g), at room temperature
3 tablespoons 80-proof brandy, plus more as desired (see Note)

In a large heavy saucepan, combine the milk, 1¼ cups (8.8 oz / 250 g) of the sugar, and the rice, salt, and zest. Cook over medium heat, stirring often, just until boiling, being careful not to let the frothing milk overflow.

Decrease the heat to low and cook at the slowest simmer for about 2 hours, stirring often and adjusting the heat as necessary, until the mixture resembles very thick rice pudding: golden brown and with very little moisture remaining. When you draw a spoon across the bottom of the saucepan, a clear line should remain, without the mixture flowing back in.

Transfer to a bowl and let cool to room temperature. (At this point, you can cover and store in the refrigerator for up to 3 days.)

In a heavy medium skillet, toast the almonds over medium heat, shaking often, until fragrant and slightly brown, about 5 minutes. Let cool completely, then coarsely chop.

Preheat the oven to 350°F (175°C). Line a 5 by 9-inch (13 by 23-cm) 8-cup loaf pan, preferably glass or ceramic, with a strip of parchment paper the same width as the pan and long enough that it sticks out on both ends.

In the bowl of a stand mixer fitted with the whisk attachment, whip the eggs and egg yolk on medium speed for 10 seconds. With the mixer running, slowly add the remaining 1/4 cup (1.8 oz / 50 g) sugar.

Increase the mixer speed to high and whip until soft peaks form, 8 to 10 minutes.

Decrease the mixer speed to medium and add the rice mixture in four additions. Scrape down the sides of the bowl after the final addition. Remove the bowl from the mixer and use a rubber spatula to gently fold in the almonds until evenly incorporated.

Scrape the batter into the prepared pan. Bake for 40 minutes, then rotate and bake for an additional 20 minutes, until the top is dark golden brown and the cake springs back when gently pressed in the center.

As soon as the cake comes out of the oven, poke it with a skewer about 15 times, making deep holes to allow the brandy to saturate the cake. Pour the brandy over the cake and let the cake cool in the pan for 30 minutes.

Run a knife along the long edges of the pan (those not covered with parchment paper), then turn the cake out on a flat surface and discard the parchment paper. Turn the cake top side up and let cool completely. Wrap tightly with plastic wrap and let rest at room temperature for at least 1 day before serving. If you can wait, the cake is even better on the second or third day.

NOTE: *The alcohol flavor in this cake should be fairly pronounced; the brandy we use is 80 proof alcohol, so don't be bashful about using more if you're not getting the brandy flavor you want.*

Pixie Tangerine Chiffon Cake with Vanilla Swiss Meringue

MAKES ONE 9-INCH (23 CM) CAKE; SERVES 6 TO 8 / HANDS-ON TIME: 1 HOUR
FROM START TO FINISH: 4 HOURS, 30 MINUTES

When James and I took our first trip to Tokyo with our good friend Jay Egami (see page 91) in 2008, the small café that was (and still is) the most thrilling for both of us was Chatei Hatou, near Shibuya Station. The coffee, as James describes on page 84, is extraordinary, and the pageantry with which it is executed and presented is unequaled. But then there is the chiffon cake.

The cake itself is delicious—a banana chiffon cake with a cinnamon and chocolate glaze. But more inspiring than the object is the process. Made by the baristas during short breaks between coffee orders, the cakes are frosted with an ease and perfection that speaks to a great deal of practice in the process. Chocolate ganache is heated in a small copper pot and applied with quick, confident strokes of the offset spatula, first on the sides of the cake, then over the top, and finally, and most importantly, on the surface of the center hole.

My interpretation of this cake takes inspiration from my hometown, Ojai, California. Ojai is a tiny citrus growing town in Southern California, and it's the only place in the world where Pixie tangerines are grown. A delightfully acidic and sweet seedless tangerine, it is perfect in a feather-light chiffon cake. While I love the ganache on the Chatei Hatou cake, one of my all-time favorite things to do is to frost a big, tall cake with a perfectly white and fluffy Swiss meringue. The magic of an enormous cake frosted with dreamlike billows of meringue and set atop a cake pedestal is pretty much my dream come true.

A few important pointers: The cake can be made up to one day in advance. After removing it from the pan, carefully double wrap it in plastic wrap and store in the refrigerator. However, the meringue must be made immediately before frosting and serving the cake.

SUBSTITUTIONS: Pixie tangerines are not widely available. Substitute equal amounts of zest and juice from any other type of small, sweet tangerine, clementine, or satsuma. Other varieties of citrus will also work wonderfully; for those, use 1/4 cup juice and 1/4 cup water. I especially love lime, Eureka lemon, or yuzu in this cake.

CAKE
1 3/4 cups (8.6 oz / 245 g) all-purpose flour
1/4 cup (1.1 oz / 31 g) cornstarch
1 tablespoon baking powder
1 1/2 cups (10.6 oz / 300 g) sugar
2 tablespoons finely grated tangerine zest
    (from about 5 small tangerines)
1 teaspoon kosher salt
1/4 cup (60 ml / 54 g) extra-virgin olive oil
7 egg yolks (4.6 oz / 133 g), at room
    temperature

1/2 cup (120 ml / 120 g) freshly squeezed
    tangerine juice
3/4 cup (180 ml / 184 g) plain yogurt
7 egg whites (7.4 oz / 210 g), at room
    temperature
1/2 teaspoon cream of tartar

MERINGUE
1 cup (7.1 oz / 200 g) sugar
4 egg whites (4.2 oz / 120 g), at room
    temperature
1 teaspoon vanilla extract

TO MAKE THE CAKE, preheat the oven to 325°F (165°C). Have ready a clean and dry, ungreased 9-inch (23-cm) tube pan with a removable bottom.

Sift the flour, cornstarch, and baking powder onto a large piece of parchment paper no less than five times. Transfer to a large bowl.

In a medium bowl, combine the sugar, zest, and salt. Using your hands, massage ingredients together, working the citrus oils into the sugar. The sugar will take on a slight orange color and very fragrant smell, maximizing the citrus flavor in the cake. Add to the flour mixture and whisk until well combined.

Make a well in the center of the flour mixture. Add the olive oil, egg yolks, and tangerine juice, and mix the liquids together to break up the yolks. Mix the yolks into the flour mixture with a rubber spatula until well combined and free of lumps. Add the yogurt and mix until thoroughly incorporated.

In the bowl of a stand mixer fitted with the whisk attachment, whip the egg whites and cream of tartar on medium speed until soft peaks form, about 6 minutes.

Transfer the egg whites to the flour mixture and use a rubber spatula to fold in them in. Work quickly and gently, and stop as soon as you can no longer see streaks of egg white.

Transfer the batter to the tube pan and smooth with an offset or rubber spatula. Bake for 55 to 60 minutes, until the cake is golden and firm and springs back when gently pressed in the center, rotating the pan midway through the baking time.

Cool upside down, atop a funnel, small jar, or bottle for at least 2 hours. Run a small offset spatula or thin knife around both the outer and inner edge, then remove the sides of the pan. Run the spatula between the cake and the bottom of the pan, then invert onto a serving plate, top side down, and remove the bottom of the pan.

TO MAKE THE MERINGUE, just before serving combine all the ingredients in the top of a double boiler or a medium metal bowl set over a saucepan of boiling water. (Make sure the bottom of the bowl doesn't touch the water in the saucepan). Whisk vigorously until well blended, then cook, stirring constantly, until the sugar has dissolved and the mixture is slightly warm, about 130°F (54°C). Transfer to the bowl of a stand mixer fitted with the whisk attachment.

Whip on medium speed until soft peaks form, about 6 minutes.

TO ASSEMBLE THE CAKE, put about 1/2 cup of the meringue in a small bowl. Using an offset spatula and working quickly (because the frosting becomes harder to work with the cooler it gets), apply a thin coating of the reserved frosting to all surfaces of the cake; this is the crumb coat, which will help prevent crumbs from appearing in the final frosting. Once the crumb coat is applied, spread most of the remaining frosting over the sides and top of the cake, and finish by applying a small amount of frosting to the inner surface, inside the hole.

Serve immediately.

From our Friends

Rose Levy Beranbaum's Coffee Panna Cotta

MAKES 6 TO 9 SERVINGS / HANDS-ON TIME: 20 MINUTES
FROM START TO FINISH: 2 HOURS, 20 MINUTES

I first met Rose Levy Beranbaum when she wrote an article about Miette for *Food Arts* magazine. I was absolutely terrified to meet the woman who had, basically, taught me how to bake cakes via her book *The Cake Bible*, but I couldn't have been more wrong in assuming that she would be intimidating and judgmental. Rose is one of the most kind and generous people I've ever met. Yet underneath all of her sweetness is a very spirited heart. She will enthusiastically walk a mile through Brooklyn with you to find a hole-in-the-wall donut shop and feast on fifteen donuts "in the name of research" and is full of fun stories from her incredible life as a fixture in the food world. We've kept up a lovely friendship and try to see each other whenever we are on the same coast.

Rose is a huge fan of Blue Bottle coffee and was the first person I asked to contribute a recipe to this book, knowing that magic would happen when she set her mind to showcasing the coffee—and magic it is! Because this recipe is made with such simple ingredients, Rose advises using "the best quality cream, the freshest possible coffee, and the finest vanilla extract" for optimum results.

SUBSTITUTIONS: You can use another coffee in place of the Blue Bottle Three Africans.

2¼ cups (530 ml / 522 g) heavy cream

7 tablespoons (3 oz / 85 g) sugar (preferably turbinado or raw sugar)

¼ cup (0.7 oz / 20 g) Blue Bottle Three Africans coffee, finely ground

1½ teaspoons powdered gelatin

1½ teaspoons vanilla extract

Whipped cream, for serving

Chocolate-covered coffee beans, for garnish (optional)

Have ready nine clean and dry 2-ounce (60 ml) demitasse cups or six small decorative dessert or custard cups.

In a small saucepan, stir together the cream, sugar, and coffee. Sprinkle the gelatin on top and let sit for at least 3 minutes.

Stir in the gelatin, then cook over medium heat, stirring constantly, just until bubbles form around the edges, between 180°F and 190°F (82°C and 88°C).

Strain through a fine-mesh sieve or a strainer lined with cheesecloth into a medium bowl. Stir in the vanilla extract. Pour the mixture into prepared custard cups.

Cover tightly and chill until set, at least 2 hours. Top with freshly whipped cream and garnish each serving with a chocolate-covered coffee bean, if desired.

The panna cotta can be stored in the refrigerator, with the cups covered in plastic wrap, for up to 3 days.

Daniel Patterson's Coffee-Roasted Carrots with Chicory Granola

MAKES 4 SERVINGS / HANDS-ON TIME: 30 MINUTES
FROM START TO FINISH: 1 HOUR, 30 MINUTES

I have been friends with Daniel Patterson, chef-owner of Coi restaurant in San Francisco and Plum and Haven restaurants in Oakland, for many years. When I first mentioned that I was dating James, he responded incredulously, saying, "You're dating that guy? The uptight, 'Oh, the water's not exactly the right temperature' guy?" The hilarious irony in this is that if anyone can rival James in uptightness, it's Daniel. James's response, macchiato in hand, was "Uptight? He is calling me uptight?" It was like a duel over whose turtleneck was more black. As you would expect, it was the beginning of a great friendship.

James and I are huge fans of all of Daniel's restaurants, but Coi is especially magical, and I've had some of the most transformative dining experiences of my life there. A typical meal at Coi is ten-plus courses, each very small and focused on one or two of the most finely curated ingredients. Where Daniel shines is with seasonal vegetables, teasing out their essence with innovative techniques and clever pairings. Amid all of the mind-blowing flavors, we are invariably in awe over the carrot course. Yes, the carrot course, which earned him the nickname the Carrot Genius from James.

Daniel makes the following recipe at Coi by roasting sweet carrots with the skin on until quite tender, then slicing and serving with crème fraîche, cilantro flowers, sea salt, a few drops of extra-virgin olive oil, a sprinkling of chicory granola, and a dusting of ground coffee. The dish is neither sweet nor savory, or is both at once, and at Coi it is served as an in-between savory and dessert course. Daniel prefers our Decaf Noir coffee in this dish, finding it to be robust without being acidic. The granola makes about 4 cups, much more than needed for this dish, but the leftovers are delicious for breakfast and will keep for up to a week if stored in an airtight container at room temperature.

SUBSTITUTIONS: You can use another decaffeinated coffee in place of the Blue Bottle Decaf Noir.

CARROTS
3/4 pound (341 g) sweet young carrots with
    tops, washed and trimmed
Extra virgin olive oil
Crunchy sea salt
1 to 1 1/2 cups (3 to 4.5 oz / 85 to 130 g) Blue
    Bottle Decaf Noir coffee, whole bean

GRANOLA
2 cups (7 oz / 200 g) rolled oats
1/3 cup (3 oz / 72 g) packed light brown sugar
1/4 cup (2 oz / 57 g) unsalted butter
2 tablespoons honey

2 teaspoons finely ground chicory root
    (see Note)
1/2 teaspoon kosher salt

1/2 cup (4 oz / 116 g) crème fraîche
Extra-virgin olive oil, for garnish
Crunchy sea salt, for garnish
Cilantro flowers or small cilantro leaves,
    for garnish
Ground coffee, for garnish

CONTINUED

TO MAKE THE CARROTS, preheat the oven to 325°F (165°C).

Toss the carrots with a bit of olive oil and season lightly with salt; their flavor should remain sweet.

Pour just enough coffee beans into a heavy Dutch oven or ovenproof roasting pot to completely cover the bottom. Add the carrots, cover, and roast until very tender, 1 to 1¹/₄ hours. Let cool in the pan; the carrots will harden as they cool.

MEANWHILE, TO MAKE THE GRANOLA, put the oats in a medium bowl. Put the brown sugar, butter, and honey in a small saucepan over medium heat. Cook, stirring constantly, until melted and simmering, then immediately pour over the oats. Add the chicory and salt and stir until thoroughly combined.

Spread the mixture in an even layer on a rimmed baking sheet and bake, stirring occasionally, for about 25 minutes, until golden brown. Let cool completely; the granola will get crunchy as it cools. Stored in a tightly sealed container at room temperature, the granola will keep for 1 week.

TO SERVE, remove the carrots from the pan, discarding the coffee beans. Slice the carrots on an extreme diagonal to make long slices. Spread 2 tablespoons of the crème fraîche on each serving plate and top with one-fourth of the carrot slices. Garnish each serving with a few drops of olive oil, a sprinkling of crunchy sea salt, and a few cilantro flowers. Top with small pieces of the granola and a dusting of ground coffee. Serve immediately.

NOTE: *Ground chicory root is available in natural food stores.*

Chris Cosentino's Braised Boar Shoulder with Gigante Beans and Baby Vegetables

MAKES 6 SERVINGS / HANDS-ON TIME: 1½ HOURS
FROM START TO FINISH: 3 DAYS

Chris Cosentino may be the most photographed person at the Saturday Ferry Plaza Farmers Market. Although a fixture on the Food Network, and possibly the most recognizable face of chefdom in San Francisco, he is still very much running the kitchen at his San Francisco restaurant Incanto and his salumeria Boccalone. An avid market shopper, he is one of the first chefs to arrive at Ferry Plaza market on Saturday mornings, loading up his cart before anyone else can come scoop him; like an organic vegetable version of the game show *Supermarket Sweep*. His young son, Easton, is usually catching a ride on his cart, surrounded by piles of fruit and vegetables. Easton is two years younger than our son, Dashiell, but the two are as close as can be. Through the kids, James and I have become great friends with Chris and his wife, Tatiana, and they are two of our favorite people to spend our Sunday afternoons with. We couldn't imagine asking anyone else to contribute a meat recipe for this cookbook, and we're delighted with this stunner.

This recipe calls for marinating the meat overnight, and Chris also prefers to let the meat rest overnight after cooking, explaining that it gives the meat a chance to suck up all the flavor and moisture from the coffee- and chocolate-infused braising liquid. Adding a potato when cooking the beans is a stroke of genius; it keeps the bean skins from splitting during cooking.

SUBSTITUTIONS: You can substitute pork shoulder for the wild boar and use another coffee in place of the Blue Bottle Giant Steps. Baby vegetables and fresh shelling beans are often available at farmers' markets. If you can't find fresh gigante beans, use 1 pound (455 g) dried large white beans, soaked overnight, but note that they will take up to three times longer to cook than fresh beans. If you can't find baby fennel and turnips, use larger ones, quartered and blanched until tender.

BOAR
⅓ cup (1.5 oz / 43 g) Blue Bottle Giant Steps
    coffee, whole bean
1 tablespoon juniper berries
3 pounds (1.4 kg) boneless wild boar shoulder
Kosher salt
Freshly ground black pepper
1 yellow onion, diced
1 carrot, diced
1 fennel bulb, chopped

1 fennel stalk, sliced ¼ inch (6 mm) thick
5 cloves garlic, crushed
2 cups (475 ml / 475 g) red wine
2 tablespoons lard
About 5 cups (1.2 liters / 1.2 kg) pork or
    chicken stock
2 ounces (57 g) dark chocolate, 72% cacao,
    coarsely chopped
2 fresh bay leaves

CONTINUED

BEANS

4 cups shelled fresh gigante beans (from
about 4 lb / 1.8 kg beans in the pod)

1 russet potato, peeled and left whole

1 onion, peeled and left whole

1 garlic head, split

1 bay leaf

1 sprig thyme

Extra-virgin olive oil

Kosher salt

Freshly ground black pepper

BABY VEGETABLES

12 mixed color baby carrots, peeled

Kosher salt

12 baby turnips

12 baby fennel bulbs

TO MAKE THE BOAR, put half of the coffee and all of the juniper berries in a spice grinder and grind to a coarse powder. Spread the mixture over the entire surface of the boar and season with salt and pepper. Massage the spices into the meat. Transfer to a pot or bowl just large enough to fit the meat and the onion, carrot, and fennel. Add the onion, carrot, fennel bulb, fennel stalk, garlic, and wine. Cover and refrigerate for at least 6 hours and up to 15 hours.

Preheat the oven to 300°F (150°C).

Remove the meat from the marinade and pat dry. Drain the vegetables, reserving both the liquid and the vegetables. Heat the lard in a heavy ovenproof Dutch oven or roasting pot over medium-high heat, then add the meat and sear until nicely colored all over, about 10 minutes.

Remove the meat from the pan, add the reserved vegetables, and cook over medium heat, stirring occasionally, until caramelized, about 10 minutes.

Grind the remaining coffee. Deglaze the pan with the reserved liquid. Add the coffee and bring to a simmer, then decrease the heat low and simmer, stirring occasionally, until the pan is almost dry, about 4 minutes. Add 4 cups of the stock. Bring to a simmer over medium-high heat, then decrease the heat to low and simmer for a few minutes. Add the chocolate and stir until melted. Remove from the heat and let cool for a few minutes. Working in batches if need be, process in a food processor until smooth. Strain through a fine-mesh sieve.

Put the meat back in the roasting pot and pour the strained liquid over it, adding more stock as needed to cover by three-quarters. Add the bay leaves. Bring to a simmer over medium-high heat, then transfer to the oven and bake uncovered until fork-tender, about 2$1/2$ hours, basting occasionally. Don't overcook, or the meat will be dry. Let cool, then cover and refrigerate overnight.

TO PREPARE THE BEANS, put the beans, potato, onion, garlic, bay leaf, and thyme in a pot and add water to cover by about 3 inches (8 cm). Bring to a gentle simmer over medium heat, taking care not to boil the beans, which will make them burst and break apart. Decrease the heat to medium-low and simmer until tender, 30 to 60 minutes, depending on the beans. Discard the potato, onion, garlic, bay leaf, and thyme. (The beans can be cooked up to this point 1 day ahead; cool completely then transfer along with their cooking liquid to an airtight container and store in the refrigerator.) Drain the beans, reserving the liquid. Stir in a bit of olive oil and season with salt and pepper to taste. Keep warm.

TO PREPARE THE BABY VEGETABLES, put the carrots in a pot of cold water with a pinch of salt. Bring to a simmer over medium-high heat, then decrease the heat to low, cover, and simmer until tender, about 3 minutes. Remove with a slotted spoon and repeat with the turnips. Keep both vegetables warm.

Fill a large pot with water and bring to a boil over medium-high heat. Add the baby fennel and blanch until fork-tender, about 2 minutes. Drain and keep warm.

TO ASSEMBLE, warm the meat, in its braising liquid, over medium heat and cook just until warmed through. Divide the baby vegetables and beans, with some of their cooking liquid, among six shallow bowls and top each serving with a chunk of the braised boar and some of the boar braising liquid. Serve immediately.

Stuart Brioza's Tuna Melt Sandwiches with Piquillo Peppers

MAKES 4 SANDWICHES / HANDS-ON TIME: 35 MINUTES
FROM START TO FINISH: 45 MINUTES

Our friend Stuart Brioza was a consultant at the Mint Plaza café between working as executive chef at Rubicon (a wonderful but now-shuttered San Francisco restaurant) and opening the incredible restaurant State Bird Provisions with his wife, Nicole Krasinski. Stuart has an amazing way of making food that is deeply flavorful without being fussy or overly complicated. In this sandwich, the depth comes from a combination of briny olives, rich homemade aïoli, and piquant peppers paired with high-quality oil-packed tuna. The recipe makes more aïoli than is needed, but it will keep for up to three days in the refrigerator and will be delicious on other sandwiches or as a dip.

SUBSTITUTIONS: At Blue Bottle, we use Ortiz tuna, piquillo peppers, and Castelvetrano olives, but if you can't find those ingredients, you can substitute other types of oil-packed tuna, roasted red bell peppers, or other mild green olives (preferably Italian).

AÏOLI

2 egg yolks (1.3 oz / 38 g), at room
    temperature
1 tablespoon freshly squeezed lemon juice
1 clove garlic, minced
2 tablespoons paprika
1 teaspoon finely grated lemon zest
3/4 cup (180 ml / 161 g) extra-virgin olive oil
Kosher salt
Freshly ground black pepper

TUNA SALAD

4 canned piquillo peppers
9 ounces (255 g) oil-packed tuna (preferably
    Mediterranean), drained
2 tablespoons capers, drained and chopped
2 tablespoons finely chopped green olives
    (preferably Castelvetrano)
Kosher salt
Freshly ground black pepper

4 rustic sandwich rolls, or 1 baguette cut into
    4 equal pieces, sliced open
1 cup (3.5 oz / 100 g) shredded provolone
    cheese, or 4 slices

Preheat the oven to 425°F (220°C).

TO MAKE THE AÏOLI, combine the egg yolks, lemon juice, garlic, paprika, and lemon zest in a large bowl and whisk until the texture is ribbony. You can also put the ingredients in a smaller container and process with an immersion blender. Starting with just a drop at a time and increasing to a few drops at a time, slowly the add olive oil while whisking or running the mixer to create a smooth, well-blended mixture. When the mixture is stable, begin adding the oil in a steady stream, still whisking or mixing constantly. The aïoli should have the consistency of mayonnaise. If gets too thick, add hot water as needed, 1 teaspoon at a time. Season with salt and pepper to taste.

TO MAKE THE TUNA SALAD, coarsely chop 2 of the peppers and put them in a medium bowl. Add the tuna, capers, olives and mix well. Stir in the aïoli a bit at a time, using just enough to hold the salad together without making it too wet. Season with salt and pepper to taste.

TO ASSEMBLE THE SANDWICHES, cut the remaining 2 peppers in half lengthwise and place one half on the bottom half of each roll. Top with one-fourth of the tuna salad and cheese. Place the open-faced sandwiches on a pan with the top halves of the rolls placed to the side of the bottom halves and bake until the cheese melts and browns around the edges, 5 to 7 minutes. Top the sandwiches with the toasted top halves of the rolls and serve immediately.

Stuart Brioza's Egg Salad Sandwiches with Arugula-Almond Pesto and Pickled Fennel

MAKES 4 SANDWICHES / HANDS-ON TIME: 30 MINUTES
FROM START TO FINISH: 1 HOUR, 45 MINUTES

At most of Blue Bottle's Bay Area shops, we serve very simple sandwiches similar to those available at French train stations. At the Mint Plaza café, we have the luxury of a small kitchen, plus cooks who know their way around an egg, so we are able to offer slightly more elaborate sandwiches. This is another beautiful recipe developed for us by Stuart Brioza. Hard-boiled eggs are combined with a savory arugula-almond pesto, layered with pickled fennel, and topped with a rich Fiore Sardo cheese (a sheep's milk or pecorino cheese from the island of Sardinia), coming together to make a delicious lunch that is both familiar and surprising. This recipe makes more pickled fennel and pesto than is needed for the sandwiches. The fennel is a great addition to other salads or sandwiches, and the pesto is wonderful with pasta or spread on crostini. Stored in an airtight container in the refrigerator, the fennel will keep for up to two days and the pesto will keep for up to four days.

PICKLED FENNEL
1 fennel bulb, cored and thinly sliced
Juice of 1 lemon
1 tablespoon extra-virgin olive oil
Kosher salt
Freshly ground black pepper

PESTO
1/2 cup (2.8 oz / 80 g), almonds
1 cup (2.8 oz / 80 g) packed arugula
1 cup (2 oz / 57 g) lightly packed Italian
    parsley leaves
1/4 cup (1 oz / 28 g) grated Fiore Sardo or
    other pecorino cheese
1/4 cup (60 ml / 60 g) water
2 tablespoons extra-virgin olive oil

Leaves from 1 sprig rosemary
1 small clove garlic
1/2 teaspoon kosher salt
Freshly ground pepper

EGG SALAD
4 eggs
Extra-virgin olive oil, as needed
Kosher salt
Freshly ground pepper

4 rustic sandwich rolls, or 1 baguette cut into
    4 equal pieces, sliced open
Fiore Sardo cheese or other pecorino cheese,
    sliced or grated

TO MAKE THE PICKLED FENNEL, place the fennel in a bowl. Drizzle the lemon juice and olive oil over the top and season with salt and pepper. Toss to combine and let sit for at least 1 hour and up to 2 days.

TO MAKE THE ARUGULA-ALMOND PESTO, toast the almonds in a heavy medium skillet over medium heat, shaking often, until fragrant and slightly brown, about 5 minutes. Let cool completely.

CONTINUED

Transfer the nuts to a food processor. Add the arugula, parsley, cheese, water, oil, rosemary, garlic, and salt and process until smooth and creamy. Season with pepper to taste.

TO MAKE THE EGG SALAD AND ASSEMBLE THE SANDWICHES, bring a medium saucepan of water to a boil and prepare an ice bath. Carefully place the eggs in the boiling water, decrease the heat to medium-low, and simmer for 8 to 9 minutes. Remove from the pot with a wide slotted spoon and plunge into the ice bath.

Peel and chop the eggs and transfer to a medium bowl. Stir in 1/4 cup (60 ml) of the pesto, drizzling in a bit of olive oil if needed to hold the salad together (but note that this egg salad is drier than most). Taste and add more pesto if you like, and season with salt and pepper to taste.

Fill each of the rolls with one-fourth of the egg salad. Put some of the pickled fennel atop the egg salad, then add sliced or grated Fiore Sardo cheese. Garnish with a drizzle of extra-virgin olive oil and season with salt and pepper.

Nopa's Blue Bottle Martini

MAKES 1 COCKTAIL

Sometimes Blue Bottle's wholesale partners have the desire to broaden their menu by adding flavors or other ingredients to espresso to make a drink in which the flavor of the espresso isn't recognizable. This we discourage. But every so often, we are persuaded by our confidence in a partner and become excited about their idea. One of those is Nopa, one of our favorite San Francisco restaurants, and a wholesale partner who continually demonstrates that serving good coffee and espresso in a restaurant setting is not only possible but can be done reliably. When Nopa co-owner Jeff Hanak asked us about serving a Blue Bottle martini that his bar manager had come up with, James was excited to try it. It's a delicious drink, and one that has so much appeal that his bartenders regularly make dozens every night. Santa Teresa Araku is a rum-based coffee liqueur from Venezuela. If you can't find it, you can substitute another rum- or tequila-based coffee liqueur. The ubiquitous Kahlua is best avoided for this cocktail given the chemical sweetness it brings to almost any drink it touches. You can substitute another espresso if you like.

1.5 fluid ounces (45 ml) vodka   1 shot of Blue Bottle Hayes Valley espresso
1 fluid ounce (30 ml) Santa Teresa Araku

Pour the liquors and espresso into a mixing glass with ice. Shake well, then strain into a large cocktail glass.

ACKNOWLEDGMENTS

We would like to thank the team at Ten Speed Press, especially our editor, Melissa Moore, and Aaron Wehner, Betsy Stromberg, and Katy Brown.

Many thanks to our friends Rose Levy Beranbaum, Stuart Brioza, Chris Cosentino, Jeff Hanak, Nicole Krasinski, and Daniel Patterson for sharing their recipes.

We are especially grateful to the family behind Rusty's Hawaiian on the Big Island—Lorie Obra, Joan Obra, R. Miguel Meza, and Ralph Gaston—for generously allowing us to visit their farm and for their help on the Grow chapter. Thank you also to Mary Diamond and Piero Bambi at La Marzocco in Italy and Aida Batlle in El Salvador.

FROM JAMES This book is dedicated to my family: my perfect, beautiful, talented, pragmatic, and serene (with dimples of steel) wife, Caitlin Williams Freeman, and my master of farty beatboxing, reader aloud of *Spy vs. Spy*, passer of cool lima beans, Dashiell Ellis Freeman. Caitlin—love is not perfunctory. Love is every second. I would also like to ask their permission to split this dedication several ways with Clay and Tara—thank you for being an inspiring and dedicated team. A book! Who knew?!

The entire crew at Blue Bottle: every time I have something delicious at one of our shops, every time I hear a thank you or a please, every time I see a gleaming steam wand, every time I hear a diplomatic explanation of a tricky drink worthy of David Lloyd George, my heart swells with pride at what we have all created. Those of you who have stayed so long and worked so hard—Katie Booser, Arno Holschuh, Mario Perez, Shaw Sturton, Vanessa Gates, Michelle Ott, Angél Argüello, Emiliano Argüello, John O'Donovan, JoEllen Depakakibo, Alex Klimek, Carmen Maldonado, Eren Ortuño—are there thanks enough?

All the people I made drinks for at the south side of the Ferry Building on Saturdays: I remember your kindness and enthusiasm. I thought about the kind of coffee book you would like to read, and then I tried to write it.

Mr. Jay Egami: thank you for being an exemplar of rectitude.

A venture capitalist? Yes! A venture capitalist: thank you John Eastburn for being smart, modest, and helpful.

Kevin Mahan, Michael Anthony, and the rest of the crew at Gramercy Tavern, you have given us the North Star of hospitality.

Everyone working so hard in coffee around the world: so many hands growing, picking, processing, shipping, serving. My hope is that the demand for good coffee makes many lives better. Aida and Lorie—thank you for letting us buy, roast, and serve your extraordinary coffee.

Thanks to three men born in 1919: Kalmen Opperman, James Monroe Freeman, and Jerome David Salinger. Also thanks to Marcel Proust, Robert Nagel, Glenn Gould, Harold Wright, and Marcel Breuer. Also, counterfactual conditionals, dependent clauses, the subjunctive case, cool old stereos, beat up French cars, San Marco Levas, and Benjamin Moore Dove Wing 960.

FROM CAITLIN What an adventure we've had, Mr. William James Freeman! Thank you for being my very best friend, my biggest fan, the person I look up to the most, and the secret funniest person I've ever met. You're the one I want to work beside every day, and to fall asleep next to every night. Thank you for bringing Dashiell into my life, and for making a family with me. I absolutely adore you and am so proud of the work you have done.

Clay McLachlan and Tara Duggan, I'm so amazed at what we did! Clay, thank you for being the genesis of this book, and for being the eyes through which so many will see Blue Bottle. Your name deserves to be on the cover of this book, and I'm sorry we couldn't make that happen. Tara, thank you for keeping us on track, for making the recipes flawless, and for making me sound much smarter than I am. You are both great friends and stupendous collaborators.

To my dad, Jay Williams. You have always been my example of hard work and determination, and to earn your pride is why I work like I do. Thank you for raising Jenna and me to be strong and ambitious women, able to create our own futures and be happy in work and in life. I love you. And, Jenna Herre, you are incredible. I am so fortunate to have you as a big sister.

To all of my pastry teams, past, present and future—thank you! Special thanks go out to Leah Rosenberg, Sarah Cox, and Alyssa Meijer Drees for all of your work in managing the three Blue Bottle pastry departments during the writing of this book. You make these beautiful recipes every day and your excellent pastry skills have taught me how to make them even better every time I do.

I turned to social media to find recipe testers for this book, and the process of getting to know each and every one of the 69 wonderful people who volunteered was more inspiring than almost anything else I've done. Some just did one or two recipes, and some devoted their full efforts, making more cookies, cakes, and treats than I would know how to get rid of. They all returned with the most illuminating questions, clever thoughts on what the home baker needs, demands for further clarification and, in the end, photos of their results. In the process, I was humbled by their generosity, wowed by their skills, embarrassed at my oversights, and so proud of their accomplishments. So, thank you, my beloved testers: Lois Mead, Sharon Grof,

Jennifer Ivanovich, Joanne Sy, Jennifer Sukhija, Zac Tigue, Emily Whitehurst, Mike Valdez, Joy Caves, Maria Saguisag-Sid, Michele Garcia, Alex Whitehurst, Sayuri Parks, Amy Cleary, Kathy Ems, Peter Mosqueda, Steven Thorne, Tami Strang, Imelda Punsalan, Betty Sun, Rose Fera, Vevina McAllister, Fred and Ellis Kuu, Hannah Rabkin, Seton Mangine, Kristine Poole, Annalea Reegan, Hidi Suen, Alicia Penzel, Luisa Barron, Lisa Scheff, Cindy Choi, Moya Magilligan, Meredith Eisgrau, Stephanie Lamar, Elizabeth Milks, Marilee Nguyen, Erik Klepper, John and Lee Joh, Ei Asada, Eddy Pak, Amy Robinson, Kimberlee Tsai, Erica Rolston, Laurie Pauker, Rhea St. Julien, Maeve Kennedy, Amanda Smith, Jenne Patrick, Angela Lashbrook, Kathleen Emma, Julie Wagne, Tammie Visintainer, Shannon Werner, Jackie B DeMille, Sandy Chan, Trevor Fischer, Suzanne Zuppello, Natasha Sanchez, Maryann Campisi, Christina Padis, Stephanie Tietbohl, Kirk & Ei-Lun Yokomizo, Valerian Hrala, Ben Lynch, Anna Gui, and Dorene Kanoh.

FROM TARA In addition to everyone above, I would like to thank James and Caitlin for bringing me on this incredible project and for inviting me into their home for fun, rewarding, and always delicious work sessions. Clay, thank you for being a catalyst and a great partner on this and many future books. Thanks also to my agent, Danielle Svetcov; Miriam Morgan and Michael Bauer, my editors at the San Francisco Chronicle; Jenna Meyer for her invaluable help in the kitchen; and Marla Simon.

At Blue Bottle, I'd like to double-thank Vien Dobui and Joseph Zohn for letting me sit in on espresso training, as well as Michelle Ott, Katie Booser, Arno Holschuh, Shaw Sturton, Alyssa Meijer Drees, Vanessa Gates, Angél Argüello, Enrique Argüello, and Sally Rather.

I'm grateful to my parents, Jane and Michael Duggan, who gave me the chance to drink a lot of Neapolitan espressi at an impressionable age, and to Dahlia and Elsie for being excited about a coffee book despite being under age 10—and for trying out all those cookies. Finally, thank you Eric Gustafson for your unending support and love, and for warming up the coffee cups.

INDEX

All rights reserved.
Published in the United States by Ten Speed Press,
an imprint of the Crown Publishing Group, a division
of Random House, Inc., New York.
www.crownpublishing.com
www.tenspeed.com

Ten Speed Press and the Ten Speed Press colophon are registered
trademarks of Random House, Inc.

Library of Congress Cataloging-in-Publication Data is on file
with the publisher

ISBN 978-1-60774-118-3
eISBN 978-1-60774-119-0

Printed in China

Design by Katy Brown

10 9 8 7 6 5

First Edition

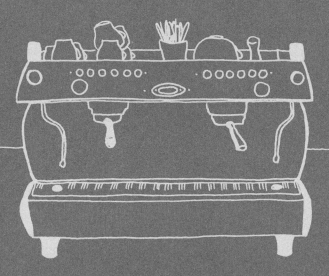